THE GREAT FAMINE

The Great Famine

Ireland's Agony 1845–1852

Ciarán Ó Murchadha

Bloomsbury Academic
An imprint of Bloomsbury Publishing Plc

B L O O M S B U R Y
LONDON · NEW DELHI · NEW YORK · SYDNEY

Bloomsbury Academic
An imprint of Bloomsbury Publishing Plc

50 Bedford Square	1385 Broadway
London	New York
WC1B 3DP	NY 10018
UK	USA

www.bloomsbury.com

BLOOMSBURY and the Diana logo are trademarks of Bloomsbury Publishing Plc

First published 2011
First published in paperback 2013
Reprinted 2013, 2014

British Library Cataloguing-in-Publication Data
A catalogue record for this book is available from the British Library.

ISBN: HB: 978-1-8472-5217-3
PB: 978-1-4725-0778-5

Library of Congress Cataloging-in-Publication Data
A catalog record for this book is available from the Library of Congress.

Printed and bound in Great Britain

Contents

Preface

Since the publication of R.D. Edwards and D.E. Williams's collection of essays, *The Great Famine: Studies in Irish History*, in 1956, an enormous body of scholarly work has accumulated on the Great Famine. Important milestones along the way include Cecil Woodham-Smith's, *The Great Hunger* (1962); Joel Mokyr's, *Why Ireland Starved* (1983); the work of James S. Donnelly Jr. and Cormac Ó Gráda during the 1980s, as well as the upsurge in research and writing inspired by the 150-year anniversary during the 1990s to which they were leading contributors.

In terms of volume, diversity of subject and sheer quality, the 'anniversary' work alone comprises an impressive body of work, transforming our understanding of so many areas: the political and economic contexts to the Famine and its medical and public health aspects; the Poor Law; evictions and emigration among others. Perhaps the most significant development of all has been the emergence of a large number of excellent local and regional studies written either by professional scholars or local historians applying professional standards to their work.

If little enough has been written of recent years, the lull furnishes a convenient moment to make some attempt at assimilating the vast corpus of Famine scholarship that now exists, for the benefit of scholars, students and general readers. To some extent this book represents an attempt to do so, in a single volume whose overall aim is to analyse in a systematic, thorough narrative exactly what happened in Ireland between 1845 and 1852, and what were the implications of these occurrences.

In one sense the vastness of the literature foredooms both objectives to failure, and in the interests of clarity and narrative continuity, discussion of many issues that deserve lengthier consideration has had to be pared down, and in some cases omitted. For the same reasons many of the lively and interesting debates engendered by the recent writing have received only brief discussion or have had to be left out of consideration altogether. Confirmation of all these regrettable necessities will be found reflected in the size of the bibliography, which even after severe restriction to works cited in the text alone, still amounts to a lengthy catalogue.

The source notes will reveal how extensively I have relied on the works of recent historians, both the leading authorities in different areas, and the authors of as many of the regional and local studies as would allow the building up of a comprehensive coverage of the entire country. Needless to say many of those scholars whose work I have consulted will disagree with many of my conclusions. All errors are my own.

Thanks are due to the various libraries and repositories whose facilities I have used: the National Library of Ireland, the National Archives of Ireland, the James Hardiman Library, N.U.I.G, the Irish American Heritage Museum, East Durham, New York. Librarians in public libraries all over Ireland were unfailing helpful, and I have imposed especially on the kind offices of Celestine Rafferty, Wexford County Library; Diarmuid Bracken, Offaly County Library; Peter Corley, Galway City Library; Mary Guinan-Darmody, Tipperary Libraries, Thurles, and Peter Beirne, Francis O'Gorman and Brian Doyle, Local Studies Centre, Clare County Library.

Over the years I have been fortunate to have had the expertise of the two leading Famine scholars available to me personally, Jim Donnelly and Cormac Ó Gráda, and I am indebted to both for their continuing interest and encouragement. In a seven-year association with the History Department of the National University of Ireland, Galway, I have benefited from the scholarly wisdom of Caitríona Clear, John Cunningham, Enrico Dallago, Niall Ó Ciosáin, Gerry Moran, Enda Leaney, Dáibhí Ó Cróinín, and Gearóid Ó Tuathaigh. I owe a particular debt of gratitude to the President of St. Flannan's College, Rev. Joseph McMahon, and the Principal, Colm McDonagh, whose warm welcome on my unexpected return in 2008 greatly eased matters for me; subsequently, in innumerable unobtrusive ways, they did everything they could to smooth my path while the book was being written.

The advice and encouragement of the following was invaluable and appreciated: Pádraig Lenihan, Willie Nolan, Perry Curtis, Matthew Lynch, Paddy Nolan, Canon Reuben Butler, Máire Ní Ghruagáin, Michael and Marie Corley, Eddie Lough, Brian Ó Dálaigh, Declan Barron, Marian O'Leary, Justin Moloney, Joe Dolan, Clare Curtin, John Jones, Daniel McCarthy, Joe Queally. My colleagues at St. Flannan's were interested and supportive, and Benny Duggan and Brendan Howard were able to render particular services. A special word of thanks is also due to Margaret Leamy, Daniel Foran, Fawn Guillfoyle, Samantha Slattery, Orla McMahon, Brian O'Reilly and Suzanne Kelly.

Of my family, who have been greatly supportive, three members were able to render specific assistance: Deirdre and Niall supplied source material I would not have found otherwise, and Cathal's technical skill rescued me from computer difficulties. My uncle, Michael Murphy, who has written authoritatively on the Famine in the midlands, drew my attention to aspects of the Famine in that part of the country; over the years my uncle, Paddy Murphy, has passed on a great deal of the *seanchas* of the west. Amidst the difficulties which beset the early stages of the writing, Michael Greenwood at Continuum (now part of Bloomsbury Publishing PLC), was extraordinarily kind and understanding; his encouragement and patience throughout the entire project has been limitless.

Prologue

THE MONSTER MEETING

On Thursday 15 June 1843 enormous crowds assembled at a racecourse outside Ennis, the county town of Clare, in a mass rally in support of the national campaign for repeal of the Act of Union, which four decades earlier had brought Ireland's constitutional independence to an end. One of hundreds of meetings organized for that 'Great Repeal Year', it was one of thirty particularly large gatherings that centred on the charismatic presence of Daniel O'Connell, the hero of the Irish masses, their Liberator, and one of the great international figures of the day. These gigantic rallies, 'monster meetings', as they were dubbed by the London *Times*, were identical in structure; each began with a staged crowd encounter with O'Connell followed by a procession, and after the open-air rally itself, concluded in the evening with a great banquet. Today, these rallies continue to fascinate, with the panoramic views they afford us of the greatest gatherings of human beings ever to take place in Ireland and fleeting vistas of the vanished world they inhabited.

Woven intricately into the fabric of the Liberator's general campaign, the Ennis rally was timetabled between larger gatherings at Limerick and Galway, the unavoidable choice of a weekday mitigated by the fact that it was also a Church holiday (Corpus Christi), on which the working population would be free to attend. In the weeks leading up to the meeting Ennis hummed with preparations set in train by the organizers, the Ennis Repeal Committee, in order to ensure that the town would be appropriately decorated for the Liberator's arrival. One of the most remarkable of these preparations was the uprooting of over 120 mature trees from demesnes in the vicinity, and their replanting in rows along the streets and the processional route outside the town boundaries. Large leafy boughs were used to decorate the facades of houses in the town, and by the time everything was in place, this lush greenery was relieved by the contrasting colours of triumphal arches placed across the streets, the transplanted trees being linked by festoons and wreaths, interspersed with flags inscribed with inspirational verse and devices of different kinds. Overhanging the southern entrance to Jail Street was a huge banner bearing the lines:

> Welcome to the Hills of Clare
> Where Freedom's voice is found to cheer you
> And honest hearts and hands are there
> To make the Saxon tyrants fear you.

In characteristic O'Connellite style, however, this bold patriotic declaration was defused by the contradictory legend on another great banner arching across the northern end of the street:

> Contempt on the minion who calls you disloyal
> Though fierce to your foes to your friends you are true
> And the tribute most high to a head that is royal
> Is Love of Repeal and Her Majesty too.

Down a short lane, the gate of Row House, the home of Charles O'Connell, the Liberator's kinsman, was buried beneath an oversized wreath of laurels and roses, overlain by an inscription in gold letters: 'Repeal! Repeal! Five Million Demand It!' In another part of the town again, an elaborately constructed chain hung across the street, a symbol of Ireland's woes, designed to be severed 'in a theatrical manner by a sword' just as the Liberator passed.

No effort was spared to ensure that the numbers passing through these impressive settings would be enormous, and the night before the meeting parish priests all over the county prepared to march their respective congregations en masse to Ennis after early Mass. Later it would be reported that contingents had come 'from an area of more than 100 miles ... travelling day and night from every village and hamlet of Clare', and from 'not only the confines, but more central parts of the counties of Limerick, Tipperary, Galway, and even King's County'. By four o' clock on the morning of the rally, Ennis was already crowded, excitement rising rapidly as one after another, hundreds of groups from outlying parishes entered the town to the brassy rhythms of their accompanying temperance bands, 'with music and banners so gay, sufficient to take Repeal by storm if it were with their reach'.

At half past ten, the procession formed in the town's northern suburbs, and in the warm, sunny weather that was to last the entire day, it slowly moved south-wards, crossing the New Bridge into the town proper, acquiring volume and formal order as it went. At its head the Ennis Temperance Band played to onlook-ers from an open carriage, followed shortly after by the Ennis Trades marching in formation, 'clean and orderly, wearing appropriate scarfs and carrying wands'. Behind the Trades came the semi-organized masses of the people; on foot, on horseback and in a variety of horse and donkey-drawn vehicles. Reaching the main square, grandly known as Exchange Place, the procession moved left down through Jail Street before debouching into the new road leading to the village of Clare and the encounter with the Liberator.

On the short journey to Clare, 'every corner, every cross-road and street poured in their tributaries to the main stream of the popular movement', and by the time the village was reached, the procession had doubled in size. After a brief halt the excited crowds moved forward again towards Carnelly Hill, where, amid scenes of near-delirium, the flags of O'Connell's escort, the Limerick Trades and escorting temperance bands hove into view in the clear summer air. As the two processions conjoined and flowed into each other, 'indescribable scenes' took place, according to the *Limerick Chronicle*'s special reporter, 'shouts long and loud rent the air, and the expiration of one was but the signal of another still louder and more enthusiastic'.

After a time this enormous melée was re-ordered into processional mode, the different contingents integrated for the triumphant return through Ennis with the Liberator and his party. Just before the town itself, the procession was joined by carriages carrying two local dignitaries: Cornelius O'Brien, M.P., and Hugh O'Loghlen of Porte, brother to the Liberator's dear departed friend, Sir Michael O'Loghlen, famously the first Catholic to be appointed to high state office after Catholic Emancipation. Behind them a great variety of gigs, jaunting cars and other vehicles scrambled to fall into position.

As the procession moved back through the town, participants and onlook-ers became possessed of an extraordinary excitement, which affected even the staunchly anti-Repeal watchers in the offices of the Tory newspaper, the *Clare Journal*, in Jail Street. At half past two O'Connell's carriage passed the *Journal*'s front windows, the Liberator sitting outside on the dickey, 'in good humour with himself and all around him'. Inside sat Dr. Kennedy, the Catholic bishop of Killaloe and the Liberator's *fidus Achates*, Tom Steele, the latter 'recognizing his friendly opponents as he passed on'. The procession took exactly an hour and a half to pass the *Journal* offices, and as it threaded through the streets, the windows and roofs of the houses were thronged with onlookers whose 'hearts, hands and voices appeared to echo in unison', their 'scarfs, hats and hand-kerchiefs . . . waved aloft' in tribute to O'Connell, who acknowledged the compliment with apparent 'surprise and gratitude'. From the open windows along the route garlands of flowers were thrown at the Liberator's carriage.

By now the procession had reached its most impressive proportions, the Ennis Trades in its vanguard standing out among their brethren from Limerick, Kilrush and other towns for colour of dress and the elaborateness and profusion of their banners. Preceded by nine war-pipers, their order of march began with the Labourers, 'a fine healthy set of men' who wore green scarves bound with red, their banners containing the mottoes, 'In God is our Trust', and 'Speed the Plough', waving high over them. Next came the Nailors, who wore crimson scarves, aprons of royal blue turned up with pink, ornamented with a heart in the centre of which was a hammer in hand in gold, with shamrocks at either side. Their banners bore the mottoes 'Trade Revived', 'United to Support but not Combined to Injure' and 'By Hammer and Hand All Art do Stand'. Following them were the Shoemakers and the Carpenters, the Painters, Sawyers, Slaters, Masons, Tailors, Smiths, Broguemakers and Bakers, each trade agleam in colourful costumes and bright banners. Last in line were the stolid Victuallers, who wore white scarves fringed with red and decked with rosettes, and held wands in their hands.

After the Trades came the Ennis Amateur Band with Mr William Shanks at the head, resplendent in blue silk scarf and white corded satin apron, bound with green silk, gold fringed and tasselled, bearing on it the square and compass in gold, along with harp and shamrock, and the words 'Ireland for the Irish'. Some distance behind rode Charles O'Connell, wearing a blue scarf, also with the motto 'Ireland for the Irish'. The town crier, John Corry, wore a costume of pink and green calico, the word 'Repeal' picked out in gold letters on his arm, and he carried in his hand a small banner on which was painted the words 'Repeal of the Union'. Well back in the procession was a carriage in which was placed a small printing press painted in the national colours, whose attendant flung Repeal squibs and ballads to the crowd as he ran them off, all to the accompaniment of an Irish Harper who sat in the front, playing national airs.

As the procession moved through the narrow streets on its journey towards the town racecourse, two miles to the north, the *Limerick Chronicle*'s special reporter counted 60 temperance bands and 150 banners, while another journalist estimated the number of horsemen present at 6,000. The noise was incredible, what with the bands and the continuous noise of marching feet and clattering vehicles, the shouts of apple-sellers, the excited screaming of children, and the cheers of onlookers on the footpaths, at the windows and on the roofs of the houses along the route.

At the racecourse, on the rising ground to the north, a great wooden platform had been erected to accommodate several hundred guests, including the Liberator and his party. From this vantage point the *Chronicle* reporter could see that by the time the earliest marchers reached the racecourse, O'Connell had not yet entered Ennis from the south, and on his arrival at the racecourse, the rear of the procession had not yet cleared the town. From the same spot a *Galway Vindicator* reporter witnessed 'interminable lines of human beings [spreading] across the country, rushing onwards in eager haste to witness the glorious sight and take part in the imposing demonstration'. As far as he could see, tents and marquees dotted the fields; jaunting cars and humbler vehicles lying scattered around in countless numbers, and thousands of respectable Tipperary, Limerick and Clare farmers on horseback weaving a path through them, many with their wives sitting awestruck in the saddle behind them.

From open flag-bedecked carriages scores of bands played the Liberator to the platform to the tune of 'See the Conquering Hero Comes', and as he climbed the carpeted stairs, 'the shouts rose to Heaven wild and solemn . . . and for minutes nothing could be heard but the hoarse murmur of the mighty multitude, which as they rolled on, reverberated in thunder on every side'. Such was the tumult that it was four o'clock before the chairman of the meeting, Cornelius O'Brien, M.P., could begin proceedings.

O'Brien's role was to introduce a number of speakers who would warm up the crowd before the Liberator was ready to address them, heedless of the fact that their words were being taken down by Constable Crean of the Ennis Barracks, who had been instructed to record all speeches for evidence of seditious utterance. Only one of the speakers, Fr. John Sheehan, came close to obliging the constable in the resolution which he proposed. Sheehan spoke with passion, mixing references to biblical retribution, military images from the Napoleonic campaigns and rhetorical reminders to England of Ireland's military prowess at battles such as Arcola, Cremona and Fontenoy. In true O'Connellite style, however, his warlike tone was abruptly reversed in concluding remarks, which denied that a 'single disposition to war existed in the minds of the people', who 'reprobated the idea of violence or bloodshed'. None of the other resolutions that followed was as lengthy or as passionately delivered, and after they had been seconded and passed, with perfect timing and a vigour that belied his sixty-eight years, O'Connell stepped forward, to be greeted by 'loud and continued acclamation'. 'Men of Clare', he began dramatically, 'I have news for you, the Repeal is coming – we are on the very verge of carrying the Repeal – it cannot be longer postponed. Clare has spoken and Ireland shall once again be free. The voice of Clare is now gone forth again on the wild winds of Heaven, and the strength of the storm and the force of the lightning belongs to that power that already proclaimed liberty to Ireland, and frightened Wellington of Waterloo and discomfited Peel of the spinning jennies'.

Expertly playing his audience, O'Connell spoke of the 'glory of Clare', which in the Emancipation struggle had been 'transcendant beyond any other county in Ireland'; Clare had 'shouted before that Ireland should be free, and Ireland threw off the shackles of religious intolerance and trampled underfoot the hated Protestant Ascendancy'. Next he drew attention to his own blood connections with the county through a collateral ancestor, Brigadier Maurice O'Connell, who had died heroically at Aughrim in 1691, and whose body slept in its tomb at Inagh. The spirit which animated the patriotic brigadier, the Liberator told the crowd, was still alive and strong, and just as he had prophesied that Emancipation would be achieved, he now pledged that they should have Repeal.

Then came the classic O'Connell about-face: in the last fortnight he had met over two million of his countrymen, who, despite their overwhelmingly martial appearance and potential, would never be used to attack others. Neither would they be attacked; and one great reason why he was leading out the physical force and power of Ireland was 'to demonstrate the folly of any maniac, any lunatic keeper, that would think of attacking so brave, so virtuous, so peaceable, and so loyal a people'. The Liberator then spoke of the role played by Irish regiments in the Peninsular War and at Waterloo, where he held, Wellington's glory was 'purchased by Irish blood'. After this came references to contemporary griev-ances: excessive grand jury cess, tithes, Poor Law rates and other burdensome impositions; finally, after exhortations to support Repeal, the Liberator concluded in a moving evocation of the beauties of Ireland's pastoral landscape.

It was a crafted, complex, and finely balanced speech, with multiple levels of appeal and meaning. Delivered with all the power of O'Connell's great voice and physical presence, its impact was felt far beyond the front rows of listeners, the only parties present who could make out his words clearly. The speech was, of course, designed to take account of these acoustic limitations, and the targeted audience of the platform party, the journalists and the foremost ranks of the crowd was more than sufficient for O'Connell's requirements. For the rest, the racecourse multitudes had to content themselves with a general intuition of what had been said; for them the sense of occasion and spectacle associated with procession and rally was a sufficient recompense for the trouble they had gone to in order to be present.

Once the Liberator had finished, it was important that a sudden deflation of sentiment should not occur, and the remaining speakers had been chosen for their oratorical punch. Next in line was Tom Steele, the affectionately nicknamed Head Pacificator, who with the Liberator's encouragement stoked the crowd's mirth with derogatory references to Peel and Wellington, whom he spoke of as 'jackeens' and 'murdering vagabonds'. Steele was followed by the forthright parish priest of O'Callaghan's Mills, Fr. Quade, who ended his speech by reading the text of a Repeal petition to be forwarded to Queen Victoria. After Fr. Quade stepped back, the chairman wound up the meeting, and O'Connell left the platform for his carriage and the journey back to Ennis, amidst the tens of thousands now streaming towards their homes.

For the homeward-bound legions, many with long journeys ahead of them, the anti-climax of the meeting's conclusion was balanced by memories of that incredible day and the stories that would later be constructed from it. For the platform party, on the other hand, the last part of the programme was about to begin; the Repeal banquet in the old town chapel. Upwards of 450 attended the banquet, for which the chapel walls were decked with flowers, laurels and other evergreens, interspersed as liberally with flags, mottoes and devices as the streets had been earlier. A decorative canopy, tastefully draped in green, crimson and white silk, had been erected over the places to be occupied by the main guests, and in keeping with O'Connell's ostentatious loyalism, paintings of Queen Victoria and Prince Albert flanked the top table, firmly counterbalanced, however, by Irish national emblems. Below the main gallery, a large representation of a harp, with appropriate inscription, was placed, the gallery itself being occupied by fashionably dressed ladies excluded by protocol from the floor. The assembled company glittered under the illumination of numerous chandeliers.

The principal guests were seated according to precedence, the Liberator and certain distinguished invitees occupying places to the right of the chairman, Cornelius O'Brien; to his left sat the Right Rev. Dr. Kennedy, Bishop of Killaloe, and other notables. Four Members of Parliament were present and eight Justices of the Peace, and, lastly, two mysterious moustachioed Frenchmen, strangers to the company who had attracted curiosity at the racecourse, and who did not seem to understand English. After the meal was over and grace said, the secretaries read out letters of apology from certain important invitees who were unable to attend. This was followed by a number of toasts, which between proposal and formal response took up the bulk of the evening. Each toast was punctuated by appropriate musical accompaniment from the Ennis Temperance Band playing from the side gallery.

Thus Charles O'Connell answered the chairman's toast of 'The People' with some remarks on the virtues of his universally celebrated kinsman, the Liberator, while the veteran Emancipationist priest, Fr. Sheehy, responded to the toast, 'Ireland for the Irish and the Irish for Ireland', with pertinent observations on the aspirations of the Repeal movement. The Liberator answered the next toast, 'O'Connell and the Speedy Repeal of the Union'. Beginning by expressing pride in the people of Clare and the 'transcendant spectacle' of the earlier racecourse meeting, he went on to liken the progress of the Repeal project to 'a mighty avalanche in the Alps . . . carrying away every matter of resistance . . . so over-whelming and resistless that it alters the face of nature, destroys the blooming and fertile villages and makes one gigantic convulsion of all'. 'Such is the progress of our cause,' he told the assembly, immediately reversing its thrust by adding, 'but such will not be its results'. Dwelling for a moment on the panic created in London by the Repeal agitation, he went on to speak dismissively of the paltry gestures of conciliation currently under consideration by London, before finish-ing to prolonged applause and cheering.

The next toast, 'The Right Rev. Dr. Kennedy and the Catholic Clergy and Hierarchy of Ireland', was answered by the bishop in a short speech that differed markedly from the Liberator's, and indeed from all others given in the course of the day. Devoid of any imagery, military or otherwise, it consisted almost entirely of a stark depiction of the 'wretched' condition of Clare, whose 'moral, industri-ous and unoffending people', long deprived of the 'protection and fostering care' of an Irish parliament, were being 'cruelly used' by their persecutors, certain unnamed landlords and 'landsharks'. These tormentors were currently engaged in a campaign of mass evictions, or 'exterminations', in certain parts of the county, which had already stretched the endurance of the people to breaking point. But for the efforts of the clergy, the bishop held, the evictions would already have led to a recurrence of the Terry Alt troubles of 1829–1831, when even 'humane and charitable' landowners were forced to flee from the 'indiscriminating vengeance of an oppressed, a starving and a maddened populace'.

Despite the cheers that greeted Bishop Kennedy's speech his intrusion of the grim realities of everyday life outside the banquet hall cast a shadow over what up to now had been a convivial gathering, and the reaction to the next set of toasts was muted. Good cheer was restored, however, when a toast to Tom Steele elicited the expected fiery outburst from the Head Pacificator, and a further set of ferocious epithets denouncing Wellington ('the sanguinary demoniac murdering villain') and Peel ('the bloody little ruffian'). Formal proceedings ended with toasts to 'Sir Colman O'Loghlen and the Repealers of the Irish Bar', 'The Press', 'The Stewards' and 'The Ladies'. Some time after midnight O'Connell and his principal guests retired from the old chapel, leaving the festivities to continue for some hours more under the chairmanship of Hewitt Bridgman, the M.P. for Ennis.

In the aftermath of the Ennis monster meeting, town residents returned to the tedium of everyday life, pondering the meaning of the Repeal whirlwind that had stormed through their county and briefly placed its little capital at the heart of a great national movement. In these discussions the size of the attendance inevitably figured, Repealers claiming an attendance of between 400,000 and 500,000, their opponents conceding one of 150,000 to 200,000. The Repeal press was naturally ecstatic, and the Tory prints as predictably condemnatory of the event. The anti-Repeal *Limerick Chronicle* editorialized sternly that 'the boastful menace of physical force was never more pointed, and especially in the addresses of a Roman Catholic Priest and his Bishop'. The Ennis Tory, John B. Knox, editor of the *Clare Journal*, was more measured, telling his readers merely that he found it distressing to see 'such misdirected enthusiasm and for so little purpose'.

The subsequent history of the Repeal movement would prove Knox correct in this supposition. His other prediction, that the Ennis meeting would soon be forgotten or 'remembered in sorrow and in anger', would prove more prescient still, but in a fashion that would have horrified him. For, within five years, tens of thousands of those who had gathered on the Ennis racecourse on that warm summer day in June would be dead of starvation or disease, or would lie half-starved in the desolate surroundings of the workhouse systems of several counties. Thousands of others would be imprisoned in the jails of these same counties or the Australian convict colony; further thousands again would suffer dreadfully in the greatest 'extermination' campaign ever undertaken by Irish landlords, unknown numbers of them dying of exposure in squalid roadside shelters or in 'scalpeens' in the bogs.

The urban poor would suffer equally with those in the countryside, and in light of what lay in store for them shortly, the proud bearing that day at Ennis of the Trades, whose colourful costumes concealed a desperate poverty, assumes a particularly affecting aspect. By 1848 Daniel O'Connell, the Liberator, would be dead, as would Tom Steele, his Head Pacificator. The great Repeal cause to which they had given such single-minded dedication would have vanished almost without trace. Those who still remembered O'Connell's rhapsodizing phrases at the Ennis banquet would surely have felt the sharpness of the irony by which his 'avalanche in the Alps' image, with its memorable impression of a force so overwhelming that it 'destroys the blooming and fertile villages and makes one gigantic convulsion of all', could now be more accurately applied to the nightmare of the Great Famine, which by that time held Clare, and Ireland as a whole, in its apocalyptic grip.

Monster Meeting at Tara, larger again than the Ennis Rally. *Illustrated London News.*

An Emerging People: The Pre-Famine Irish

We must always remember that these are but an emerging *people, civilising a little too rapidly to improve* equally *as they proceed.*

— *DIARY OF ELIZABETH SMITH, 12 JULY 1846*

In the mid-nineteenth century, Ireland was proverbial all over the western world for the extraordinary poverty of its people. 'Misery, naked and famishing,' remarked the French traveller Gustave de Beaumont in 1838, 'that misery which is vagrant, idle, and mendicant covers the entire country; it shows itself everywhere, and at every hour of the day; it is the first thing you see when you land on the Irish coast, and from that moment it ceases not to be present to your view.' According to the German travel writer Johannes Kohl in 1841, no mode of life anywhere else could seem pitiable to somebody who had witnessed the misery of Ireland. 'I see much here to remind me of my former condition,' wrote the recently escaped American slave, Frederick Douglass, deeply shocked by scenes he witnessed on his arrival in Cork in October 1845. So profound is the picture of deprivation painted by these and other writers, that had we no other sources for the period, they would be sufficient to establish that on the eve of the Great Famine, Ireland was a very poor country indeed.[1]

De Beaumont's sense of being overwhelmed by poverty from the moment of arrival on the quayside was the common experience of visitors, who, as they ventured further into the little and great streets of the city surrounding the port at which they had landed, became aware of the numbers of poorly dressed or ragged people, especially noticeable where fine buildings and the elegant clothing of the well-attired supplied a revealing contrast. The respectable as well as the unrespectable poor were represented in the public thoroughfares; unemployed labourers and craftsmen and their children, as well as beggars and other street people. Glimpses down side-streets revealed what appeared to be veritable swarms of the very poor.

Disabled beggars descend on mail coach in Irish town, early 1840s. Hall's *Ireland*.

Ireland's urban spaces were all like this, and in each of them the rumbling of the mail coach to a halt at the official stop provided the signal for beggars to descend on it in numbers, importuning the passengers as they alighted, and often following them for some distance along the streets. Huckster stalls were one of the most common sights glimpsed by these visitors as they shook off the beggars, and became aware of the aggressive salesmanship of vendors selling apples or cheap trinkets, ribbons and tawdry brass rings. Visitors would also have noticed the many cheap whiskey shops and illegal shebeens that proliferated everywhere despite the work of the temperance crusader, Fr. Theobald Mathew, reflecting the drunkenness that was the national vice and the concomitant of Ireland's desperate poverty.[2]

City and town misery served as a prelude to that of the countryside where over two-thirds of the population lived, and to which the visitor was introduced via the extended single-streeted suburbs that radiated out from every urban centre, the one-roomed cabins lining them growing ever more dilapidated before they petered out in rural landscape. One-roomed cabins abounded here also, either standing alone or clustered together in countless hamlets that dotted the landscape, and usually lying at the centre of a crosspatch of tiny cultivation plots. 'Imagine,' asked de Beaumont, creating a representative archetype, 'four walls of dried mud, which the rain as it falls, easily restores to its primitive condition; having for its roof a little straw or some sods, for its chimney a hole cut in the

Typical fourth-class house. Note the dungheap beside the gable. Hall's *Ireland*.

roof, or very frequently the door, through which alone the smoke finds an issue'. This 'wretched hovel', home to several generations of one family, had no furniture, apart from a single communal bed of straw or hay:

> Five or six half-naked children may be seen near a miserable fire, the ashes of which cover a few potatoes, the sole nourishment for the family. In the midst of it all lies a dirty pig, the only thriving inhabitant of the place, for he lies in filth. The presence of the pig in an Irish hovel may at first seem an indication of misery; on the contrary it is a sign of comparative comfort. Indigence is still more extreme in the hovel where no pig is to be found.

Real-life versions of de Beaumont's generic cabin were to be found in every corner of Ireland. Local contributors to the Poor Inquiry of 1835–1836 have left us with descriptions that vary in detail only, as in the two following examples from the widely separated counties of Tipperary and Cavan. In Tipperary, cabins were just ten feet wide, and between sixteen and twenty feet long; cabin furniture consisted of 'a rude bedstead, straw and a blanket or blankets for one bed which suffice for the whole family, an iron pot, a small table, a large box and two or three chairs with hay-rope bottoms'. In Cavan, cabins were of 'stone, mud walls or sods'; badly thatched, they were seldom glazed or plastered, the clay floor and walls 'for the greater part of winter, wet with rain falling through the roof'. The family slept 'on some dried rushes or straw thrown on the floor in the chimney-corner, as the warmest place in the house'. Stools were strategically placed 'to keep the bed from taking fire'; day clothes were thrown over them along with blankets.

More than any other aspect of everyday life, these poor dwellings exemplify the chronic poverty of pre-Famine Ireland, and, when combined with the appearance of the occupants, the neglected or unimproved state of agricultural land, and the down-at-heel appearance of the houses of the relatively well-off, many landowners' residences included, they complete an even larger panorama of rural misery. There were places in Ireland, to be sure, where prosperity was the rule rather than the exception and where the landscape displayed neat, whitewashed cottages and trim, tended fields. This was so over great stretches of the north-eastern counties, and in the fertile country of south-east Leinster. But even in these better-favoured locations there were pockets of intense deprivation, such as the Fews district of Armagh, for example, or at Taghmon, an island of desperate poverty set in the rich farmlands of County Wexford. Even in parts of County Down, 'the most thriving and best-conditioned quarter of Ireland,' according to one account, in 1845 there were many roadside dwellings that resembled 'abodes of extinguished hope, forgotten instincts, grovelling, despairing, almost idiotic wretchedness'.[3]

The senses of visitors were bombarded by so many images and impressions of poverty, and from so many angles at once, that they tended to perceive it as a single undifferentiated mass. That it was, in fact, a multilayered, highly structured entity was something that tended to escape casual observers, who frequently failed to notice its many anomalies and deceptions. Only the more perceptive realized that poor clothing, weed-grown thatch and dunghill-dominated farm-yards were often deliberately designed to deflect the attention of landlord or agent from any indication of material progress, however slight, that might lead to a crippling increase in rent.[4]

Contemporary statistics, likewise, delineate the complexities of pre-Famine poverty in an approximate fashion only. The one-roomed cabins we have been describing belonged to the category of 'fourth-class house', one devised by the 1841 Census Commissioners to describe the meanest sort of dwelling. Fifty-one per cent of houses enumerated were of this kind, and in especially deprived areas the figure rose as high as ninety per cent. In such dwellings more than three million of the poorest sections of Irish society lived, about two-fifths of the total of almost 8.2 million recorded by the census.

But a great many poor persons, hundreds of thousands of them, lived in 'third-class' houses that were only a little better in quality; some fourth-class houses were much better appointed than others, and there were many elements in Irish society who do not appear to have lived in dwellings that could be formally

Beggars. Hall's *Ireland*.

classified at all. Largely undetectable to the historian because they existed below the radar of written documentation, such elements included the urban underclass of beggars, petty offenders and prostitutes who lived on the streets, and in the countryside, itinerant dealers, the intractable boccoughs (Irish: *bacach*, lame person) or roving vagabonds, and others who like them avoided official notice if they could. Probably the most elusive group of all were the beachcombers of the western seaboard counties, who lived almost solely through gathering seaweed and selling it inland to farmers as fertiliser. At the beginning of the Famine, in County Clare, so many of these shy, reclusive people were concentrated in coastal districts that their exclusion from the census was believed to have led to a serious population underestimate in 1841.[5]

At any rate, the fourth-class house, in all its gradations, was the abode of the lowest order of landholders, the cottiers and labourers who formed the pyramidal base of rural society. About 300,000 individual cottier households existed on the eve of the Famine, and something over twice that number of labourer households. Cottiers were in effect bound labourers, who cultivated tiny holdings whose average size was about five acres, and who lived in a formal landlord-tenant relationship with those from whom they rented their land, whether this was an actual landlord, a middleman or a large farmer.[6] Part of their arrangement entailed working for the 'landlord' for set wages, which were offset usually against rent for their plots; limited access was also given to turf-bogs and/or commonage. Without the protection of leases, cottiers lived largely at the whim of those to whom they paid rent.

The position of the unbound or 'landless' labourers was even more precarious, in that they had no tenure rights at all to the cultivation plots on which they subsisted. These minute plots – average size of just one acre – were rented ready-prepared and manured for the reception of potato seed, and only for the growing season. Known by many different names in different counties, this notorious system was everywhere recognized under the term 'conacre'. For the labourer, as for the cottier, rent for conacre plots was usually delivered in wage labour, and a pig reared during the year took care of any further expenses that might arise over the growing period. The importance of the pig to the domestic economy of cottiers and labourers is reflected in the fact that it was reared indoors with the family, and it is for this reason that it features so prominently in the accounts of travellers and travel writers.

Above labourer and cottier levels was a stratum of about 250,000 tenants who rented small holdings (average twenty acres) from landlords or middle-men. These were rent-payers rather than labour-providers, and among them family members attended to agricultural tasks, without hired assistance. When circumstances made it necessary, they might labour for farmers or rent out some conacre land. Above them again was a group of about 150,000 well-off farmers, men whose average size of holding varied between fifty and eighty acres, entitling them to the designation 'snug', 'rich', or 'large'. But there was a wide divergence as to what constituted a snug, rich, large or comfortable farmer, and the Devon Commission, which investigated the Irish system of land tenure just before the Famine, heard many witnesses employ the terms to describe 'occupiers of twenty, thirty or forty acres'. In the coastal districts of Mayo, in 1846, the occupier of three acres was generally known as 'comfortable'.[7]

The system of land occupancy was a highly evolved one, of a complexity such that one individual might at the same time be a smallholding tenant, a wage labourer and a conacre man, and it was not uncommon for a tenant with a paltry twenty acres to rent out some of his land to cottiers. The system was sustainable only because of the fertility of the potato and its remarkable dietary qualities. No other crop has such a high yield that it can afford sustenance to an entire family on such a small area of ground, and it is, in addition, virtually the only food that can be eaten exclusively all year round without leading to serious nutritional deficiency.[8] A potato-rich diet meant that the Irish poor enjoyed rude good health, and visitors from abroad often compared their good skin tone, strong dentition and well-developed physique with the pallid, listless, appearance of the rural and urban proletariat of their own countries. There is also evidence that the Irish poor were taller in stature and lived longer than those of other western European countries, and a wealth of contemporary anecdotal commentary on the Irish indicates admiration for their general good looks.

The extent of dependence on the potato is impossible to gauge precisely, and there were wide geographical variations as to the availability of supplements such as oatmeal or fish. But we do know that by 1845, the majority of smallholders and those below them had become exclusive potato-growers and eaters, no longer being able to afford to devote even part of their tillage ground to alternatives such as beans or oats. On the eve of the Famine, just short of three million people were completely dependent for subsistence on the potato, with a further several million heavily dependent on the plant. At higher societal levels, potatoes were central to the dietary regime of large farmers and other well-off groups to whom other foods were readily available; potatoes featured prominently even on the relatively more sophisticated tables of landlords.[9] As much as one-third of the entire tillage acreage in Ireland was given over to potatoes, and the signs of potato cultivation were evident in virtually every part of the country.[10] Travelling across country it was easy to read the agricultural calendar by the changing colours visible at ground level, from the brown or red of newly planted fields, to the heavy green of maturing potato fields, and the progressive yellowing that bespoke plants ready for harvest.

In the decades leading up to 1845, access to land, and land for potato-growing in particular, was becoming ever-more difficult, and those at the lower levels of society were increasingly desperate to obtain it. As early as 1833, one Mayo land agent described the hunger for land as 'incredible', stating that 'there is no rent you ask that will not be promised'. In 1844 numbers of witnesses before the Devon Commission spoke of the common practice whereby vacant holdings were auctioned off to the highest bidder. Accepted bids were often far greater than the bidders could possibly pay; and they did so out of the desperate calculation that once possession was achieved, it would be less bothersome for the landlord to negotiate on the rent rather than initiate eviction proceedings.

At the lower levels of society, the practice of subdividing holdings was one of the most chronic problems of land occupancy. Portions of a holding might be sublet in order to supplement income by renting out conacre, or the holding itself divided to provide for children. Subdivision and subletting had been even worse in previous decades when landlords had connived at the practice in order to create extra vote-carrying freeholds, or when middlemen converted leased farms into a great number of minute holdings, which yielded a hugely profitable rental, uncaring of the damage done to the land in the process. In 1845 Irish rents in general were extremely high relative to the value of the land, much more so proportionately with regard to smaller holdings.

Changing circumstances, however, both electoral and economic, removed the advantage of smallholding tenants, and from the 1830s the tendency was increasingly to hold for pasture land previously set out in smallholdings and conacre, thereby driving up rents and aggravating the problems of smallholders and conacre men. This reverse process reflected the conversion of many landlords to managerial virtue in the practice known generally as consolidation. Realizing the economic benefit of ending subdivision and subletting, such landlords henceforth sought to increase the size of holdings by removing a proportion of the tenants and redistributing the land among the others, 'squaring' the enlarged holdings in neat contiguous units. A major concern of consolidators was the elimination of the ancient Rundale system of collective tenancies, which was very prevalent in the marginal lands of the west.[11] For those landlords and agents involved in its suppression, the ending of Rundale was pursued with almost religious zeal.

Another consolidator priority was the recovery of middleman farms held on long leases, some of them made more than sixty years previously. A great number of these leases expired in the decade before 1845, which gave the consolidators the opportunity of eliminating the smallholder or cottier 'warrens' left by the middlemen, either by 'voluntary' surrender, eviction, or, in a small number of cases, by subsidised emigration. Under this pressure, the middleman system suffered a rapid decline that eventually became irreversible, although it was still a major feature of Irish landholding right up to the Famine.

Such were the contradictions of Irish rural life that in the same area, subdivision and subletting might be still taking place on some estates while systematic consolidation was occurring on others. At the same time, the creeping shift from tillage to pasture meant that across the countryside, the cultivation rectangles of cottiers, labourers and smallholders were increasingly juxtaposed with the untrammelled grass of stock farms. And as potato ground became ever scarcer, land previously considered marginal came into production for this kind of potato production. Rocky terrain, upland, mountain scrub and cutaway bog were, in any case, much more easily adaptable to the spade cultivation of the growers than to the plough or to grazing. Potato ridges could be built with ease around rocks and other protrusions, on steep slopes and on uneven ground, and where this was done, a striking visual neatness was achieved.

In the years before 1845 the regular patterns of potato plots climbed ever further up mountain slopes and across bogs, their patchwork greenery an agreeable sight to the distant eye as the growing season advanced. Cottiers and conacre men were often accused of being lazy and slovenly; but this was methodical, exacting work, often carried out after a hard day's wage labour. It was rewarding too, and brought out in the cultivators a kind of creativity for which they had few other outlets. Potato growers observed their own rituals in preparing and maintaining their ridges; they used special long spades known as loys and took an aesthetic satisfaction in the shape and strength of their ridges, enjoying each stage in the growth of stalks up to the point when the stalk tips broke into delicate blossoms that lasted a matter of days, their fall signalling the approach of the time for lifting.

Pre-Famine rural streetscape. Hall's *Ireland*.

Issues such as access to conacre and tillage land, rents, consolidation and eviction all tended to bring the lower orders into conflict with the landlords, middlemen and wealthier farmers, whose influence was felt in these aspects of rural life. There were in all about 10,000 landlords, whose ancestors had been the beneficiaries of the seventeenth-century confiscations that had transferred nearly the entire land-stock of Ireland from Irish Catholic to British Protestant hands and left only a fraction in the hands of the original owners. By the mid-nineteenth century descendants of the original grantees still enjoyed an almost exclusive possession of the country's land, and all others occupying land were their tenants or subtenants.

A great gulf divided the fifty or so wealthiest landlords, mostly titled English absentees, from those with more modest properties, the average being about two thousand acres. Landlords who were comparatively far down on the scale found themselves obliged to supplement their rental income from other sources in order to sustain a style of living that would not otherwise have been possible. A great number were also large-scale occupiers of land leased from their wealthier peers, and to them also went the spoils of county government, with its many opportunities for contract graft. Others had mercantile interests, others again were in the professions, or held public office. These financial expedients reflect a generally poor level of estate management, the tendency to squander capital badly needed for investment, and the encumbering of properties with expensive family settlements. Landlord indebtedness was the rule rather than the exception and many estates, especially the smaller ones, operated close to bankruptcy. On the eve of the Famine, indeed, a great number of properties had already been taken over by the exchequer or chancery courts.[12]

Because of the complexities of Irish land tenure and the enormous divergences in the circumstances of persons so described, middlemen are notoriously difficult to distinguish as a group. The most successful middlemen, indeed, followed lifestyles that were identical to landlords, and, like them, lived in large houses set in walled demesnes, and were accorded gentlemanly status within society. The greatest attributed sin of the middleman was the crowding of farms with subtenants, and the consequent wrecking of the agricultural value of the land, all of which made them easy to stigmatize as villains. Antipathy to middlemen amounted to a moral value on the part of the consolidating landlord – who in some guise might himself be considered one – which allowed him to displace culpability for brutal treatment of the subtenants, now dehumanised by the label of 'squatter'. It was, after all, the middleman who had created the squatter problem in the first place, and his, therefore, was the odium when the landlord evicted them.

At the best of times neither landlords, middlemen nor large farmers were beloved of those who paid rent to them; on particular issues and occasions, a murderous hatred might exist between them. But the real rift in Irish rural society, one that was longstanding and all-pervading, was that between landlords and tenants of all grades and classes. 'You cannot imagine the hatred that exists between the landlords and the people', the Kilkenny lawyer J.P. Prendergast commented to Alexis de Tocqueville in 1835, agreeing with him that if Britain's protection were removed from the former, 'violent revolution' would instantly take place. Few commentators were as blunt as Prendergast, whose views were informed by an unrivalled understanding of landlordism – he was later to achieve fame as the historian of its Cromwellian antecedents – but few would have disputed his claims either. The Devon Commission, whose members were all landlords, did not address the question directly, but the landlord–tenant dichotomy was, of course, implicit to the entire exercise.

Popular hostility towards landlords derived from long experience of the behaviour and attitudes of an oppressive élite that was alien in ethnicity, language, and religion, and was greatly exacerbated by current issues of rent, access to land, consolidation of farms, and the ejectment of smallholders and 'squatters'. Landlord attitudes towards the people derived from assumptions of social, ethnic and religious superiority; generally despising those among whom they lived, even those they favoured were seen as wilful children, to be indulged on occasion, certainly, but to be ruled ultimately by dominance. But landlords feared their tenants also, and almost a half-century after the bloody national uprising of 1798, which had pitted landlords against their tenants, the cloud of fear and suspicion of the Catholic masses it had engendered had not dissipated. Violent acts of resistance to landlord actions were seen as part of a pattern of untrustworthiness and treachery dating to 1798, particularly in those localized troubles that occurred from the 1820s onwards.

By 1845 little substance was left of the solidarity some historians have seen as linking landlord and community in a nexus of mutual respect and co-operation in the late eighteenth century. Some traces remained, to be sure, and in local sporting occasions, estate improvement projects, church-building schemes, electoral contests and political 'interest', landlords still exerted considerable public power, but apart from those districts of the north-east where landlords and tenants shared a common Protestantism, political allegiance and customary agreement on tenants' rights, these were largely superficial points of contact. And, finally, the emergence of a dynamic middle-class Catholic nationalist leadership meant that the 'country people' (the term 'peasant' was not in general use) were steadily drifting away from landlord control. The emergence of the cold, dispassionate principles of estate consolidation, with its absence of human feeling for those affected by it, must be seen as marking the end of any emotional engagement between landlords and those who paid them rent.[13]

For their part, tenants had at their disposal a set of tradition-sanctioned modes of proceeding against the perpetrators of oppression or injustice. These operated mainly through the agency of what were known as the secret societies. Where injustice was widespread enough, or where it was compounded by more general economic grievances, the troubles might spread beyond the local scene into broader, regionally based movements sustained over periods of years. Agrarian 'outrages' associated with very distinct groups and movements in widely separated parts of the country shared the common ground of anonymous violent action that terrorised their targets, and made it difficult for the authorities to apprehend them. Colourful names hid a very deadly intent, and the Carders, Rockites, Terry Alts, Lady Clares and other groups owed their success to general community support and fear of their actions among potential offenders, who might equally be a smallholder or a landlord.

Authorities and the public knew all this activity under the name of Whiteboyism, after the movement that had convulsed the southern counties of Munster and Leinster during the 1760s and afterwards, and established many of the classic methods of secret agrarian organizations in the nineteenth century. So-called after the white sheets or smocks worn by participants (partly for ritual purposes, partly for disguise), the Whiteboys had formed a loosely organized movement reacting against a variety of grievances, including tithes, enclosure of common land, high rents and local taxes. So widespread did Whiteboy activity eventually become and so threatening to civil order that the Irish Parliament resorted to enacting a series of extremely severe measures known as the Whiteboy Acts in order to suppress them.[14]

Latter-day Whiteboys observed similar quasi-legal procedures to their eighteenth century predecessors; 'tried' their intended targets in secret night-time meetings, and carried out sentences imposed by these 'courts'. Usually the victims had been warned previously by letter or posted notice to desist from whatever activity was deemed malfeasant, and this was usually sufficient of itself to ensure compliance. Their motivating grievances were similar to those faced by their late eighteenth century predecessors, with the addition of such offences as refusal to let conacre, the carrying out of clearances and most common of all, the renting of a smallholding from which the previous occupier had been evicted. In case of non-compliance with their demands, activists were prepared to burn down farm buildings, assault houses, dig up pasture, and maim cattle.

Individuals were physically assaulted, fired upon and, as an ultimate sanction, assassinated.

Such acts were done by night, the participants dressed in white sheets, or women's capacious dresses; combined with the blackening of faces such outlandish costumes achieved anonymity and bred maximum levels of fear. Where assassination was decreed by the 'midnight legislators', it was often carried out by individuals hired from outside the community who could carry out the task efficiently and depart, leaving authorities with no leads. Despite the violence of the Whiteboys, in no sense did they constitute a sort of Irish rural mafia; outbreaks disappeared with the abatement of immediate grievance, and in the meantime the threat of retribution did much to restrain the behaviour of the predatory, whether middlemen, large farmers, landgrabbers, or the plague of rural Ireland, the gombeen man, or parish moneylender.

Constabulary and civil authorities tended to exaggerate Whiteboy violence in order to justify their own actions in suppressing them, and statistical returns inflated the level of 'outrage'. Certain counties were assigned particularly fearsome reputations, and in the pre-Famine years, Tipperary was presented as being the most disorderly and dangerous place in Ireland. There is no doubt that a number of particularly violent incidents did occur in Tipperary in the decades before 1845, but if one examines the outrage tables, it emerges that the county's dominant position in them was in no small measure due to the particular incidence there of two of the most common offences, the minor, non-violent categories of posting threatening notices and administering unlawful oaths.[15]

To what extent, therefore, was pre-Famine Ireland a violent, dangerous place, and to what extent were the prosperous classes living, as they often perceived themselves to be, on the back of an unpredictable beast? Certainly, anyone resident in a region convulsed by an agrarian outbreak, such as the Rockite uprising of the early 1820s, the Terry Alt commotions at the end of the decade, or the Tithe War of the 1830s, would have been justified in feeling constant apprehension for their personal safety; the same is true of anyone caught up in one of the more localized disputes over rents or evictions. However, that said, all but a tiny fraction of the violence of rural Ireland was related to agrarian issues and the appalling pressures bearing on the lives of those at the lowest levels of society. Away from disturbed districts, or in districts where outbreaks had just ended, the level of violence was low, and recent research has shown that the homicide rate in general was not markedly different in Ireland from any other western European country. And even in disturbed times and districts, strangers were greeted with warmth, and afforded hospitality rather than suspicion, while women of all classes were able to travel the country at all hours of the day or night without fear. It is surely significant that not one of the literary travellers and writers who passed through Ireland in the decade and a half preceding the Famine period reported feeling personally threatened or their lives endangered.

The one form of popular violence likely to be encountered by visitors took place on social occasions, especially where strong drink was available. Affrays might occur at fairs, markets, 'patterns' (assemblies at holy wells and the shrines of various saints) or 'goals' (hurling matches), or indeed wherever people gathered in large numbers.[16] It also occurred as part of the culture of faction-fighting at fairs and other occasions, between opposing groups with names such as Caravats and Shanavests, Reaskawallaghs and Coffeys, Cooleens and Black Mulvihills, Wrenboys, Bogboys and Tobbers. Here, however, much of the group violence was ritualized, featuring clearly understood rules of engagement, such as where one faction leader trailed his coat before the opposing group, inviting them to step on it so as to provide a pretext for commencement. In these conflicts particular specifications were insisted upon for the sticks used for weapons, which were classified precisely as either 'cleahalpeens', 'shillelaghs' or 'wattles'. To a great extent, faction-fighting was spectacle as much as altercation, and it is not surprising, therefore, that travel writers, particularly, were attracted by this kind of colour, and anxious to include a fight in their various narratives.

Among the people, social activities were bracketed within the agricultural calendar, which alternated between periods of intensive labour at planting, harvest and other points, and periods of relative leisure. On Sundays and Church holy days no labour was done (this was why political meetings were scheduled for these days, notably Daniel O'Connell's Repeal rallies). Winter presented the longest period of relative idleness, and its long dark months provided fertile soil for the maintenance and transmission of Ireland's unique culture, its ancient linguistic and literary traditions and its heritage of music and dance. The linguistic/literary/oral tradition was substantially an illiterate one, yet it was one that held learning in awe, and was propagated in nightly 'cuaird' sessions, when neighbours gathered in each other's houses to trace genealogies, recreate old mythologies, recite or sing works by living or long-dead poets, and to exchange and embroider news. The census of 1841 is reckoned to have been skewed to a certain extent by reason of the fact that it was taken on a Sunday night in June, in the course of which a great proportion of the population was engaged in these 'visitings'. Tradition was richest in Irish-speaking districts, informing, therefore, the consciousness of well over three million persons in the early 1840s, aside altogether from English-speaking areas still influenced by the language.[17]

In Irish-speaking areas, or those where the language was declining, elements of a venerable scribal tradition survived, now maintained by isolated networks of teachers, tradesmen and day labourers, who often found themselves transcribing material they did not fully understand. One indication of their commitment to their task is found in the colophon written on a collection of folk-tales transcribed by one Micheál Ó Raghallaigh in Ennistymon, County Clare, and finished as the district was being ravaged by starvation late in 1846. Apologizing to the reader for the flaws in his manuscript, Ó Raghallaigh excuses himself on the grounds that 'is cearduidhe mé agus am aimsir díobhuinn do sgríobh mé an saothar so.' [I am a tradesmen, and it was in my free time that I wrote this work.] The same year, a copyist in Ballynoe, east Cork, included a message to a local patron on his completed manuscript apologizing for its defects: 'Gaibh leathsgeal na locht do cidhfir annso am dhíaig da bhrigh gur tré bhuaireamh aígne, agus ríachtanas an tsaoghuilsi mé féin agus mo mhuirrear air easba bídh agus eadaig do scriobhas an beagan seo.' [Please excuse the errors you see in what follows,

Barefoot Irish dancers performing to flute music. Hall's *Ireland*.

because it is on account of mental distress and the necessities of life that I have
written this little amount.]

Irish forms of music and dance, highly distinctive as they were, informed
social occasions and activities: weddings, wakes – a great source of fascination
for visitors – patterns and sporting events, performances taking place also
during house-based occasions; in public house entertainments, or in the street
or green during fairs and markets. Such was the passion for dancing that it was
common for passersby to pair off spontaneously in various figures at crossroads
where people encountered each other on summer evenings. Wherever dancing
took place, observers were struck by the manner in which music and dance
together seemed to meld into a single creative expression, integrated by the rapt
participation of musicians, dancers and audience. One visitor, J. Stirling Coyne,
who was immensely taken with Irish dancing and music, quoted with enthusiasm William Carleton's dictum that dancing was 'little else than a happy and
agreeable method of enjoying music', and that its 'whole spirit must necessarily
depend upon the power of the heart to feel the melody to which the limbs and
body move'.[18]

In this self-contained cultural world, a set of beliefs that predated Christianity
still held sway among the people. Its core comprised the world of the Good
People, or fairies, a diminutive but lordly race, who resided within the pre-
historic ringforts that dotted the landscape, supernatural beings who in their
way were as capricious as landlords, and had to be placated by stratagems that
were not dissimilar. Belief in this alternative world derived from the ancient
European folk tradition; its very Irish manifestation was found in all parts of the
country. Flourishing in the face of clerical opposition and the tolerant dismissal
of young Catholic professional scholar-literati such as John O'Donovan and
Eugene O'Curry, these beliefs may well have had a role in managing the nagging,
constant anxieties of everyday life and maintaining what outsiders saw as the
feckless and fatalistic cheerfulness of a people who, in reality, had no other choice
but to live as they did.

Without any sense of contradiction, the people balanced belief in fairy magic
with the official magic of the Church, whose message they imbibed with devotion
in packed churches on Sundays and holy days, from a clergy whose members
were treated with the greatest deference and respect. The massive population
increases of recent decades was reflected in hundreds of newly-built churches,
large barn-like buildings featuring wide transepts and shaky wooden galleries,
the standing congregations in the naves jammed into spaces without pews or
any consideration of safety. For the most part, the poor lived their lives entirely
within the bounds of the Catholic parish community, or in the sub-parish defined

by one of its churches, the great world beyond being an unknown, intimidating quantity that impinged on them only at intervals.

No matter what the depth of their poverty, these were far from being a degraded people. Cabin interiors, damp and miserable and shared with animals and poultry though they might be, were kept as clean as possible; personal cleanliness was a particular preoccupation with the poor. A strict code of morality prevailed, and all commentators who remarked on the subject reported that female chastity was extraordinarily cherished.[19] In the tiny one-roomed households, family modesty was preserved in orderly sleeping arrangements known in parts of the country as 'sleeping in stradogue', whereby the female children slept side by side by the wall farthest away from the entrance, followed by the mother and father, and then the male children and visitors being accommodated immediately inside the door.[20]

In the context of the poverty and harshness of the lives they led, the ease of the people with themselves, in the intertwining of family and community, is striking. In a countryside that teemed with people in a manner that it is difficult to conceive of in today's empty landscape, these things were expressed in a host of ways: in a universal welcome for children and in uninhibited displays of feeling between adults of both genders; in the abandon of social occasions; in the embrace of placatory superstitious acts and even in the overindulgence in alcohol.

It was these aspects of life precisely that elicited the contempt of landlords and the stern disapproval of evangelically minded Protestants who wished to bring the people to more industrious, sober ways. On the other hand, it was these aspects that made Irish life so interesting, and caused visitors of such very different backgrounds as Henry Inglis, Anna and Samuel Hall, Asenath Nicholson and William Thackeray to fall in love with the country and its people. It was these things also that fascinated the armchair travellers of the British reading public who read travel literature on Ireland with such avidity. The grandeur of Ireland's scenery, alternating with vignettes of its astonishing poverty and the quaint ways of its people, were an endless source of fascination. Or rather, these things were a source of fascination up to the point when emigration threatened to visit Ireland's poverty and backwardness on the other island.

From the second decade of the nineteenth century, the rising Irish population had been a source of growing concern to Britain. The census of 1841 with its revelation that the Irish population was now slightly over half that of England and Wales, and close enough to one third of the United Kingdom as a whole, was startling indeed. Serious inadequacies in the census, in fact, may mean that the

Irish population was even larger, and by 1845 not far short of the nine million insisted on by Daniel O'Connell and his supporters during their great campaign for repeal of the Union with Britain in the early 1840s. For O'Connell, the rising population was a positive sign, a source of strength and a symbol of pride for the nation his oratory consciously willed into being. In speeches delivered at the 'monster' rallies of the campaign, he reiterated the figure again and again, his statistical extrapolation no doubt causing the civil authorities on occasion as many sleepless nights as did his political agitation.

Even more alarming was the fact that Ireland seemed to be exporting its poor to Britain in escalating numbers, a scare that had begun decades earlier in 1829, when Thomas Malthus warned a British parliamentary committee that unless something were done the Irish 'must shortly fill up every vacuum created in England or Scotland, and to reduce the labouring classes to a uniform state of degradation.'[21] By 1841, the prediction seemed to have been realized, since the English census of that year recorded over 400,000 Irish-born residents in English cities, exclusive of the tens of thousands who were of Irish parentage. Northern cities, such as Liverpool and Manchester, had particularly high Irish populations, amounting to between one-fifth and one-third of the working population there.

In fact, worries about Irish population and the Irish emigration to Britain were largely misplaced, and those perusing the census returns should have been comforted by the fact that they also furnished clear evidence that the rate of increase of the Irish population was slowing rapidly, just 5.6% over the 1831 figures, a rather modest increase compared with the hefty English and Welsh rise of 13.4% over the same period.[22] There was little recognition either of the fact that the British poor did not seem at all demoralized by the Irish influx, or that assimilation of earlier Irish immigrants into the larger British population, while fraught with difficulties, was already taking place.

A great many other misconceptions about Ireland were current in Britain, where little or no understanding existed of the profound changes that the country was currently undergoing. Ireland's economy, for example, believed by many writers and political economists to be a mere subsistence one, was in fact a complex blend of the barter system of the labourer, cottier and smallholder levels, and a modern commercial and financial economy that intersected with it at many points, most noticeably in the spanking new business and bank premises that were beginning to appear on the main streets of the large towns. Ireland's economy was also increasingly becoming integrated with that of Britain, not just in regard to the corn and livestock exports that fed two million of Britain's population, but in the textiles sector (admittedly in recession during the 1830s) and other proto-industries of the country, notably the north-east, where the basis of a major industrialised zone in the Lagan Valley was already being laid down.[23]

Ireland's infrastructure was also undergoing major change, and thanks to the county Grand Juries and the Board of Works (the latter operating relief works schemes since 1831), the country's main roads were of a generally high quality. A whole tracery of minor roads also began to appear, opening up districts hitherto inaccessible to markets. A rapidly expanding railroad network snaked across the countryside, connecting the principal cities, backed by investors who were confident about Ireland's commercial future. A major project by the Ordnance Survey saw the country mapped to the highest international standards by the early 1840s, the Survey bringing with it not just cartographic accuracy, but also an invaluable (if too ambitious) attempt at recording the country's rich heritage of cultural antiquity. Ireland's educational systems, in addition, had taken a great leap forward with the inauguration of free elementary education in 1831, and although secondary education remained the preserve of a burgeoning sector of private academies, the 1840s would see the inauguration of state-sponsored university education with the establishment of Colleges in Galway, Cork and Belfast.

Those who profited most from the new educational possibilities comprised a rising educated middle-class of all religions, but they disproportionately benefiting Catholics, to whom many career possibilities had been opened since the Emancipation Act of 1829. The emergence of an educated Catholic middle-class is one of the major developments of this period, bringing with it a new intellectual leadership to nationalist Ireland, whose views and interests were reflected in a range of historical and literary magazines, the *Nation* newspaper and the journalism of a number of others at provincial level.

Although the poor benefited from educational reform only on a patchy basis, their world was being transformed also. Faction fighting, long past its heyday in any case, had largely been suppressed by the late 1830s by the Irish Constabulary, a recently formed national gendarmerie, which also went a long way towards putting an end to Whiteboy activity whenever it surfaced in the wake of estate consolidation and clearance. The rowdy scenes at hurling matches, patterns and fairs were rapidly disappearing also under the combined onslaught of constabulary and Catholic clergy. Partly because of their association with these sporting occasions, the traditional dance and music of Ireland also came under disapproval; dances became less and less frequent, and at parish level the musical impulse was increasingly represented by the brassy sound of temperance bands.

The temperance movement was one of two extraordinary mass phenomena which had a profound effect on social behaviour from the late 1830s. As the movement's charismatic founder and promoter Fr. Theobald Mathew crisscrossed the country, presiding at indoor and outdoor ceremonies, enormous numbers of the poor and the prosperous took the pledge in public, in scenes where religious exaltation vied with public spectacle. And although many drinkers returned to their intemperate behaviour in a short time of taking the pledge, a great many did not, and right up to the Famine itself, the public houses trade suffered a steep decline, the demand for illegal liquor drying up also.

The second of the two movements, Daniel O'Connell's Repeal campaign, benefited from Fr. Mathew's temperance achievement and borrowed from its organizational methods. O'Connell's *modus operandi* was to assemble great concourses of people in hundreds of mass meetings around the country and thereby to pressurize the British government into repealing the Union of 1800 by sheer force of popular will. These monster meetings, especially those attended by the Liberator himself, were extraordinary spectacles, enormous open-air operas of choreographed crowd movement, accompanied by much waving of banners, by rousing speeches, and magnificent banquets for which the locally notable scrambled for places. Excitement was engineered weeks before each meeting and maintained for days after the dispersal of the crowds.

The authorities were in two minds about the temperance campaign, but they were unremittingly hostile to O'Connell and Repeal, and much concerned in both cases by the way in which the rural masses were being inflamed to a high pitch of powerful emotion. Temperance activists and Repealers, for their part, considered their achievement had been to instil a sense of social discipline into a people egregiously lacking in this quality previously. From whatever stance it was considered, and regardless of their eventual failure, it could not be denied that both campaigns had been attended by extraordinary achievement. O'Connell's Repeal campaign had been stupendously successful from an organizational point of view, in that between 1843 and 1845, he and his lieutenants were able, repeatedly, and almost at will, to marshal gigantic crowds into orderly public meetings without so much as a single incident of public disorder or drunkenness.

For those schooled in the ways of traditional Ireland, all the changes of the period leading up to 1845 were disconcerting and difficult, a dissatisfaction that is perhaps personified in the figure of Rory Oge, the blind uileann piper encountered by Anna Maria and Samuel Hall at a fair in Killaloe in 1841. The Halls go to some trouble to present the piper, whose last name we are not told, as one of the last of his kind, and in a colourful conversation that takes up seven pages of text, and which includes a roguish illustration of Rory Oge in his tent, they allow him vent his spleen on the current age. Rory Oge resents the fact that 'faction-fights have altogether ceased, and [that] dances are now-a-days few and far between', and is 'wrathful exceedingly' on issues ranging from the disappearance of illegal stills and the decline of dancing to what he sees as a general

The blind uileann piper, Rory Oge, at Killaloe. Hall's *Ireland*.

loss of spirit among the 'boys'. His particular *bête noir*, however, consists of the temperance bands, which appear to him to be the harbingers of a new tame orthodoxy among the people that was killing off the old, wild cheerful anarchy of Ireland. For the new disciplined Ireland in the making Rory Oge has nothing but a withering contempt.[24]

The Halls themselves were acutely aware that a transformation was taking place among the people, and even though they admitted that Ireland was becoming a far less interesting place as a result, they believed the changes were to be welcomed. Elizabeth Smith, a landlord's wife from Baltiboys, County Wicklow, whose contact with the lower orders were less sympathetic than the Halls, was also conscious of a change in the nature of the people, one that she considered to be an improvement. In July 1846, just before famine brought devastation to her part of the country, we find her reminding herself in a diary entry of just how far they yet had to go. 'We must always remember that these are but an *emerging* people', she wrote, 'civilising a little too rapidly to improve *equally* as they proceed. We consider them too much as if they were further advanced – more on a par with ourselves than it is possible for their intellect to become under many generations.'

Whatever similarities may have existed between the attitude of the British government towards the 'emerging people' and that of Elizabeth Smith, the approach of the former to Ireland's poverty was decided largely by the advice of certain political economists, few of whom had any deep knowledge of Ireland. Three of the six members of the Poor Inquiry of the mid-1830s were political economists, including the chairman, the eccentric Protestant Archbishop Whately of Dublin, recently professor of the subject at Oxford, a man who did know his Ireland. Whately's Inquiry was significant in that it laid out in detail for the first time the exact dimensions of the problem; perhaps the most sobering statistic to emerge from its deliberations was that nearly two and a half million people were in severe want in Ireland for the greater portion of each year because of the seasonal nature of employment.[25] But this was its only significance, since its recommendations – a series of long-term measures aimed at expanding demand for 'free and profitable labour', including large-scale land reclamation; the provision of state-assisted emigration; extensive investment in agricultural education, and a major expansion of public works schemes – were never implemented. For reasons of cost, the Whig-Liberal government opted for the cut-rate solution proposed by another political economist, one George Nicholls, who recommended the one solution the Poor Inquiry specifically rejected as entirely inappropriate to Ireland, that is, the extension to the country of the new Poor Law operating in England.

Nicholls, a senior functionary of the English Poor Law (bitterly detested by the poor in that country), made his determination after a tour of inspection in Ireland that lasted a mere six weeks – according to Archbishop Whately, before he had left England at all. Like other doctrinaire political economists, Nicholls's concern was less the humanitarian one of solving a social evil as the prevention of the social instability he believed would take place if poverty were not controlled and regulated. Indeed, in his later *History of the Irish Poor Law*, he specifically mentions Irish emigration to Britain as a reason for introducing the Poor Law to Ireland. However, even Nicholls was clear on the fact that his proposed Irish

Poor Law was intended for the management of 'ordinary' poverty, and that it could not cater for major subsistence crises.[26]

Following the acceptance of Nicholls's plan, legislation was passed in 1838, extending the Poor Law to Ireland and adding an extra member to the Poor Law Commissioners in England. The new Commissioner was to be based in Ireland, and along with a number of Assistant Commissioners would have responsibility for the Irish section. The structures of the English Poor Law were borrowed *in toto*, the basic unit being a union, a combination of parishes that was at once the relief catchment area and the district on which taxes which would fund the whole operation was to be levied. This land tax, or Poor Law rate, was to fund the operation of the workhouse that lay at the centre of each union where those who were 'proper objects of relief' would be accommodated. No relief was to be afforded outside the workhouse (the English system did allow this), and conditions within workhouses were to be 'less eligible', that is, materially worse than those prevailing outside, in order to ensure that only genuinely destitute persons would seek relief, and only for a short time. In the context of Irish poverty this represented a fearsome depth of deprivation indeed.

In pursuit of the 'less eligibility' principle, every aspect of workhouse life was deliberately made repellent. Once they had entered the workhouse, destitute

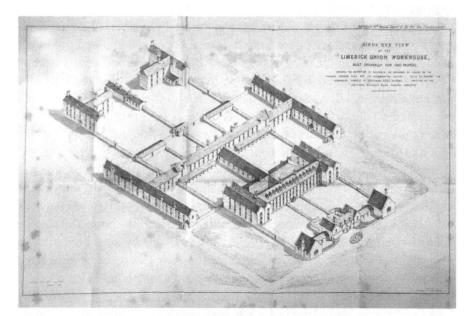

Plan of Limerick union workhouse, one of the larger of its kind, built for 1,600 inmates. *Thirteenth Report of the Poor Law Commissioners.*

families were separated, boys from girls, husbands from wives. Most cruelly
of all, children over the age of two were separated from their parents, and saw
them afterwards only at very restricted intervals. An ill-fitting uniform had to
be worn by all; the food was made unpleasant but consistent with nutritional
adequacy, and for the adults long monotonous days of work were required, the
work deliberately designed to be 'irksome'. Refractory persons could be confined
in punishment cells, and those leaving the workhouse while wearing the uniform
could (and routinely would) be arrested for theft of its property.[27]

Quite purposely, therefore, the Poor Law was made degrading, humiliating
and psychologically devastating, in line with Nicholls's dictum that the workhouse regime should be so repellent for the poor that 'the reproach for being
an inmate of it extend downwards from father to son'. With the passing of the
1838 Act, the word 'pauper' entered currency in Ireland, acquiring connotations
of institutional dependency, effective loss of citizenship and human dignity,
and social and familial failure, all of which were deeply wounding to a people
so gregarious and full of social pride as the Irish. Those who could not bring
themselves to accept workhouse conditions were deemed not to be require relief
at all, either for themselves or their families; in this manner the 'workhouse test'
allowed the system to function by deterring the majority of the destitute from
applying to it for relief.

Opposition to the new Poor Law was widespread in Ireland, but it was incon-
sistent and contradictory in motivation. Daniel O'Connell opposed the Bill in
Parliament; the lot of the poor would not, he believed, be improved by treating
them like criminals, and 'boxing them up in a workhouse'.[28] But the Poor Law
was not a priority issue for O'Connell, and he and the other Irish M.P.s who
voted against it did so for different reasons and with varying levels of conviction.
Among the public there was much hostility to the measure also, but for two
opposing reasons. The first, a humanitarian impulse, is reflected in a meeting held
in Strabane, County Tyrone, where one speaker suggested that a tax on absentee
landlords would be a more just means of tackling poverty; at Ennis, County Clare,
a speaker at another meeting expressed outrage at the callousness of Poor Law
officials and the injustice the system promised to visit on the poor. The second,
self-interested reason we find in comments such as that by a landlord print in
Armagh, the *Newry Telegraph*, which slated the Poor Law as being 'concocted
by theorists who know little or nothing of the people for whom they propose to
legislate'; the 'people' referred to by the *Telegraph* were tax-paying landlords. The
Cork Constitution, also a landlord organ, declared that the proposed workhouse
diet was so luxurious for the inmates that the pauper would 'as soon go purgatory
as quit the workhouse'.[29] But objections, from whatever quarter, were futile, and

with the steady introduction of the Poor Law to parishes all over Ireland, by late 1845 when 122 of the projected 130 workhouses had opened, the oppressive ethos of the Poor Law quickly took hold in all of them.

Apart from a few which had been converted from the precursor Houses of Industry, Irish workhouses were of a standard design, adaptable for capacities varying between 600 and 800 inmates. Some of the city workhouses were built to accommodate much larger numbers. The English architect responsible for the basic design, George Wilkinson, had been instructed that they were to be inexpensively built and without ornamentation. Despite his ingenuity in subverting his brief by including 'pleasing and picturesque' Tudor-style hood-mouldings, window mullions and tall chimneys, the newly completed workhouses were forbidding buildings; internally they exuded a bare institutional bleakness, their external appearance somewhere between barracks and prison.[30] Exterior appearance and internal conditions soon engendered a loathing so deep for the workhouses among the people that even in the harshest periods leading up to 1845, nowhere were they more than half-full; resorted to chiefly by those already socially outcast, professional beggars and street prostitutes.

As they became accustomed to these gaunt, bare new landmarks on the outskirts of their union towns, the poor went about their business, unaware of how hugely they would soon loom in their lives. These lives continued to centre around the cultivation of the potato, a precarious existence, since, for all its nutritional properties, this 'luxurious esculent' was extremely vulnerable to climatic variation and disease. Late-occurring frosts in spring could retard or destroy an early crop, while wet, windy weather might flatten developed stalks in a late one, stunting the growth of the tubers beneath; growing plants were susceptible to a number of diseases, notably the damaging 'curl'. Attempts to strengthen the potato's resistance to disease and overcome another drawback, its inability to sustain prolonged storage, led to the breeding of new varieties, and on the eve of the Famine the most popular types included the Crow, the Cup and the succulent Apple. But the poor saw little of these varieties, for by this period, only the high-yielding but watery and tasteless Lumper, first developed as a feed for horses, was sufficient to keep their families fed.[31]

Between 1800 and 1845 the potato had failed on a local or regional basis many times, causing subsistence crises that ranged between severe hardship and actual starvation. Serious regional famines occurred in 1822 and 1831, while 1817, 1819 and 1834 were also difficult seasons in some places. The immediate pre-Famine years saw the potato crop fail in many areas on an almost constant, alternating basis, a particularly bad season being 1842, when food riots broke out in many towns and cities. In some western counties, in 1843 and 1844, certain districts underwent crises that were considered locally severe.[32] As they struggled to survive through these difficult times, none of those affected by them could have had any suspicions that far from improving, their travails would soon descend to the level of unrelenting nightmare.

A Long Farewell to the White Potatoes: The Coming of the Blight

Mo mhíle slán do na fataí bána
Ba shubhach an áit a bheith in aice leo
Ba failí soineannta iad ag tíocht chun láithreach,
Agus iad ag gáirí linn ar cheann an bhoird
[A long farewell to the white potatoes
How great the happiness they could afford
How glad they made us when they came before us
With faces smiling at us from the board]

— *NA FATAÍ BÁNA*

The memory of recent failures ensured that throughout the growing season of 1845 the potato fields were watched with greater anxiety than usual. More potatoes had been sown than for many years past, and throughout the spring and summer, in addition to the long-use plots of smallholders and labourers and the commercial farms, hillsides and cutaway bogs all over Ireland were carpeted in the light green foliage of growing plants. With the passing of the weeks, the tension of the watch-keeping was maintained as the weather alternated between warm sunny periods and intervals of cold heavy rain; uncertainty was sharpest in early July when heavy downpours flattened the stalks in their ridges, threatening the growth of the tubers.

The securing of the early crop in the course of the month, however, was the occasion for relaxation, and towards its end the *Freeman's Journal* declared that the potato, 'the poor man's property', was 'never before so large and at the same time so abundant'. Optimism dipped briefly with a sudden fall in temperature and more rain, but soared again with the return of settled weather in mid-August, which seemed certain to continue into September.[1] In this fine interval local newspapers rose to the occasion in lyrical prose about prospects for the main crop, now forming invisibly beneath sturdy stalks in fields and haggards and due for lifting in mid-October.

Three-legged pot in which potatoes were typically boiled, and basket in which they were placed. Hall's *Ireland*.

In the watching and waiting, little attention was at first paid to news that began to emerge from the early weeks of August regarding the widespread destruction of growing potatoes in the south of England by an unknown plant disease. Unable to assign a cause, puzzled British commentators referred to the disease as the 'murrain' or 'blight'. The latter term eventually became the one to enter common usage; the scientific label *Phytophthora infestans* would only be bestowed several decades later when all aspects of the disease were finally understood. Scientific opinion was, however, quick to recognize that the new disease appeared to be the same as that which had appeared in America the previous year, and when on 20 August, Dr. David Moore, the curator of the Botanical Gardens in Glasnevin, observed similar symptoms in potatoes cultivated there, he recognized at once that the 'blight' had arrived in Ireland. But this fact was not known to the general public, which remained largely uninformed and unconcerned over subsequent weeks, even as gardening and farmers' magazines and newspapers began to carry reports identifying instances of blight from various parts of the country. Part of the reason for this lack of concern was that these publications downplayed the significance of the blight, both because they feared causing undue alarm and because they dared not believe it themselves. After insisting for weeks that a bumper harvest was still in prospect, as the evidence of destruction mounted they turned instead to counselling patience and a postponement of judgement until the main crop was ready for harvesting.

A similar resolute optimism was displayed by the constabulary, which had been instructed by government in mid-September to gather data regarding the state of the crop from the localities. The earliest police reports from Tubbercurry and Ballymote in Sligo, for example, and Ballinrobe in Mayo, refer respectively to 'small failure in a few instances', 'every appearance of most abundant return in this part of the country' and 'ample and good'. To the north, in County Derry, the county inspector reported on 20 September that apart from one district, the potato disease 'does not exist to any extent' in the county.[2] Well into October, almost everywhere in Ireland, the constabulary, along with journalists, magistrates and clergy, were still maintaining that the potatoes were safe and that the harvest would be good.

When the main crop was dug out in mid-October, the full extent of the destruction became apparent, the shock of its extent all the greater for having been understated for so long. From all parts of the country, a rising and frightened clamour reflected an identical story, repeated endlessly: wrecked cropfields, withering and slimy potato stalks, the tubers beneath blotched and ulcerated, their sudden decomposition producing a strong, foul stench that assailed the nostrils of cultivators and passersby alike. On 15 October, an agitated *Nenagh Guardian* reported that the 'awful plague' had appeared in the locality, and the following day, Joseph Grogan, Lord Ponsonby's agent at Philipstown (Daingean), County Offaly, wrote that all along the canal line in that and adjacent counties, potato haggards that very recently had 'not the least appearance of damage' were now showing definite signs of infection. On investigation, his own potatoes, which he had believed safe, were found to be badly infected, the damage having been done 'in a very short time'. From County Waterford, three days later again, a Resident Magistrate wrote that the potato crop appeared 'to be universally blighted', and on the twentieth the Dungarvan Board of Guardians warned that if the 'very general' failure of the potatoes were not checked, 'the worst consequences as regard provision to the people' were to be feared.[3]

Most frightening of all was that the potatoes seemed to be almost visibly rotting as they were dug out, and it was common that a 'potato field tried today may be good and sound and in three days after in a state of melancholy putrefaction'. Potatoes pitted in a healthy condition were found to be absolutely rotten shortly afterwards. On 20 October, the chairman of the Ballina Guardians, George Vaughan Jackson, dramatically displayed diseased potatoes from his best fields to the Board, taken from what had at first appeared to be 'a most healthy crop'.[4] From Swinford, Sub-Inspector Edward Hunt reported that 'a general panic of all classes, both of farmers and householders' was taking place as a result of the failure, an assertion that could have applied anywhere in the country where the potato had been heavily sown.

Not even the northern counties, which would ultimately be spared the worst of what was to come, escaped the destruction. In Inishowen, in northern Donegal, the blight had made 'frightful ravages' by 22 October, while in the south-west of the county potatoes planted along the coastline near Killybegs were reported to have been affected by the fungus sooner than those planted on upland farms.[5] In Tyrone to the east, the Strabane area lost an estimated one-third of its potatoes, although other parts of the county fared considerably better. Much of County Antrim was devastated, as were parts of neighbouring County Down, the situation made worse there by the fact that the turnip crop in that county had also been ruined, it was incorrectly supposed, by the same rot. In Fermanagh, which experienced what was probably the first authenticated case of major destruction by potato blight anywhere in Ireland (near Florence Court on 20 September) the damage was also extensive.

From early November, to fear was added discomfort and misery, as weeks of persistent heavy rain made the harvesting and storage of the remaining potatoes a physically difficult and highly frustrating and unpleasant experience. At Coolcronane, near Foxford, one magistrate was shown 'acres of potatoes that were entirely covered with water and ruined'. As the rain pelted down, he witnessed local people struggling in waters 'nearly up to their knees' as they tried to dig out the unseen potatoes from muddy waterlogged ridges.[6]

Those who went to such frantic lengths to save their potatoes were not, of course, the well-off farmers and commercial growers, who could afford to sustain the loss, but the poorer smallholders, and the bound and unbound labourers. The anguish endured by them and their families as a result of the loss can be inferred only since they did not commit their feelings to paper, and journalists and other commentators showed little interest in canvassing them.

We know a great deal more about the reactions of those at higher levels of society, notably landlords and others associated with land management who were only indirectly affected by the failure. The original alarm of this sector in October and November was succeeded by calmer reflection in which the dire predictions made earlier were revised. One-third to one-half of the potatoes had certainly been destroyed, according to this thinking, but the remainder had been salvaged from a sowing that had, after all, been much greater than usual. In early December, when it was noticed that the blight did not seem to be progressing any further, this was also seized upon as an indication that things were not as bad as feared, as was the fact that diseased potatoes were still usable or could be fed to animals. The poor, it was held, would not therefore face a crisis of subsistence, at worst calculation, until the following March, when the potatoes that had survived the blight had been consumed. And at that point, the authorities would have intervened, just as they had done during recent local harvest failures.

In public such views were articulated at formally convened county meetings, where they were most forcibly supported by those who, sensing imminent tenant demands for rent abatements as well as the inauguration of relief schemes for which they would substantially bear the cost, had consistently denied the existence of a crisis. Privately expressed views show a similar pattern, and thus, at the end of November, Elizabeth Smith, the chatelaine of Baltiboys, whose diary had earlier revealed great anxiety about the crop, was writing that the potato failure had been greatly exaggerated, the blight 'by no means as far spread as was supposed and the crop so over-abundant that the partial failure will be the less felt'. In Philipstown, we find the land agent, Grogan, revising his earlier pessimism, and writing to a correspondent that the potatoes 'were not getting any worse, thank God'.[7]

But these were dangerous rationalizations that misrepresented both the damage done to the potato crop as well as the condition of the poor, and above all they ignored the fact that the blight had not, in fact, been checked at all. Throughout the winter potatoes left in ridges (a common ready-made form of storing them) or pitted under the usual conditions continued to rot, especially during a spell of unseasonably warm weather in January 1846. The deterioration, in fact, would persist right through to the point where no more edible potatoes from the October harvest were left. In some districts this was in mid-February, much sooner than had been anticipated.

However, not everybody had been guilty of complacency, and by late autumn of 1845, even as the rhythms of normal life were resuming and the attention of the comfortable classes turning again to the seasonal cycle of legal/administrative processes, public occasions and entertainments that were now moving towards their usual winter phase, there were those who remained deeply worried about the poor and their immediate prospects. Among them was Fr. Philip Fitzgerald, the Catholic curate at Callan, County Kilkenny, who wrote to the Repeal Association in mid-December that some weeks before 'the panic had subsided with, it was thought, the progress of the disease'. 'Now, indeed,' he added, 'the prospect is far more gloomy. A very contrary and alarming impression prevails.'[8] Another was Rev. James Garrett, Church of Ireland vicar of Emlyfad in County Sligo, who petitioned the Lord Lieutenant late in November regarding the situation of the conacre tenants in his vicinity. 'These poor beings', he wrote, 'cannot obtain any employment at this season. They have already few sound potatoes and will probably be destitute before the first of March.'

Another again was Rev. Robert Traill, Church of Ireland rector of Schull Parish in West Cork, who had expended a great deal of energy since late October in devising and promoting a type of potato pit which he was convinced protected potatoes against blight. In early December, Dr. Traill was still trying, without success, to persuade local landlords to allow tenants to keep their grain so as to spare their potatoes for seed, and was lobbying government on the urgency of introducing public works.

More outspoken than any of the above was John Busteed Knox, editor of the Ennis-based conservative newspaper, the *Clare Journal*. A staunch Tory and long-time admirer of the Prime Minister, Sir Robert Peel, throughout November and December, Knox used his editorial columns repeatedly to denounce Peel, the Lord Lieutenant, Lord Heytesbury and their respective administrations in London and Dublin for what he saw as an abject failure to address the needs of the poor.[9] Knox was equally scathing of interest groups in his own locality: landlords, Boards of Guardians, Grand Juries and others whose abiding faults he saw as procrastination and apathy. Several days after Christmas he was still editorializing gloomily on the impossibility of organizing meetings that might thrash out possible modes of action, especially the controversial proposal to repeal the Corn Laws, or 'almost any other subject'.[10]

The letters of Fr. Fitzgerald, Rev. Garrett and Dr. Traill and John B. Knox's sulphurous editorials represent the tail-end of a vast body of data relating to the potato failure reaching the British cabinet from Ireland. Individuals and bodies which had made such representations, across the political spectrum from Repealers to Irish Tories, were, however, disconcerted to find government strangely unresponsive to their concerns. Newspaper editorials went unchallenged; letters and petitions elicited curt and uninformative replies, followed usually by an enduring silence. The impression of official indifference that this created was confirmed for many when early in November, the Lord Lieutenant, Lord Heytesbury, accorded a brusque reception to a deputation from a committee of Dublin Corporation convened to urge solutions to the crisis on government which were informed by personal witness. The snub – Heytesbury had merely read out a prepared statement outlining in general terms what government proposed to do before ushering the delegation to the door – caused mortal offence in Ireland and to a much wider public than that of the Repealers and Liberals who comprised the delegates. In a withering comment, the County Clare Tory John B. Knox informed his readers that Lord Heytesbury had told the 'first men in the country' that 'he has appointed scientific men to make experiments how rotten potatoes can be made sound and how long pigs can live on blackberries ... they may retire and rest calmly as his efforts will be directed to secure food for the people. There now, gentlemen, good morning.'[11]

But, in fact, the government was not indifferent, merely immobilized by uncertainty as to how it should proceed; and although the summary treatment of pleas from Ireland arose partly out of the impossibility of dealing at individual length with the avalanche of such material, the vacillation of Prime Minister and cabinet was undoubtedly the major factor. Peel, who was famously antipathetic to Ireland and its people ever since a stint as Chief Secretary three decades before, distrusted news from across the Irish Sea as being by definition exaggerated. It was some weeks before he fully accepted the scale of the potato failure, and by that time he and several of his ministers had become influenced by a depressive providential interpretation of the failure espoused by his Home Secretary, Sir James Graham.[12]

Like many other prominent figures in British life, Graham, who was no more popular in Ireland than his Prime Minister, was the holder of pre-millennial evangelical views. Pre-millenialists believed that the destruction of the potato harvest was a providential judgement on both countries, but especially Ireland, for a range of moral failings that were as variously and vaguely defined as they were wholeheartedly subscribed to. For Graham, who read apocalyptic doom into every new report from Ireland, active governance was not to be contemplated, at least not yet. Only repeal of the Corn Laws, which kept the price of grain artificially high in Britain and Ireland, would constitute an atonement of sufficient weight to turn aside divine wrath and retribution. If this viewpoint is understandable as a convenient marriage between evangelical and Free Trade principles, two entirely different but eminently compatible forms of faith-based belief, held with similar fervour by their devotees, the fact that abolition of the Corn Laws might actually be of some practical benefit to the poor in the form of falling grain prices, was a bonus benefit, and not one directly intended. Although Peel was more rational than his Home Secretary on the issue, there is little doubt that his initial reluctance in tackling the socioeconomic fallout from the potato failure in Ireland was shaped to some degree by providentialist belief.

Peel was already committed to the repeal of the Corn Laws, and his conversion some years previously had divided his party and left him with a fragile hold on office, one that depended on a Free Trade Tory rump together with the contingent support of the Whig-Liberal opposition. In these circumstances, it was inevitable, if politically cynical on his part, that he would use the Irish crisis in order to force a path in the desired direction. The Corn Laws controversy would have led to political upheaval in Britain had there been no harvest crisis in Ireland, and its significance, therefore, was medium- rather than short-term, in that it hastened the fracturing of the Tory party and the arrival in office the following year of a Whig-Liberal administration, with all that would entail. Since repeal of the Corn

Laws would not be accomplished until that time, the issue had no short-term impact at all on what was happening in Ireland.

At any rate, amid the political uncertainty, by late October all that had been done by government was the dispatching to Dublin of a special Scientific Commission which was instructed to investigate the nature of the blight and recommend remedial measures. The work of the Commission was hampered by the fact that none of its three members, the eminent English scientists, Lyon Playfair and John Lindley, and the Irish-born makeweight, Robert Kane, possessed the requisite expertise in plant biology. Lindley, indeed, had already foredoomed the Commission by his earlier rejection of a fungal origin for the blight, which expert opinion elsewhere – in Ireland, even amateur researchers – had already identified as the cause. Lindley's view was accepted without argument by his fellow commissioners, who collectively attributed the blight to a 'wet putrefaction', an egregious error which ensured that their subsequent recommendations would be utterly useless.[13]

Growers who implemented the Commission's recommendations (the major one being the construction of ventilated storage pits) enjoyed precisely the same level of success as the smallholders of Loughrea, south Galway, who 'left off the digging' of their potatoes in November to travel twenty miles to Scariff in East Clare, where a priest was reported to have a charm cure for the blight. Also in Clare, one commercial grower would later tell a journalist from the *Freeman* newspaper that he had carried out the Commission's recommendations with meticulous care on his extensive acreage, commenting with resignation that, 'of course I lost all my potatoes'.

One further, rather macabre, comment on the Scientific Commission's deliberations comes from a report in a Kerry newspaper describing the proceedings of an inquest supposedly held by one grower in Schull Parish, in Cork, early in 1846 on a 'deceased' pit of potatoes. According to this story, the grower gave evidence to the inquest that he had followed the Commissioners' instructions to the letter, despite which his pit had 'died'. The jury returned a verdict of wilful murder against the three Commissioners.[14] Spoof though this report undoubtedly was, the 'inquest' findings prefigured uncannily something that would later become commonplace from late the following year, that is actual inquests where juries would attribute starvation deaths directly to members of government.

It was well over a month after the Scientific Commission had embarked upon its futile labours that the first active government measure took effect. This was when a Relief Commission, under whose umbrella all government relief operations in Ireland would proceed, began to meet. Among its earliest duties was the supervision of the purchase and transportation to Ireland of about 20,000 tons of

American corn, or maize, at a cost of £100,000, whose purchase Peel had authorized some weeks before. Also known as Indian meal, American corn was chosen
despite its nutritional inferiority and difficulty of preparation, for the reason
that its importation would not interfere with ordinary commerce, since it was
unknown in Ireland as a food and no trade in it therefore existed in the country.
In order that markets might not be disturbed by such a large purchase, secrecy
was maintained throughout the complicated procurement procedure (organized
through Baring Brothers, the international bankers) and its transportation to
Ireland. It was several months before the public became aware of the purchase.

Estimated by one official to be sufficient to feed one million people for forty
days, the quantity purchased was not remotely sufficient to bridge the gap in
food supply left by the potato failure. But that was not its purpose; feeding the
people was never the intention of government; and had such a proposal been
made it would have been dismissed as socially undesirable and well outside the
proper functioning of government; the expense alone would not have borne
contemplation. The imported meal was intended rather as a dampener on food
price inflation in the localities where it was to be distributed. It was, moreover,
not to be given gratis to the poor, but to be sold to them or to relief committees
at cost price, and only at times when grain prices were rising locally. Stringent
regulations were laid down forbidding free distribution except under the most
impossibly restrictive conditions.

Under the direction of the army Commissariat, thirteen main depots were
to be established for storage and distribution of the meal: at Limerick, Kilrush,
Galway, Westport and Sligo for the west; at Waterford, Clonmel, Dublin and
Dundalk for the south and east, and at Banagher, Athy, Tullamore and Longford
for the midlands. Sub-depots were to be set up in 105 other locations where no
relief committees existed or where they had insufficient funds; these were to be
operated either by the coastguard or constabulary. However, only in February
were the depots and sub-depots in place; only in the last days of March did sales
of meal begin and then only in some locations where want made it necessary
to do so in advance of the appointed date of 15 May. It was June before all the
depots were finally open.[15]

The slow pace at which all this took place was a matter of quite deliberate
planning, distribution being carefully graduated to match the advance of distress
as perceived by official eyes. In the event, however, a series of unforeseen difficulties combined to make the distribution of the meal to the poor even more
protracted, among them the inadequacy of the roads to carry large quantities
of meal to remote locations where want was severest; the insufficiency of naval
transport in carrying it by sea, and the fact that the poor did not know how to

cook it, and did not possess the simple hand-milling technology to grind it down from the raw, flint-hard state in which it was received. Failure to grind the meal, steep it overnight in water, or to cook it adequately led to bowel complaints in the initial stages of its consumption by the poor. In some locations, there were disturbances when the poor became dissatisfied with or refused to accept what became known as 'Peel's Brimstone'.[16]

Together, all of these factors limited the effectiveness of the American corn/ Indian meal as a mechanism either for controlling prices or alleviating the worst distress. In many cases, indeed, by the time the meal arrived in the stores or depots, the situation of the poor had deteriorated to the point where they could not afford it at any price. The one measure that would have had an immediate and dramatic effect on prices in the crucial short-term period, the closing of Irish ports to the export of grain and other agricultural produce, was rejected by government, despite the great clamour from Ireland that this should be done. Government justification of its refusal at this and all subsequent occasions during the Famine was founded on the same free-market ideology that prevented a more generous attitude with regard to the direct distribution of meal. An even more compelling, if understandably less publicized, reason related to the implications of a port closure for the supply of food to Britain where there was such a dependency among the lower orders on imported Irish produce.[17]

In Galway, where one-quarter of the population was reported to be in a state of 'absolute pauperism' when the city depot opened in April – prematurely because of reported distress – crowds immediately besieged it in their anxiety to purchase what they could afford, while the local papers helpfully printed recipes for its preparation, adapted from the diet of American slaves. In Cork, the opening of the city depot around the same time saw large crowds of the 'humblest description' descend upon it, who became 'so turbulently inclined as to require the immediate interference of the police,' who remained there for the entire day. Very few sales were, however, made. North of Galway city, on 19 May, when a coastguard officer in Conamara, the appropriately named Captain Helpman, arrived at Cleggan to stock the new sub-depot there he found large crowds, 'many from long distances', awaiting his arrival, their money ready to purchase meal. After a time his stock ran out, leaving many 'in tears as a result'.[18]

However, the lesson the authorities drew from reports they received of these and similar occurrences elsewhere related not to the hardship which the would-be purchasers were undergoing, but the fact that these very poor persons still had money. From this it was concluded, wrongly, that they were not as destitute as supposed, and, accordingly, from June meal supplies were ordered to be sold at the higher prices of the local markets. Injunctions against the gratuitous dispensation of food were maintained rigorously, and wherever local committees or coastguard and constabulary personnel defied instructions and connived at this 'demoralizing' practice, they were reprimanded.[19]

From the beginning, government intended that local relief committees should play a central role in the relief of distress. However, for the same reasons as the delays in meal supply, apart from a disastrous pilot project in Kilkee, west Clare, they were not permitted to function until mid-February, when instructions governing their operation were issued. Over the ensuing months hundreds of committees came into existence, and at the summit of their activity in August 1846, just before they were replaced, there would be some 648 of them altogether. The organization of the committees was very loose, and based usually either on the Catholic parish, its civil equivalent, which had different boundaries, or on the administrative unit known as the district electoral division. While each of these bases had individual advantages, problems arose when used together in a given county or district, the result being a territorial gap where no relief coverage was present. The earliest committees to be formed were in those areas of the west and south which had extensively suffered in previous local crises, and which were therefore most familiar with administrative procedures. In areas which had not known much pre-Famine distress, the situation was different, and in Offaly, for example, the absence of experience told in early wrangling for dominance between landlords on the one hand and Catholic and Protestant clergy on the other.

As the committees emerged, however, the membership eventually did encompass a wide spectrum of respectable society, from clergymen of both denominations to shopkeepers, county officials, landlords and middlemen. A notable problem was encountered in that many landlords were reluctant either to accept membership or to contribute to funds.[20] Committees varied greatly in their levels of efficiency and commitment; where they were most effective, the work was carried out by a small core of active members, much as in local bodies everywhere in pre-Famine times. At their best, the active membership was dedicated and painstaking in their duties, and equal to the task of challenging government bureaucracy which sought to restrict entitlement to relief. Many committees went to great lengths to do so, and in the general process of their work developed a high level of administrative expertise as well as ingenuity in soliciting local and government financial contributions. Becoming adept in discerning the needs of genuinely poor people, in many instances they provided their own work schemes where the public works were late in beginning. At their worst, committees were negligent and lazy, failed to meet regularly or adequately collect subscriptions, or consumed their energies in factional political rivalry. Some committees selfishly disputed responsibility for especially destitute districts which they insisted belonged to other committees. Members of a few committees were corruptly involved with contractors.[21]

No local relief committees were formed in Counties Armagh, Derry, Fermanagh and Tyrone, and while this is generally indicative of much lesser distress in these areas than elsewhere, in certain districts it also reflects an unwillingness on the part of local property interests to recognize the extent of deprivation. In these northern counties, such a reluctance usually had a sectarian basis; where it occurred elsewhere in Ireland, as in the relatively well-off regions of counties of south Leinster, its origins relate more probably to pre-existing social tensions between landlords and labourers. In Wexford, for example, in April, the Gorey relief committee chose not to apply for government grants at all on the demonstrably false grounds that destitution was no worse there than in previous years, that meal was available and 'employment more ample and better paid for'.[22]

The most important role assigned to relief committees related to what was the core responsibility of the Relief Commission, the provision of public works schemes which would secure employment and wages for the poor. This was essentially a reprise on a massive scale of what by now was a well-worn state response to localized subsistence crises; as before it would centre on repairs to and extensions of the roads network. The legislative package passed in early March after an unhurried passage through Parliament did, it is true, provide for land drainage projects and the construction of piers and slipways, but in the event few schemes of the kind survived official ideological preference for 'un-reproductive' works, those, that is, that were clearly not of benefit to private individuals.

Road schemes were of two types. The first was to be administered locally through the county Grand Juries and carried out by private contractors, the costs being borne by a loan advanced by the Treasury. The second type was to be carried out by the Board of Works, the cost to be shared equally by local sources and government.[23] Bureaucratic procedures attached to both schemes, however, and their failure to dovetail as planned with the emergence of relief committees led to many delays. Eventually and very unevenly, schemes began to come into operation from the end of March, multiplying during April and May. At the same time, over considerable stretches of the country, including districts where all remnants of the October harvest were long gone, and where the price of alternative foods had risen sharply, the people would be without works provision even in mid-June.

All these delays served to accelerate a slow deterioration in the physical condition of the poor that had commenced with the winter and progressed slowly
ever since. As the months went by the bureaucratic euphemisms of 'want' and
'distress' began to feature more frequently in newspapers and official documents.
Official sources tended to soften these phrases even further by referring to them
as imminent possibilities, rather than the actual realities we know them to have
been in so many cases. The intention of this kind of circumlocution was to
reassure the public and enable official agencies to preserve a necessary detach-
ment when setting about implementing remedial action. Too often, however,
it could also serve as a barrier behind which a detached indifference might be
preserved.

In January, in Kells, County Meath, a survey carried out by a County Deputy
Lieutenant had revealed that the destitution of the poor was 'far worse' than earlier
reported. Whole families were living on a single daily meal consisting of diseased
potatoes, and one case was noted where seven persons had sat down to a morning
repast that consisted of a half-stone of bad potatoes, their first meal since the previous day. Some weeks later, similar stories emerged from Gallen, County Offaly,
where country people had been subsisting for months on 'the worst description of
food' and where the Church of Ireland vicar, Rev. Holmes, wrote that large numbers
of families were in distress 'through want of food and labour'. By mid-March, in
north Tipperary, an area supposedly better off than most other counties, potato
prices were 'enormously high', well out of the reach of the poor, according to the
Tipperary Vindicator, which pleaded, 'in God's name, let something be done to avert
starvation.'[24] A few weeks later, around Gurteen, County Sligo, even diseased potatoes were no longer available; and fever had made its first dread appearance. With
the exception perhaps of Gurteen, none of the above areas were those traditionally
associated with pre-Famine subsistence crises; at this time even in south Wexford,
'want and destitution' were reported to be 'impending'.

Most relief committees responded to developments such as these by redoubling their energies in raising subscriptions, in purchasing and distributing meal
and providing stopgap employment for labourers, cottiers and tradesmen, hoping
thus to provide a bridge until the commencement of government works. Some
landlords organized estate relief schemes for their tenants; but very many who did
also refused to subscribe to relief committees they believed to be 'irresponsible',
and whose extravagance they feared would see them saddled with liability for the
support of other men's tenants, or, worse still, for 'squatters'.[25]

One very unusual local response to government inaction emerged in west
Clare, which had endured several very recent difficult seasons, and where the
authorities were as a result closely attuned to the rapidity with which the deepest

Pre-Famine artist's impression of landlord's agent being begged for rent reduction by tenants, a common occurrence in the early part of the Famine. Steuart Trench, *Realities of Irish Life*.

Potatoes were often stored in the cabin roof-space, as in this illustration from February 1846. *Pictorial Times*.

human suffering could follow on a harvest shortage if early relief measures were not taken. At the end of January, magistrates in the Kilrush area decided that instead of waiting for the promised government works, they would instead exercise their powers of requisition to activate a little-used Public Works Act from 1837, allowing them to provide local employment relatively quickly. Presentment sessions were accordingly held and road schemes approved, and within the space of little over a month, actual works were commencing. The Kilrush initiative was soon copied all over Clare, projecting the county well ahead of all the others in the provision of relief employment. So satisfied with the progress of these works were the Clare authorities that, when the government public works package became available at the end of March, the county Grand Jury re-assembled specially after the spring assizes in order to reject it as being too cumbersome, and, in any case, unnecessary.[26]

Where the people began to show restlessness at work delays, magistrates, clergy and other community leaders sought to reassure them by reminding them of the benefits public works would eventually bring, and the danger of jeopardizing the relief employment by any act of violence or disorder. For the most part this message was received trustingly by the poor, and for some time popular unease was manifested merely in the anxious thronging of food stores and depots, in the spreading of wild rumours of rioting and food plundering elsewhere, and in a scattered posting of threatening notices in some districts.[27] From this point, for the first time, we also find the poor assembling in large numbers to march on the homes of magistrates, clergy and officials in search of food or simply for intercession with government in regard to public works.[28] At the end of April, one hundred or so labourers marched through Skibbereen in west Cork, preceded by a man holding up a spade to which was affixed a loaf of bread, the traditional manner in which impoverished communities indicated the presence of starvation in their midst.[29]

As government continued to stall on the public works, popular frustration and anger became impossible to contain fully, and acts of hunger-inspired lawlessness inevitably took place. These increased rapidly in frequency in those parts of the country where food shortages were already serious. In addition to a surge in petty food-stealing offences and a further rash of threatening notices, there were also the beginnings of attempts to keep food supplies in localities and to obtain food by force. As early as January farmers in south Donegal had been prevented from bringing corn to market by 'persons who live on the road they have to pass with it'. Off the coast of the same county, at the end of March a party of twenty impoverished men attempted to steal and plunder a fishing vessel, *Mariner*, which had just taken on board several hundred tons of potatoes. On the Fergus estuary in Clare a few weeks later, another large party made a successful raid on a smack, *Maria*, which was carrying grain, the raiders carrying off hundreds of sacks under the eyes of the captain and crew. Slightly later again, a hunger-crazed crowd composed of persons with 'hollow eyes', whose bones 'protruded through the skin which covered them' attacked the grain mills owned by the Quaker firm of Grubb, Malcolmson and Hughes in Clonmel, only to be driven off by a mixed force of artillerymen and dragoons.[30] In Carrick, some miles away, over several days in April, disturbances took place as a result of a sudden rise in the price of food.[31]

By and large, however, incidents of this kind were still not of significant proportions, and even official sources acknowledged that since the previous year 'outrages' had increased in volume in only five counties, while actually declining in all the others. For this period outrages peaked in the spring with the incidents described above, and faded away afterwards with the gradual opening of the public works.[32] For the remainder of the summer, they would recur only where there were difficulties with works or in the odd case of conflict over land. In June, for example, labourers who were refused places on preliminary works schemes in Ballinrobe, County Mayo, forced themselves on the works, declaring that if they were not afforded employment, 'they would break into houses for provisions'. In the same month, in Rosmead, County Westmeath, when a gombeen man broke a Whiteboy-organized strike against the taking of conacre, the rent for which was so high that local labourers could no longer bid for it, he was shot dead.[33] But even if they were so far relatively confined, incidents such as these constituted another foreshadowing, of two different kinds of survival and protest action that would become endemic from the following autumn.

In the great majority of cases, wherever and whenever public works schemes opened, they transformed the living conditions of the poor. Thanks to the wages paid for roads labour, food could now be afforded; rents could be paid and other obligations discharged; anxieties were dispelled, and a semblance of normal living was restored. Frightened pleas for assistance abruptly ceased wherever public works opened and cheap meal became available to relief committees. At the height of their operation in mid-July, the public works were of crucial importance to the survival of the 140,000 or so labourers who toiled on them daily and to their families, who together comprised a total dependency of perhaps 700,000 persons.

However, there were many problems with the works, the major one being that for the short time they operated they were never sufficient to the prevailing level of distress in the worst affected districts. There were many complaints that schemes operated by private contractors tended to favour better-off persons rather than the destitute labouring poor, and that employment went by favouritism or 'interest'. There is also a certain level of evidence that, even at this point, persons who had been physically debilitated by prolonged hunger were already physically too weak to work. In Galway City, for example, in May, a labourer who was dismissed for idleness was later found to be weak from starvation; a little later the 'shambling gait' of another was found to be due to debilitation. Where even a few instances of this were reported, they point to a much wider level of deprivation throughout the general community.

The greatest difficulty with the works, however, arose out of commencement delays, and the fact that there were so many distressed areas which saw no works at all during the period of Tory government.[34] The former problem arose out of the tedious administrative procedures attaching to the legislation, the latter most frequently where no relief committees had been formed or where jurisdiction for a particular district was disputed between committees. In late June, in Clareabbey, County Clare, where no works had yet begun, a Catholic clergyman, Fr. O'Gorman, wrote of 'the awful state' of the labourers of his parish and of the 'ravages made by hunger, so visible in their countenances, distracted manner and wild expression', all of which had 'rendered them furious'. About the same time the relief committee at Coolaney, Sligo, complained that no works had opened in the desperately distressed upper half-barony of Leyney for which it had responsibility. By 12 July, some works had been approved, but none had yet commenced, in a district where 'destitution and starvation' were now reported to be spreading rapidly. By the end of the month, indeed, work on one of only two schemes to open in the half-barony, at Kilmacteige, had no sooner begun for 600 labourers than the county surveyor intervened and dismissed 400 of them, in what seems to have been a dispute over jurisdiction.[35]

From about this time also, the sources disclose the first references to deaths by starvation during the Great Famine, most of them well-attested, indisputable instances. As early as 22 March, several persons were reported to have died of hunger at Baylough, near Athlone; in mid-April, William Smith O'Brien, one of the County Limerick Members of Parliament, told the House of Commons that coroners' juries in Kilkenny, Clare, Cork and Waterford had returned starvation verdicts; while considerably later, in June and July, a cluster of starvation deaths figure in press reports relating to a remote, upland part of west Clare where the parishes of Inagh and Miltown Malbay converged. In early July, several cases were reported from Partry (Mayo), and Tubbercurry (Sligo).[36] The common factor in all these cases, widely scattered as they were, is that they took place where no public works were in place or where works had been delayed.

In view of all this, and what has been said generally of conditions at this time, it is perhaps surprising that a number of contemporary or near-contemporary assessments of Tory relief policy should have been positive, particularly so in view of the origin of some of these encomia. In June, Fr. Theobald Mathew wrote to Charles Trevelyan, the Treasury official with the greatest influence on relief policy, expressing thanks for the 'wise and generous' measures taken by government, which he considered had succeeded in warding off what might otherwise have been 'a frightful famine'. The following year, Isaac Butt (later to achieve fame as the founder of the Home Rule movement) was to declare that Peel's relief provision had been 'made with consummate skill', and the leading nationalist newspaper, The *Freeman's Journal*, would contend of Peel that 'no man died of famine under his administration'.[37] However, Fr. Mathew's letter was penned during that short illusory period in the summer of 1846, when it seemed that the crisis was over, and drenched as it is in the relief of calamity averted, the language in which it is couched is understandably extravagant. The accolades of Isaac Butt and the *Freeman's Journal* came in April 1847, at a time when Whig-Liberal mismanagement of a renewed crisis was already of such proportions as to make virtually any other government, no matter what its shortcomings, shine by comparison. In effect, therefore, Robert Peel's reputation in Ireland was saved by the misdeeds of his successors.

Since then, most historians have accepted that Tory relief measures were in fact prompt, generous and effective in preventing starvation, many of them relying on these well-known evaluations of Fr. Mathew, Isaac Butt and the *Freeman's Journal*, which have been persuasive precisely because they emanate from sources that were not normally sympathetic to Peel and the Tories. Some of the more recent historians have praised Peel in effusive terms, and qualifications have been few and very moderate.[38] In the absence of any detailed study of exactly what did happen on the ground in the first half of 1846, evidence of community-wide suffering and instances of starvation mortality, where noticed at all by historians, have been taken as isolated and unrepresentative. It has been easy to overlook also that the £850,000 spent by the Tories on relief was far from being as generous as was (and is still often) maintained, in that almost sixty per cent of this sum consisted of loans that would have to be repaid. In fact, three-quarters of the money spent on food supplies was recovered in sales.[39] Peel's antipathy towards Ireland is not something that historians have emphasized too much either; nor has it been very much stressed that during the early months of 1846 his pre-occupation was less with relief than with the suppression of a mass disorder in Ireland that he was almost alone in anticipating, and which never emerged; nor again that his departure from office in the summer came as a result of losing a vote on a harsh Irish Coercion Bill which he had been attempting to push through Parliament.

Writing during the 1960s, Kevin B. Nowlan concluded that Peel 'went out of office without having accomplished anything to make the Irish people better able to meet the calamity that lay ahead of them'. What Nowlan seems to have been hinting at here is something that is apparent from a close reading of the sources for the first half of 1846, that a major outcome of the Tory approach to relief was that the poor became effectively stripped of the ability to resist the slightest further disruption to their lives. The meagreness of the relief afforded and the purposely scheduled delays in its dispensation drove the urban and rural poor to liquidate their every last resource in order to provide for their families. With little to pledge or sell in any case, and the conacre system on which they depended severely disrupted, cottiers, labourers and the poorer smallholders nevertheless divested themselves of anything that could produce ready money. This included whatever furniture remained; domestic animals; tools, boats and fishing tackle for those who combined potato cultivation with other occupations; bedclothes; and the good clothing reserved for Sunday Mass. At a very early point, hypothermia arising out of insufficient clothing, amounting to near-nudity, would become the first hardships of the Famine to affect the very poor, even before the onset of actual hunger.[40]

All over Ireland fourth-class houses were reduced to the condition of their worst examples, leaving just the four walls and a handful of pots and crocks on the earthen floors, where the occupants slept or huddled beside meagre fires of branches and wet turf. In some places, families were reported to be shutting themselves off in their cabins to hide the shame of their destitution; in others once safe smallholders were now reduced to a meal a day.[41] In the wake of the Tory relief programme, the 'hungry months' of the early summer were hungrier, perhaps, than they had ever been. At this point the future of the very poor rested almost totally on two factors: the public works, which now in mid-summer were spreading rapidly; and on the yield of the growing potato crop.

Over large parts of the country, the early potato crop of 1846 had been sown many weeks sooner than usual in order to lengthen the growing season. However, the volume of potatoes sown was significantly lower than in the previous year – according to one estimate by as much as one-third.[42] This was because the blight had discouraged so many growers from again engaging in the massive effort that had gone into the cultivation of marginal land the previous year, and because the conacre system had come under enormous strain since the failure. Labourers and cottiers experienced extreme difficulty in paying their rents, and many conacre plots were abandoned or taken back by farmers. Potatoes normally kept for seed had been ruined by the blight, leading to a chronic shortage and inflated prices; poorer growers were often unable to obtain seed potatoes at any price. And out of sheer necessity others again had eaten potatoes they would normally have set aside for sowing.[43]

In the public prints and in official circles, however, there was little discussion of these issues, and throughout the spring newspapers were as poetic in their descriptions of the growing crop as they had been the previous autumn, and as euphoric about harvest prospects. If such optimism was to some degree a product of the warm sunny weather of May and June, it also reflected a collective will that after all that had been endured up to now, the new potato harvest must not – could not – be anything but bountiful. Scattered early signs, in February and April, of potato blight in very early potatoes passed almost unnoticed in the press, or perhaps were subconsciously ignored, and on 3 June the *Cork Examiner* was exulting in 'a most cheering promise of an abundant harvest', a prediction repeated in almost exactly the same words by the *Freeman's Journal* three weeks later.[44]

But the optimism was short-lived, and from the middle of July onwards it became evident that *Phytophthora infestans* was once again attacking the growing potatoes, renewing its advance this time by an assault on the early crop, in a manner that was markedly more aggressive than the previous year. This time around the attack was even more rapid, leaving a strange disconnected overlap in the sources between urgent pleas for the opening of public works schemes, and descriptions of potato fields newly ruined by blight.

3

One Wide Waste of Putrefying Vegetation: The Second Failure of the Potato

I passed from Cork to Dublin, and this doomed plant bloomed in all the luxuriance of an abundant harvest. Returning on the third instant, I beheld with sorrow one wide waste of putrefying vegetation. In many places the wretched people were seated on the fences of their decaying gardens, wringing their hands and wailing bitterly [of] the destruction that had left them foodless.

— FR. THEOBALD MATHEW, 7 AUGUST 1846

The blight recurred with the reactivation of dormant fungus spores in the soil when conditions became favourable – ironically the same warm, humid weather that had given rise to optimism. Released upwards into growing potato tubers and stalks, the spores produced a new pattern of destruction, and instead of the gradual east–west geographical advance of last year, the blight seemed to strike, frighteningly, everywhere at once. One of the earliest references to the recurrence dates from 11 July, when growing potatoes in Castleconnell, County Limerick and in O'Briensbridge, just across the Shannon, in Clare, showed clear signs of the disease. Within days, blight had made its appearance in gardens around Ennis, where newspaper editor John B. Knox noted with anguish that it was occurring much earlier than the previous year, and that it was much 'deeper in the potato' and likely to be more prevalent.

In the coming days Knox's remarks would be repeated by scores of other commentators throughout Ireland, many of whom seemed awestruck by the rapidity with which the blight was spreading, and by the awful portentousness of the thunderstorms, heavy mists or strange, chilling, 'bitter' or 'noxious' dews that so frequently accompanied it.[1] At Glendalough, County Wicklow, on 19 July, the onset was preceded by a dense white fog that rose from the sea in the direction of the mountains, where the Catholic curate, Fr. John Gowan, was toiling downhill towards the coastline. The next morning, according to Gowan, the entire crop in the area was blighted; the leaves were 'blackened and hanging loosely on their stems, and a disagreeable odour filled the air'. In Laois, the land agent William Steuart Trench, who had sown 160 acres of potatoes on a reclaimed mountain property near Cardtown, was at first relieved to see his crop 'as luxuriant as ever, in full blossom, the stalks matted across each other with richness, promising a splendid produce'. Within a few days, however, among the still luxuriant stalks, a rank odour was now perceptible, indicative of rot below, and within a few days more the stalks and leaves had withered, his entire crop ruined.

Those journeying through the rural landscape had a particularly vivid perspective on the extent of the devastation. In a letter written on 7 August, Fr. Mathew, an inveterate traveller, wrote of his shock in witnessing the spectacle of a crop which so recently had promised 'the luxuriance of an abundant harvest' being reduced over the space of a few days to 'one wide waste of putrefying vegetation'.[2] Less than a week later, on a journey from Ennis to Limerick, John B. Knox noted that virtually all the potato fields he passed were devastated by blight, the one exception standing out in its unsullied green foliage. On his return journey two days after, 'this field had, in the meantime, been attacked and . . . the disease was rapidly spreading through every part of it'. Early in September, Lord Monteagle, the prominent Liberal and Munster landlord, described a journey of 160 miles from Dublin to his country seat in County Limerick, in which he did not see 'one single potato field that was not blighted'.

The failure of 1845 had been partial, and it had been many months before its full extent was apparent. This time the destruction was near-total, with over ninety per cent of the growing potatoes being ruined, early and late crops alike, over a very short space of time, hardly a month in all.[3] Unlike 1845, virtually all that remained sound of the two harvests would be blighted in the ensuing weeks, either in the ground or in the process of digging out. If the failure of 1845 had been unprecedented in scale and very difficult to come to terms with, this time the people were left either numb with disbelief and unable to take in the scale of what had happened, or in a similar state of mind to those 'wretched people' found by Fr. Mathew, 'seated on the fences of their decaying gardens, wringing their hands and wailing bitterly [of] the destruction that had left them foodless'.

Failure of the potato on this scale meant that one of the two props on which hopes for recovery from the grinding misery of the previous twelve months had rested was now gone. Cottiers and labourers, who had exhausted all resources remaining to them over the previous eight months, were now left totally exposed by the new failure, their precarious hold on potato ground evaporating as the conacre system began to crumble. Smallholders a little higher on the socioeconomic scale were under similar threat, and for the first time, tenant farmers once considered comfortable began to feel the pressure because of the twin losses of conacre rents and their own potatoes. Neither commercial growers nor middlemen were immune either, and the land agent, Trench, would soon be forced to surrender his Cardtown property as a direct result of having to write off expected profits from his potato acreage and the cost of reclamation of the land which he had hoped it would finance.

All would now depend on the public works, the second source of this year's hope, so agonizingly slow to materialize, but so important to the preservation of life when they did; these would surely be expedited in areas they had not so far reached, and expanded to deal with the scale of the new crisis. A strong, if vague, confidence prevailed in the new Whig-Liberal government, which was expected to prove more generous than its Tory predecessor. 'We expect good measures from the British parliament,' wrote one elderly Kerry smallholder, James Prendergast, in an unworried letter to his children in the United States in mid-August, 'but we must wait to know the issue.' According to the ranking Commissariat officer in County Limerick, Colonel Pine-Coffin, as unfortunate in his name as Captain Helpman in Conamara had been happy in his, the most common remark made to him regarding the potato failure by the country people was that 'we know your honour will help us again.'[4]

But rescue by government action was by no means a foregone conclusion. The limited measures introduced by the Tories to deal with the failure of 1845 had been set at nought by the new failure: all the intricate planning, the clever time-tabling of different aspects of the programme to coincide with anticipated levels of destitution was now irrelevant, swallowed up in a new crisis that, if it was to be addressed properly, would require a level of expenditure and state involvement with its population that had no precedent anywhere. If Peel's performance in 1845–1846 made it uncertain as to whether he would have been equal to the challenge, a combination of factors made his successors entirely unfit for it, and it was, therefore, to the profoundest misfortune of the Irish poor that the recurrence of the blight coincided with the arrival in office of a Whig-Liberal government headed by Lord John Russell.

Russell's administration was a rickety one whose survival was contingent on the continuing divisions between the two squabbling Tory factions. He came to power (without a general election) at the head of a party that contained a wide divergence of tendencies and vested interests that had to be catered to. Even more than their Tory predecessors, the new cabinet was influenced by Christian providentialism and the unyielding tenets of political economy, with a particularly rigid laissez-faire attitude with regard to private enterprise and the markets. Wealthy country gentlemen or noblemen all, and far removed from the life experience of the Irish poor, they had an instinctive suspicion of relief expenditure, which they believed encouraged waste and dependency; had a 'demoralizing' effect on the recipients, and should therefore be confined to the strict minimum necessary and for the shortest possible period. A number of the most influential party members and office-holders were great landowning magnates with extensive Irish properties, among them Lords Palmerston, Clanricarde, Stanley, Lansdowne and Bessborough, individuals whose interests were diametrically opposed to those of Irish labourers, cottiers and smallholders, and whose hostility to any relief effort involving financial liability for themselves, no matter what the circumstances, was guaranteed.

Above all, the new government was influenced much more strongly than its predecessor by the Treasury, whose head, Assistant-Secretary Charles Trevelyan, had been closely involved in the Tory relief programme by virtue of his control over the purse strings. Trevelyan, who was also a man of evangelical views and an adherent of political economy, was a workaholic, arrogant individual still in his thirties, much frustrated by the subordinate position to which the Tory Prime Minister had firmly relegated him, as he had been by the many shortcomings of the Peel administration, and the pervasive inefficiency, cronyism and abuse he considered to have bedevilled their relief programme. On the other hand, he and the senior figures of the new administration were mutually congenial to an extraordinary degree, and the approval of Lord John Russell and Sir Charles Wood, the new Chancellor of the Exchequer, from the outset lent Trevelyan an influence on policy that was much greater than normally permitted a civil servant. Although he was never able to dictate Whig relief policies to the extent that was once believed, the most recent historian of the topic, Peter Gray, has shown that very close relationships with his political masters would henceforth make Trevelyan the 'lynchpin of relief operations', a role he would occupy while the Famine lasted.[5]

None of this was yet apparent when the new regime took over in mid-summer, and with the exception of the militant young nationalists associated with the *Nation* newspaper, in Ireland the changeover was greeted with general enthusiasm. The Whig-Liberals, after all, were the old parliamentary allies of Daniel O'Connell and his Repealers, and during the 1830s the alliance had borne such rich fruit as Ireland's unique national system of state-sponsored elementary education in 1831, the Poor Inquiry of the mid-decade, and the pragmatic resolution of the tithes question in 1838; it was not yet held against the Whig-Liberals that they were responsible for the Poor Law of the same year. Lastly, it was a Liberal-Repeal parliamentary combination that had driven the Tories from office.

The accession to power of the Whig-Liberals promised a renewal of the old alliance, clinched by a speech by Russell in Parliament in which he announced his intention of pressing ahead with long-sought Irish reforms, including a franchise-widening bill, a landlord and tenant bill, and a programme for the reclamation of wasteland. For the longer term, further reforms were in prospect.

For much of the summer, to the extent that the new administration concerned itself with Ireland, it was in terms of these planned reforms rather than the crisis precipitated by the second successive failure of the potato harvest, which Russell first broached to Parliament on 18 July, four days after he had been informed of the return of the blight, and a week after it first became current news.[6] Trevelyan's initial reaction to news of the resurgent blight was typical of the man; the Peelite relief programmes must, he believed, be closed down as soon as possible, since if they were still in operation as a new food crisis was unfolding, the poor would become permanently conditioned to having the state take care of them. In full agreement with this view, on 21 July, Sir Charles Wood ordered the shutdown of all public works, whether completed or not, from 8 August, and the closure of the meal depots and the dissolution of the Relief Commission by 15 August.[7] For those depending on the works or those who were still waiting for works schemes to open in their particular district, this would prove to be the worst possible government decision, made at the worst possible moment.

Nevertheless, Irish realities could not be totally ignored, and even as the meal depots were closed and the public works shut down as ordered, plans for a new relief programme were being drafted. These were based on a memo presented to government by Trevelyan on 1 August, and elaborated on by Russell in Parliament on the seventeenth. Russell's parliamentary statement began with a reference to the 'great pain' he felt in informing the House that prospects for the potato harvest were 'even more distressing than last year', and continued with an outline of a series of proposals, involving a great programme of public works, supplemented where necessary by the emergency provision of food. At first sight it seemed to amount to no more than a re-structuring of the Tory measures that had just been terminated, the resemblances hardly surprising given the ideological assumptions shared by Tories and Whig-Liberals, and the continuity afforded by Trevelyan's central involvement.

However, the more extreme commitment of the Whig-Liberals to laissez-faire principles is reflected in important areas that were initially easy to overlook, chief among them a much-enhanced preoccupation with economy; with the elimination of waste and abuse, and strangest of all to modern eyes in a famine situation, with value for money. Even though ground-level relief operations would again combine the efforts of government officials and local relief committees, the Treasury would henceforth exercise much tighter control over finances, and, through officers of the army Commissariat, over the distribution of food. In the interests of cost-efficiency, it was not considered necessary to appoint a new Relief Commission.

The new government was also determined not to purchase any further quantities of grain on the international markets, leaving the supply of grain instead to merchants, who Trevelyan insisted – rather more strongly than the merchants themselves – would not import supplies if the government was seen to be doing likewise.[8] Only in remote and impoverished areas of the west where normal market structures did not exist would supply depots be established, and the government was adamant, despite the distress present in such areas, that no depots would be opened along the south coast or in impoverished areas of the east. No matter how harrowing the circumstances of the poor in eastern districts became, there would be no relenting on this last decision. The western depots were to be supplied by the stock in hand at the time they had been closed in August and, in accordance with the changes of June, food would be sold to the poor at the prices of the local markets, with an added loading factor of about fifteen per cent to ward off speculative purchase.

In the context of a second, much graver food crisis, these policies were woefully restrictive, and only in regard to the purchase of meal would worsening circumstances lead to any significant revision. This came about when, after many weeks of representations from senior Commissariat officers and certain public figures, government finally accepted the necessity of purchasing limited quantities in Britain and abroad.[9] However, by the time agents acting on behalf of government attempted to buy the meal in agreed amounts, they came up against an international grain shortage. Ultimately, only a small quantity could be sourced, and had to be purchased at much higher prices than would have been the case had it been purchased a few short months earlier.

In addition, the inevitable months-long delay between the sourcing, purchase and transportation of the supplies meant that the stocks in the western depots remained very low. Meanwhile, a flotilla of small naval steamboats puttered through coastal waterways and in around isolated headlands all along the western seaboard, moving supplies of grain that were inadequate to the purpose from one place to another in an effort to make up the deficiency, while coastguard personnel busied themselves making quern stones available for grinding. Fearful of the implications for the poor of the approaching winter, in September and again in October, Sir Randolph Routh, the head of the army Commissariat, would tentatively suggest to Trevelyan that Irish-produced grain now being exported to Britain in increasing quantities might suffice to bridge the gap in supplies, or might help to do so.

For Trevelyan, this was a heretical proposal and on the second occasion it was made, he rounded on Routh, telling him not to 'countenance in any way the idea of prohibiting exportation', which he believed would 'inflict a permanent injury on the country'. By December, only 22,000 tons of meal had been purchased abroad by government agents, and of this only a pitiful 4,800 tons had yet arrived in Ireland. When the depots were finally opened in December, they were insufficiently stocked, and throughout the winter as they sought to add to their supplies, government ordered even closer regulation, and maintained their insistence on grain sales at local market prices.[10] All these decisions would impact very severely on the poor in the east of Ireland, which would have no meal supplies at all, and on those in the west, where they were available on such restricted terms.

But the emergency supply of food was a relatively minor aspect of the Whig-Liberals' relief strategy, and considerably greater importance was attached to the role of relief committees, both in regard to the collection of local contributions, and as indispensable adjuncts in the operation of the proposed new public works. New rules drafted by Routh were aimed at exercising a tighter control over the committees, which were to be appointed by the lord lieutenant of each county rather than allowed to be organized locally; their powers were much reduced, and their proceedings were subject to examination by inspecting officers. The new rules meant a substantial changeover in membership, in which Repealers who had dominated town-based committees were excluded for political reasons and Catholic curates for reasons that never became clear. Repealers and Catholic curates had been particularly effective on committees, the latter having laboured 'like tigers', according to Lord Monteagle, who declared that without them 'we could not do a stroke'. In addition, government contributions to local relief funds were to be reduced to half the total amount collected locally, although as mass starvation spread across the country towards the end of the year, further sums would be allocated on a case-by-case, though stringently monitored, basis.[11]

The Whig-Liberal public works programme was set forth in the legislation that became known as the Labour Rate Act, passed on 28 August. Under this Act, all works were to be integrated under the Board of Works and funding was to be an entirely local charge, based on government loans repayable through the county tax, or cess, but levied according to the rating mechanism of the Poor Law. By making the cost of works a local charge, it was hoped much of the supposedly wasteful, inefficient and corrupt practices believed to have marred the Tory works schemes could be eliminated, as well as the foolish financial excesses of the presentment sessions.

As it was laid out, the working of the Labour Rate Act promised to be even more hidebound by bureaucratic procedures than the earlier works legislation. As before, only works selected at presentment sessions by magistrates and cesspayers in each district could be pursued, but with the difference that presentment sessions now had to be authorized by the Lord Lieutenant, whenever he judged that want in a given locality had reached a critical point. Following the presentment sessions, the approval of the Board of Works for individual schemes was first required, followed by the sanction of the Treasury. After these procedures were followed, Board personnel for each district were appointed and supervisors hired, and the approved routes surveyed by engineers. Only when these time-consuming preliminary tasks had been completed could relief committees begin to select persons needy enough to require employment.[12]

At the Treasury, Trevelyan was not perturbed by delays he admitted would be extensive, but saw them instead as providing the opportunity for Board of Works managers to 'restore their establishments on a scale proportional to the magnitude of the task about to devolve upon them, and to prepare, through their district officers, plans and estimates for the assistance of the baronial sessions'.[13] As for the labourers, he envisaged them happily taking advantage of what he called the 'breathing-time' to harvest their own crops and carry out wage-producing harvest work for large farmers.

Satisfactory as all this might have appeared on paper, it failed to take account of the fact that the return of the blight had deprived labourers of any crops to harvest and farmers of agricultural work to give to labourers. Seismic changes had taken place in rural society since the previous autumn, in which the relationship between conacre labourers and farmers had been shattered, and by August of 1846, as they contemplated their blight-ruined potato gardens, the former had little reason to fulfil the labour obligations of their conacre agreements. Labourer domestic economies faced collapse, not least because the wherewithal no longer existed to feed pigs. Farmers, who were themselves beginning to feel the economic pinch, would henceforth insist on prior cash payment for conacre, a development that effectively excluded labourers from access to potato land in the future.[14]

As the conacre system began to disintegrate, farmer families, themselves beginning on a process of impoverishment at a pace that varied with their previous circumstances and local conditions, would in future carry out the agricultural tasks which had previously been delegated to labourers. With the evaporation of harvest work, therefore, the labourers and cottiers that together formed one solid stratum at the base of Irish society were without the means of sustaining themselves, and any reserves they once had were now long gone. The time was not far off when many of them would be faced with the choice between squatting in their cabins until physically removed from them, or of abandoning their plots altogether.

It does not appear that Trevelyan ever came to an understanding of these matters, or that the implementation of his relief programme, regardless of the 'approaching calamity' (his own phrase), was bound to lead to enormous suffering. Of the 'breathing space' so crucial to his strategy, his self-serving account of the period, *The Irish Crisis* (1848), tells us no more than that it 'was not obtained'. Despite this there would be no departure from the schedule for the opening of public works laid down in late August, and this meant that the new public works would not come into operation before mid-October at the earliest. For over a month and a half after the closure of the Tory schemes, therefore, apart from supplies issued by a few meal depots that remained open in the west, some few works sites left functioning for a time, and the distracted efforts of the membership of a number of committees who remained at their posts, almost nothing in the way of relief reached the vulnerable poor.

For labourers and their families, the loss of their potatoes followed by the closure of the public works was extraordinarily disheartening. 'The cup has been held to the lip of the most patient peasantry in Ireland,' wrote the Rev. James Garrett from Sligo to the Under Secretary on 30 August, bitterly protesting the shutdown of works in Ballymote, just three days into a newly sanctioned phase of operation, 'and is dashed suddenly from their grasp without slaking their hunger or thirst.'[15] For thousands of discharged labourers, in Sligo as elsewhere in Ireland, the closures opened up, for the first time, the real and terrifying prospect of death by starvation. In this period, there can be no doubt that numbers of people certainly did perish, although for the most part they died without leaving much of a trace in the evidence. Among them were persons living on their own and/or in remote areas; elderly persons whose deaths were misattributed to old age or illness, or younger persons whose deaths were concealed by families shamed by their inability to provide for them.

The earliest recorded instance that it has been possible to find in the literature for this period dates from mid-August, and concerns the death of a public works labourer in Skibbereen, County Cork; it was followed a few weeks later by the death of a young man named Anthony Donnelly, whose body was found on the twenty-fifth near Massbrook, a remote location between Pontoon and Crossmolina in Mayo. We are not told the identity of the Skibbereen victim, and of Anthony all we know is that for ten days before he died he had been on the public works; at the inquest held on his body, it emerged that his food in the interval had consisted entirely of rotten potatoes. If we add to this scattered evidence of starvation what we know of the physical appearance of the poor, it is clear that as autumn loomed, over a great portion of the west and south of Ireland many communities were now at the beginning of a painful descent into mass debilitation, and that the public works, when they eventually came into operation, would serve merely to slow the process rather than to reverse it.[16] In a proportion of instances, as we shall see, it would hasten it.

The prospect of starvation elicited a variety of responses from those who faced it, ranging from a reflexive violence to a fatalistic, passive pleading with civil and ecclesiastical authority. As far back as July, the brutal policy of shaking labourers off the public works prior to shutdowns by wage reductions had led to a spate of attacks on officials and supervisors. In County Limerick, in early August, labourers informed of an imminent works closure tore up a section of road which they had just constructed, while in Roscommon at the end of the month, wage reductions on the Clover Hill works saw three hundred labourers storm into Roscommon town and threaten to sack it and steal beef, mutton and bread if their pay was not restored to its full amount. Terrified, the local Board of Works inspector complied.[17]

The mere existence of a great assembly of people was enough to create a sense of threat to civil order, no matter what their overall disposition. However, the great majority of labourer protests and marches that emerged at this time were peaceable affairs, at least initially. Whatever aggression the participants displayed was belied by the pleading tone of the petitions they subsequently put together for forwarding to government by local magistrates. For the most part, they showed a willingness to disperse under the soothing promises made by authority figures. Such was the case with the five hundred or so discharged labourers, 'poor, wretched, emaciated human beings', carrying loys and shovels, who assembled outside the residence of a magistrate, in Islandeady, County Mayo, in mid-August. The several thousand poor persons who marched into Westport in the same county, to the residence of the Marquis of Sligo, took exquisite care to avoid walking on his gravel driveway, 'lest their doing so might injure the grass of the demesne'. They departed, satisfied, after Sligo promised them he would not harass them for his rents, and that he would do 'as much as any Mayo landlord' to assist them.

Nevertheless, over time, increasing desperation gave an edge to public demonstrations, and the hundreds of labourers who marched into Unionhall, south-west Cork, some weeks later, demanded food and employment in much

Food demonstration in Dungarvan, County Waterford, October 1846. Note the loaf of bread attached to the pole. *Pictorial Times*.

more strident tones, vowing that they would not allow themselves to starve. Even more agitated were the 7,000 smallholders and labourers who crowded around the sessions house at Clifden, Conamara, on the day of presentment sessions on 23 September, and murmured agreement when one of their number called out, in good English, 'We will not die of hunger: on this point we are all agreed – we will slaughter every beast in Connemara – we will not do the thing at night, but openly in the light of day. The cattle belonging to the landlords must be first'.[18]

If such scenes were played out mostly in the western half of Ireland, the labouring population was suffering even in districts close to Dublin. So appalled did the new Lord Lieutenant, Lord Bessborough, become by the sights he was now witnessing on a daily basis close to his own environs in the Phoenix Park, that on his own authority on 6 September, he ordered the immediate resumption of all the discontinued works, hardly a week after the last of them had closed. But Bessborough's maverick gesture cannot have made much difference: no funds had been allocated and the Board of Works was undergoing a reorganizational metamorphosis that would leave it immobilized until mid-October, when new works would be laid out under the Labour Rate Act.

Many of the early, peaceful labourer marches featured the symbolism noticed in the previous chapter of an individual at the front holding aloft a spade or pole to which was attached a loaf of bread. Such was the case on 8 September in County Tipperary, where labourers from Loughkeen parish marched in procession to Birr, in Offaly, in search of food and work. At another march about the same time between Doneraile and Mallow in County Cork, the foremost marcher held up a pole on which a diseased potato was impaled.[19] This kind of symbolism had faded by the end of September when labourers had lost faith in the promises of authority, and mass marches that began peaceably increasingly degenerated into disorder. In County Cork, full-blown riots were taking place by the last week of the month, with great crowds of starving people from the country rampaging through towns such as Cloyne, Castlemartyr, Midleton and Fermoy, looting bakeries and grain stores. In Castlemartyr, the crowd seized as much food as they could from shops and stores, before gathering at the residence of the earl of Shannon, and threatening to pull down his castle 'over the head of his lordship'. On 25 September, immense crowds gathered on the hill above Youghal with the intention of sacking the town, and were only prevented from so doing by the intervention of parish clergy.

The Cork disturbances were, significantly, concentrated in the easterly, less distressed districts, rather than in the stricken west. Similarly, across the border in Waterford, it was the more prosperous western portion of the county that was convulsed by the outbreaks of late September.[20] In Clare, most of the disturbances took place in the centre of the county, around and to the south of Ennis rather than in the distant parishes west of Kilrush, which were already sinking mutely into the horror of mass starvation. In Galway, it was in the congested city centre that sustained rioting took place in early October, and fears that the turbulent boatmen of the Claddagh might join the townspeople in their disorder caused the authorities to position armed vessels on the Corrib River, separating them.

A noteworthy feature of these disorderly marches and the riotous incidents that arose out of them, was that apart from a handful where crowds were fired on, police intervention, which in pre-Famine food riots had tended to be brutal and bloody, resulted in comparatively little injury. In many cases, indeed, the police seem to have exercised restraint, to the extent of avoiding even direct physical contact with the gaunt and hunger-inflamed rioters. Few, however, can have shown the same compassion as the Waterford constables who, rather than apprehend several men caught breaking into a city store in November, instead offered them the money in their pockets. The response of the men was equally surprising; in their pride they refused to accept it.[21]

In many of these disorders crowd action was focused primarily on preventing the outward movement of grain. As far as it is possible to judge this seems to have arisen as a spontaneous collective impulse, and the manner in which it was repeated in town after town and city after city across the country is very striking. In these occurrences, typically, crowds stood in the path of grain-carrying vehicles, which were often forced back to the warehouses from which they had come.[22] In Galway, meal carts leaving for different parts of the county were turned back as they exited the city limits, their drivers obliged to take an oath that they would not carry grain out of town. In Enniscorthy, County Wexford, in December, crowds of poor people assembled for the purpose of preventing grain carts moving northwards in the direction of Wicklow. For the last two months of the year, collaboration between south Clare crowds and elements within the narrow confines of the city reduced the supply of grain to Limerick to a mere trickle.[23]

In the countryside, armed parties strove to retain grain supplies within different communities by preventing farmers from bringing their grain to town markets. Newspapers identified these anonymous disguised groups as being from the labourer-smallholder social strata, and farmers responded by adopting a system of armed convoys. Such events inevitably aggravated hostilities between farmers and labourers, already at a heightened level because of the conflict relating to the now worthless conacre plots. Over a broad region of Munster, including parts of Clare, Limerick and Tipperary, the enforcement of this 'moral economy' was carried out with precision, according to the old secret society traditions of the province. Participants referred to themselves as Whiteboys, Molly Maguires or Terry Alts, and acted in accordance with the old long-standing rituals established generations previously. Threatening notices were issued, signed by the pseudonymous Captain Starlight, Captain Moonlight or Lady Clare, to farmers sending grain to markets outside the locality, and an escalating sequence of sanctions was developed for dealing with those who refused to abide by their interdictions. Ignored warnings were succeeded by the formal escorting of grain vehicles back to their point of origin by individuals clad in the traditional disguise of blackened face and white sheets or women's shifts. Repeat offenders had their horses shot, while those seen as incorrigibly persistent faced the ultimate sanction of assassination.[24]

Although secret society activity would continue well into 1847, fluctuating on a seasonal basis in autumn and winter for several years more (in some districts intermittently until 1849) food-related protest was at its height from September to November of 1846. It took place in the context of an escalating incidence of sheep and cattle stealing; plundering of grain carts and coastal vessels; threatening letters and posted notices; arms raids on big houses; assaults on farmers, landlords and their servants; and attempted and successful assassinations. As hunger turned to actual starvation for scores of thousands of labourers and cottiers, all this activity formed the fraught background against which the presentment sessions of the new public works proceeded.[25]

The settings for presentment sessions varied from the formal surroundings of urban courthouses to the modest 'sessions houses' of rural villages and hamlets. Proceedings were directed by authority figures; landlords, relief committee members and clergymen. In accordance with regulations, Boards of Works personnel were invariably present to help guide presentments towards realistic objectives. Great crowds attended these sessions, and everyone present showed the deepest interest in the proceedings; from the landlords and cesspayers who would ultimately bear the financial burden, to the labourers, cottiers and smallholders who formed the overwhelming majority of the attendance, and whose survival depended on their ability to find employment.

The atmosphere at these presentment sessions was usually one of great tension, manifested in the volume of noise made by the labourer audiences, the many loud interruptions from the floor, and, most ominously of all, in the silences which sometimes greeted proposals from the chair. Humorous exchanges were frequent, and entire meetings sometimes dissolved for a time in bouts of laughter that carried more than a hint of hysteria. In few counties were sessions calm and orderly, and in most areas rapidly worsening conditions stretched the tension to almost unbearable levels. This was the case in the east of Ireland and throughout the northern counties, just as in those of the west and south. Sessions held in Counties Tyrone and Armagh, in fact, furnish some of the most turbulent scenes witnessed anywhere in Ireland, and in Down, according to James Grant, they were characterized by 'anxiety, menace and even violence'.[26]

Regardless of how early the presentment sessions were held, however, or of what transpired at them, they could not translate into actual public works until the required administrative procedures had been complied with, and even then not until after 8 October, when the activities of relief committees were sanctioned by the publication of their official instructions. In the weeks that followed, altogether 1,097 committees came into existence across the country, including counties where they had not previously been formed; in all nearly 450 more than under the Tory schemes. Prolongation of procedural matters caused many delays in commencements, thereby inflicting great injury on the poor who waited so desperately for them, although in a surprising proportion of districts and counties, works opened within just a few weeks of presentment sessions. At any rate, from the middle of October, very slowly at first, then with ever greater rapidity, public works sites opened across the country. Within weeks of the first presentment sessions, some 26,000 persons were in the employ of the Board of Works on schemes under the Labour Rate Act and by 21 November more than 250,000 were so employed. By the end of December this had risen to 441,000.[27]

The Labour Rate Act favoured the same 'un-reproductive' works that had characterized the Tory schemes, and despite the furore that culminated in the famous Letter issued by Chief Secretary Labouchere allowing 'reproductive' schemes, the vast majority of those undertaken consisted, as before, of road-widening, hill-cutting and hollow-filling, and the construction of new roads, many of them involving the reopening of sites abandoned the previous August. Some benefits certainly attached to the construction of most of these roads, but under normal circumstances their priority would have been so low as to make them almost pointless. The exercise as a whole was one that, to put it mildly, amounted to an extraordinarily inefficient use of funds, the irony being that it was brought about by a government supposedly wedded to the virtues of efficiency.

The first presentment sessions had begun at that point when the entire cottier/labourer stratum, the underclass below them and a sizeable portion of the smallholders directly above, had reached the brink of starvation. As the works commenced persons at this level of society were dying in significant numbers; as the public works at last began to reach into the parishes, starvation mortality became a torrent that would continue throughout the winter and the early months of 1847. The works would certainly save many thousands of lives, but they would also hasten the ending of thousands of others whose health had broken under months of food deprivation. Public works labourers and their families would therefore become the first mass casualties of the Famine.

Even in the present state of our knowledge, the first deaths in this first great wave of starvation mortality remain difficult to pinpoint; however, the three unnamed persons stated to have died of hunger at Cong, County Mayo, in the first week of October, certainly figure very early. The first death of a person to whom we can assign a name and identity comes from County Clare on the ninth, a widow named Conlon, from Cloontohil, near Dysart, who dropped dead from hunger-related exhaustion as she set out for Ennis, five miles to the south, in search of food for her children. From two weeks later, on 25 October, comes the case of Dennis McKennedy, from Caheragh, near Skibbereen, County Cork, who was found dead on the roadside near his home.[28]

The spread of starvation mortality in the country as a whole is usefully illustrated in the experience of north County Mayo, for which an unusually full documentation is possible, and from which the following catalogue is taken. It begins with reports from the end of September relating to the villages between Pontoon and Foxford that 'entire families' were 'lying and many dying', the appearance of disease exacerbating their situation. In the first week of October parents in Castlebar were reported to be putting their children to bed during the day, in order 'to sleep off the hunger which was gnawing at their hearts'. During the same week, the three starvation fatalities from Cong, mentioned above, took place.

On 26 October, the *Tyrawley Herald* carried an inquest report on a man named Hugh Daly who died 'in consequence of insufficiency of food' near Ballina, and three days later another on a woman named Bridget Thomash, a public works employee, who died at Ballycastle 'having eaten a bare meal a day for the fortnight before her death, and sometimes nothing'. Hundreds of 'poor creatures' were reported to be similarly circumstanced in the same locality. On 6 November, a woman named Melody died of starvation near Palmerstown. The night before her death she had procured shelter in another woman's cabin, where she consumed a small mixture of meal and water. The following morning, after attempting to rise from the straw on which she was lying, she fell dead from exhaustion. Post-mortem examination revealed her stomach to be much shrunken, with no food at all in the large intestine.

On 17 November four persons were recorded as having died of starvation in the parish of Attymass. On 5 December the relief committee at Claremorris reported that on one works some labourers 'from extreme hunger are not now able to crawl to work'. These individuals were clearly close to death.[29] By 11 December in Ballaghadereen, where only one-fifth of the working population had succeeded in obtaining public works employment, numbers of deaths were also reported to have taken place. From this time forward, the sources contain details of inquests on the bodies of Martin McGever, Crossmolina; John Barrett, Cloomalagh, Killala; Anthony Malley, Notlish, Crossmolina; John Munnelly, Ballymoholy; Pat Loftus, Knockfall; Catherine Walsh, Robeen; John Ruane, Lacken; and Bernard Regan, Crossmolina.[30]

Of these we know that Pat Loftus had been carried into the house of Anthony Walsh at Straide by neighbours on the evening of Friday, 11 December. After struggling to digest the warm milk, gruel and bread given him by his host, he died about 12 o'clock that night; the only property found on his 'miserably clad' body afterwards was one half penny and a pair of spectacles. Catherine Walsh was an elderly woman, who worked on the public works until 'from her age' she was no longer able to withstand the onset of a winter that would prove the coldest in living memory. At the inquest on her body held on 16 December, the examining doctor concluded that she had died of starvation. The body of John Ruane, on which an inquest was held two days later, was found by a little girl on the pavement near the church at Lacken. Ruane came from 'a colony of fishermen', who were 'comfortable in their own way before the present calamity'; his death, the jury ruled, came about through starvation. Bernard Regan, a young boy, was the son of a Limerick butcher, who, having lost his employment, was refused entry to both Limerick and Galway workhouses (having walked the intervening distance along with his seven children). The family subsequently begged its way to Crossmolina, where the boy died.[31]

Indications are that similar catalogues could be compiled for other counties without much difficulty.[32] A systematic examination of printed and manuscript sources would without any doubt hugely increase the number of known instances of death by starvation, but even this would provide a mere impression of the true picture, since mortality of this kind was documented in a small proportion of cases only; at no stage during the Famine would any attempt be made at an official tally. Even the relatively plentiful source material that survives regarding hunger deaths on the Mizen peninsula of west Cork, the best-documented of all distressed locations in Ireland at this time, understates their full extent by a considerable factor.

We know more about the Mizen district because of the writings of a number of clergymen, journalists, newspaper sketch artists and philanthropic visitors to the locality. Through their efforts, parishes such as Skibbereen and Schull would become bywords for the horrors of Ireland during this period and for much of 1847. Like so many of the districts of the western half of Ireland, where tens of thousands would perish so miserably, south-west Cork was a place of stunning natural beauty. It was densely populated by smallholders, cottiers and conacre men, and its land was predominantly owned by a small number of absentee landlords. No commercial infrastructure existed, although parts of the region, especially Schull and Skibbereen, had until recently been major suppliers of potatoes to the Cork markets. Despite mounting distress, the relief depot at Skibbereen remained shut, and the public works did not open until the poor were at starvation level, in mid-October.

Starvation mortality began in October with the death of Dennis McKennedy, mentioned above. Dennis's death, which was once believed to represent the earliest known starvation death during the Famine, attracted attention because on the day he died he had been labouring on the public works. Post-mortem examination of his body revealed no food at all in the stomach or small intestines, a 'portion of undigested raw cabbage' found in the large bowel indicating his last meal. The coroner's jury, which subsequently brought in a starvation verdict, attributed his death to the 'gross negligence' of the Board of Works.

A gap of several weeks followed before details emerged of the death of another public works labourer, Jeremiah Hegarty, also of Caheragh, on 10 November. Head of an extended family of nine, Jeremiah had been labouring for eight days on the works, until at two in the afternoon, he sat by the ditch, 'apparently very weak', and died shortly thereafter. Medical evidence given at the subsequent inquest revealed that 'want of sufficient nourishment was the remote, and exposure to the cold the direct cause of his death'. His daughter's affecting testimony revealed that on the Friday night, Jeremiah had given his own food to his grandchildren 'because they used to be crying of hunger'. The family had a little haggard of barley, but the landlord had 'put a cross on it', marking it off for his rent. Her father's bed, she told the court, 'was a little straw scattered on the ground and some packing for his covering', and the rain was 'down though her house'. The family also had no turf for the fire, 'because they had no food for the people that would be required to cut it'. Her father had pawned all his good clothing two years earlier; and her husband's greatcoat and a quilt which might have warmed him had just been pledged in order to help pay for the manuring of the garden.[33]

On 15 December, a Cork magistrate named Nicholas Cummins entered some cabins in what he at first thought was a deserted hamlet near Skibbereen. In the first,

> six famished and ghostly skeletons, to all appearance dead, were huddled in a corner on some filthy straw, their sole covering . . . a ragged horsecloth, their wretched legs hanging about, naked above the knees. I approached with horror and found by a low moaning that they were still alive – they were in fever, four children and a woman and what once had been a man . . . in a few minutes I was surrounded by at least 200 of such phantoms, such frightful spectres as no words can describe. By far the greater number were delirious, either from famine or fever. Their demonic yells are still ringing in my ears and their horrible images as fixed upon my brain.

In another cabin, Cummins's clothes were 'nearly torn off' when he tried to bolt from 'the throng of pestilence' that gathered around him; a tight grip on his neckcloth forced him to turn about and confront 'a woman with an infant just born in her arms and the remains of a filthy sack across her loins – the sole covering of herself and baby'. The same morning, according to Cummins, the constabulary opened a house on the adjoining land 'which was observed shut for many days, and two frozen corpses were found, lying on the mud floor, half devoured by rats.' A mother, he tells us, herself in fever, 'was seen the same day to drag out the corpse of her child, a girl about twelve, perfectly naked and leave it covered with stones.'

No-one was more aware of what was happening in south-west Cork, and indeed in Ireland as a whole, than Charles Trevelyan, a man who refused to filter his correspondence through secretaries, insisting on reading it all: such was the volume of information reaching him from Ireland, indeed, that his private papers constitute one of the most important sources for Famine history. In addition to official documentation concerning west Cork, press reports were also available to him, and in early December the personal testimony of a delegation of Protestant clergymen from the area, not to mention the published account of Nicholas Cummins. Yet Trevelyan's thinking at this time still challenges analysis. Was his refusal to allow the opening of the relief depot at Cork until the end of December due to his own knowledge that stocks of grain were so very low that they were totally insufficient to feed the poor there, or indeed anywhere else? For weeks he had been refusing pleas from Donegal and Mayo to open the depots in those locations, or to establish stores in Monaghan and Wicklow. Routh's letter on 12 December, informing him that he had authorized the opening of the Skibbereen depot three days a week, elicited a warning from Trevelyan that regulations must be observed, and that grain could not legally be dispensed from government stores there. The irrelevancy of their exchange was lost on both men: hardly any meal was sold from the Skibbereen depot in the event because the starving inhabitants did not have the money to purchase it.[34]

Trevelyan's unconscionable rigidity in clinging to the letter of regulations which he himself had drafted might be said to bespeak something that went pathologically beyond mere bureaucratic intransigence, but if this is the case, its nature is something we cannot know. At the very least, he had bungled the emergency food supply situation unbelievably, yet at no stage does he reveal any level of self-doubt that might accompany a realization of personal failure. And although the dreadful developments in the parishes of west Cork, together with similar events elsewhere, were crucial in the abrupt subsequent government decision made on Trevelyan's advice to abandon current relief strategies altogether, he was able to extricate himself from the situation without attracting significant criticism or lessening government faith in his abilities.

Starving children in potato field at Caheragh, County Cork, February 1847. *Illustrated London News*.

The Blessed Effects of Political Economy: Public Works and Soup Kitchens

*On yesterday, all without exception were dismissed from the public works . . .
the new committee has not as yet . . . distributed a single ration to the starved
multitude who have been for weeks waiting on them. This district will be one
vast graveyard and afford a most beautiful illustration of the blessed effects of
political economy.*

– FR. PHILIP FITZGERALD, CALLAN, MAY 1847

By early March 1847, when the public works were at their greatest extent, Ireland's
roads network had become a gigantic construction site. On five thousand separate works around the country, some 734,000 persons toiled, six days a week. The
works represented the sole economic support of over three million people, more
than one-third of the country's pre-Famine population. Twelve thousand officials,
from engineers and overseers to check-clerks and pay-clerks, were employed in
organizational or supervisory capacities. On one level the creation of employment on such a scale and at such short notice was an administrative achievement
that historians have justly considered astonishing. On the other hand, over its full
range of operation, from October 1846 to July 1847, the public works are more
astonishing still as a reflection of the lengths to which the ideologically driven
government of Lord John Russell was prepared to go rather than actually feed
the starving.

Such a colossal programme was possible at all only because the labour requirements were very basic and very similar everywhere. Roads were of a standard
Board of Works design, of an average width of twenty-one feet, flanked on both
sides by simple drains. Construction and repair presented no real technical challenge; neither machinery nor draft animals were in general use, and the labour
of the workers was virtually identical on every works. 'The men are put in gangs
to excavate the hills and remove the earth to the hollows', the young Westmeath
engineer, John Keegan, newly appointed to a district in Offaly noted in his diary

in January 1847, 'six to eight loosening, four filling the barrows, and four men wheeling. A double run of twenty five or thirty yards back.'[1] Such work practices varied hardly at all on roads from Antrim to Waterford.

In terms of geographical distribution, public works employment was skewed towards a number of counties in the west and south, reflecting the regional imbalance of human suffering as well as a wide divergence in local skills in the working of public works legislation. The daily average of persons employed in Cork and Galway stood at something over 42,000 and 33,000 persons respectively, while the smaller counties of Clare and Limerick held a greatly disproportionate respective daily average of 31,000 and 26,000. By contrast, the daily average in Down, at just 335, and Antrim at 270, reflects a much lesser level of destitution in these counties.

In each county, works were monitored by Board of Works superintendent engineers and inspectors; smaller districts were supervised by junior engineers, while individual sites were in the charge of stewards or overseers. These lower-ranking employees, along with check clerks and pay clerks, tended to be young men whose attire, educational attainment and position of authority was sufficient to set them off sharply from the labourers, apart altogether from the fact that their presence was a matter of career choice rather than the stark matter of survival it was for the latter.[2]

The great majority of those who toiled on the public works were labourers, cottiers or smallholders, or practitioners of trades for which there was now no demand. In northern counties, weavers predominated among the latter group; elsewhere fishermen and town artisans featured. One in fifty public works labourers was female, mostly women from households that had lost menfolk to starvation, fever or work exile to England. Although women were frequently assigned the same duties as male labourers: digging, wheeling barrows or carrying loads on their backs, more often they were put to work in groups that included disabled persons and children at the side of the road, breaking down stone with small hammers into sizes suitable for road surfacing. A not uncommon sight on works in many districts was that of young mothers labouring alongside their male counterparts, their infant children bobbing on their backs behind them. Children were also widely employed, so many, indeed, that in some rural parishes the national schools were obliged to close.[3] In October 1846, a newspaper correspondent in Dungarvan, County Waterford, found it 'very affecting' to see so many ten- to thirteen-year-olds breaking stones, their hands blistered from hammer work, making him wonder what could have induced their parents 'to have taken them from the schools of the Christian Brothers, that nursery of virtue and morality'. In March 1847, on one north Mayo site, a visitor noticed 'poor neglected children . . . crouched in groups, around the bits of lighted fires in the various sheltered corners of the line'.

Even though the works did provide essential subsistence for those who managed to remain healthy while they laboured, from the outset the programme as a whole was plagued by difficulties. The greatest problem throughout, one of enormous magnitude, was that regardless of the scale of work provided, it was still not sufficient to cater for the numbers applying. At all stages of the programme a great many chronically deprived and suffering labourer families were entirely unprovided for, and as late as mid-January 1847, one-third of those returned as destitute by local relief committees were without work.

Board of Works personnel blamed the relief committees for foisting persons on them who were not needy, for reasons that varied from corruption to self-interest and politics, and they convinced themselves that rampant abuse and fraud among labourers and committees was the true reason for the huge demand for places. Board of Works inspectors, accordingly, spent a great deal of their energies revising lists and striking off workers considered not needy enough. Whether refused places in the first instance, or struck off later, rejected applicants were effectively abandoned to their fate.

The shortcomings of committees were, of course, manifold. Apathy and internal quarrelling marred the efforts of some, while the membership of others were negligent in raising subscriptions and compiling relief lists, or in purchasing meal for those in want. On some committees landlord, middlemen or large farmer members conspired to have their own tenants placed on works in order to secure their rents to the exclusion of absolutely destitute persons.[4] For their part, labourers, in many cases, exhibited a tendency to avoid strenuous work, which was understandable given the physical condition of many; even the genial John Keegan recorded instances in his district where he came unexpectedly on men standing idly in groups, who 'then, of course, become very diligent'. When engaged in task work, some labourers invented ingenious ways of ensuring double payment for the same stone pile on successive days. But these failings were small-scale and to be expected in such a huge operation, and the vast majority of committees, or at least the core of active members, undoubtedly displayed concern for the labouring poor they served and genuine commitment to their relief, just as labourers were happy to perform a day's work for a day's pay where health and proper wages allowed them. Significantly, in their report for 1847, the Commissioners for Public Works themselves acknowledged that abuses, in general, had been 'greatly exaggerated and the exception taken for the rule'.[5]

Only labourers, of course, had any real grievance, since only they suffered on the works, as they did from the very beginning, and often their suffering was grievous. The first casualties were those who were refused places, so many of them being so desperate for work that they turned up on site regardless, and laboured, sometimes for days at a time, alongside labourers who had obtained work tickets, in the vain hope that they too would be paid. Site invasions by large groups of rejected applicants were frequently on such a scale as to swamp works, leading to their closure and the laying-off of the entire workforce.

For those who succeeded in obtaining places, nowhere was public works labour anything other than a harsh, grinding experience that over time sapped both spirit and physical strength. By the time works opened in many places, prematurely severe weather had set in, which deteriorated into the coldest, hardest winter in half a century; early in 1847, exceedingly wet weather followed, succeeded later by heavy snowfalls. Having pawned or sold their good clothing and coats months earlier, most labourers had to face these conditions barefoot and clad in the tattered remnants of old garments. In Berehaven, County Cork, in February 1847, it was reported that 'the men on the roads are now going barefoot ... their feet suffer, and the checked circulation falls with double effect on the vitals'. According to this witness the men believed they were 'doomed to die'. At Coloney, County Sligo, in May, after a winter spent on the works, 'men and women' were reportedly 'reduced to a most pitiful state of nudity; men's coats worn over tattered petticoat on our women and the men somewhat indecent in their torn garments'. Not surprisingly, exposure to the cold became a widespread condition, and in combination with hunger, work-exhaustion and, later on, fever, swept thousands to their deaths.[6]

Another great problem related to wages, which were initially pegged at a level slightly below those obtaining locally, averaging between eight and ten pence per day, never enough to sustain labourers and their families, and their purchasing power eroded progressively as food prices rose over the autumn and winter. Attempts to replace the day wage by 'task' payment in this situation caused the greatest resentment. In theory task work incentivised labourers to give value for money by allowing them to earn much more than they could by daily labour, but for people in poor physical condition it was a dreadful hardship and led to rapid and dramatic physical deterioration among those obliged to engage in it. Where pay was delayed through the inefficiency or corruption of pay-clerks the result was similar, as in the case of Dennis McKennedy, referred to in the previous chapter, a labourer who was owed a fortnight's wages when he died. The general inadequacy of wages produced thousands of cases like that of Dennis McKennedy, and indeed those of Jeremiah Hegarty and Bridget Thomash, the other labourers we have mentioned as perishing under these conditions in the autumn of 1846.

Public works labourers who still had the strength reacted against the many grievances bearing upon them in a number of ways. Peaceable representations made to Board of Works officials were sometimes successful on minor issues, as were organized marches through towns to places where relief committee meetings were in session. Threatening notices served on offending officials, or physical attacks made on them, could also have their effect, especially where they were associated with the dreaded Whiteboys, who made their appearance on many works. Regardless of the incongruity of their traditional garb in the surroundings of a modern civil engineering programme, the Whiteboys still retained the power to intimidate and impose their edicts, as they sought to lay down and enforce minimum wage levels, to discipline officious stewards or remove 'strangers' from supervisory positions. A number of attempted assassinations took place, and such an air of tension hung around works generally, that even in relatively tranquil areas Board of Works inspectors and engineers furnished themselves with pistols. In disturbed districts, none ventured forth alone and unarmed.[7]

Little of this outrage activity had any motivation that could be said to be criminal, and the serious assault on two clerks in County Longford in late December 1846 by two men dressed in women's clothes was remarkable less for the Whiteboy guise of the assailants than the robbery of the payroll money in the victims' custody. The overall level of public works violence, in fact, was probably far lower than is suggested by the grimly beleaguered tone of despatches sent by Board of Works officials from certain areas. From the end of August 1846 to the beginning of February 1847, just 140 separate incidents of outrage or violence were reported to the Board of Works, most of them concentrated in counties badly affected by hunger distress, with Clare, Limerick, Kerry, and parts of Cork and the midlands figuring more frequently than other areas.[8]

On major issues, relating especially to wages and conditions, labourer protests ran up against the wall of Board of Works regulation and the Treasury in distant London, and failed completely. Here it was the Board of Works inspectors, or rather a significant element within their ranks, who displayed the greatest obduracy and who created the perception of rampant outrage and lawlessness that was used to justify official intransigence at higher levels. Most notorious in this regard was Captain Edmond Wynne, Board of Works inspector for west Clare. By his antagonistic conduct towards relief committees and labouring forces, all of whom loathed him, Wynne sowed resentment and disruption wherever he went, while at the same time acting out the persona of a conscientious officer struggling gallantly in the face of unreasoning opposition and social disintegration. Trevelyan, for one, was only too eager to be persuaded, and Wynne's highly coloured reports were a major factor in legitimizing the appalling official response to outrage, that is, the immediate closure of works. Wynne himself describes the result on one community:

I confess myself unmanned by the extent and intensity of the suffering that I witnessed, more especially amongst the women and little children, crowds of whom were to be seen scattered over the turnip fields, like a flock of starving crows, devouring the raw turnips, mothers half-naked, shivering in the snow and sleet, uttering exclamations of despair, while their children were screaming with hunger.

Wynne's apparently emotional reaction to this dreadful scene is belied by the fact that he was responsible for the closure that gave rise to it, and that within weeks he was using it as an object lesson for all public works labourers in his district.

It is difficult to know to what extent Wynne and a few other egregious figures of his kind were representative of the general run of officials. The correspondence of most officials at this time does show, however, that they were severely harried by responsibility and intimidated by labourer anger, none of them that we know of pondering the realities confronting them daily. Far from questioning instructions, they tended to fall back on the safer formulae of 'abuse' and 'imposition' which fill most official correspondence from this period. This was especially the case with Board of Works inspectors who came from British army or naval backgrounds, men without knowledge of, or sympathy with, Ireland, and whose service experience was a positive hindrance to relief work.

On the other hand, service personnel figure among those few officials who managed to win the entire trust of labourers. One such was Captain Oldershaw, Board of Works inspector in Tyrone, who listened to labourer grievances; gave extra allowances for particularly hard work; had a high opinion of labourers under his supervision; and enjoyed excellent relations with relief committees. But Oldershaw operated in one of the least distressed counties in Ireland. In distressed and disturbed districts, labourer attitudes were more complex, and officials might be seen alternately as villains and heroes by the workforce. In December 1846, for example, an engineer named Michael Keating was attacked by a Whiteboy band at Shanid, County Limerick, for an offence that is not specified in the sources. Barely a month later, at Shanagolden, Keating was dismissed for failing to attend a relief committee meeting, his defence being that providing employment for 200 men in his care was of greater priority. When the relief committee met to consider Keating's case, six thousand labourers abandoned their workplaces throughout the district in order to protest outside the building in which the meeting was taking place. Keating was reinstated.[9]

Where representations of grievance failed or were not attempted, labourers simply endured. Those with families sacrificed their own nutritional needs to those of their children, as in the case of Jeremiah Hegarty in Skibbereen, who

Removing the dead for burial at Skibbereen, January 1847. *Illustrated London News.*

worked for days without food, the result being a rapid breakdown in physical health, followed by death. Even young men, healthy until obliged to work for some time while hungry, succumbed; at the end of February, the superintendent engineer in Wicklow noticed that after a few weeks on the works young men who arrived with a 'stout appearance' were already fainting from hunger. According to Mrs. Asenath Nicholson, an American evangelist who travelled widely through Ireland in the Famine years, labourers who began work in hunger often died before the end of their first week, many being 'carried home to their wretched cabins, some dead and others dying, who had fallen down with the spade in their hands'.

Eyewitness accounts that describe persons staggering on the works through exhaustion abound, and inquest documents feature innumerable cases where labourers spent their final moments crawling along the roadsides or across fields in the direction of their homes. Sometimes, however, physical debilitation was not instantly recognizable, especially in a person encountered every day, and in Offaly, John Keegan described his shock in one diary entry when inquiring after certain absent labourers, on being 'coolly told' they were on the point of death or had died since he had spoken to them the week before.[10] In old age, the Cork land agent Samuel Hussey remembered vividly an occasion in his youth during the Famine, when returning home along a relief road near Bantry, where a work gang had been busy two hours earlier, he found 'three of the poor fellows stretched corpses on the stones they had been breaking'.

It was in the period after Christmas that disease began to spread rapidly on the public works. In January, dysentery and dropsy were widely reported from Wicklow, while in February, on one site in Ardee, County Louth, dysentery was reported to be very prevalent, with fever 'daily increasing'. Some weeks later, in south County Cork, labourers were seen to 'drop off the roads into a low malignant fever, which consigns many to an early grave, leaving their families in a worse condition'. In May, in Westport, County Mayo, one physician spoke of a type of fever that was common locally. It began with racking pains, headaches and shivering, with sufferers becoming, after a brief respite, 'prostrate, dozing', finally sinking after four or five days, when 'no vital power or means of reaction appears in them'. The 'greatest mortality' from this fever was 'among the labourers, men and women, on public roads, in cold, wet, boggy hills'.[11]

If we can never know exactly how many died unnecessarily of starvation, fever or exposure on the works, individual instances afford some startling indications. In February 1847, County Wicklow's superintendant engineer referred to thirty labourers having recently died in the Arklow district, while at the end of March, the secretary of the Schull relief committee told of one hundred cases in the previous eight days where widows of public works labourers had replaced their recently deceased husbands on the lists, and of six instances where he had 'altered the name of the father to that of the son, and from the son to the widow, and from the widow to the daughter, all having died'. Anecdotal evidence of this kind is all we have in identifying geographical and social patterns to mortality on the works, and overwhelmingly relating as it does to western and southern counties, suggests that it was the already starving cottiers and labourers who succumbed first after the opening of the public works, and that it was in the period after Christmas that the attrition began to tell on labourers from smallholder backgrounds.

Labourers employed on landlord schemes, rather than the official works, fared little better, if one is to go by the evidence of an English journalist named Alexander Somerville, who travelled around the country in the early months of 1847. On one occasion in Longford, in March, Somerville watched seven men working in a field of newly sown oats on a scheme funded by their landlord, whom he does not name. At a distance the men seemed to be working 'very indifferently', the seven of them 'doing less than one man's work'. Up close, however, Somerville realized that far from displaying laziness as he had first supposed, the men were 'staggering among the clods' or leaning on their implements, 'from sheer weakness and hunger'. One, who he had supposed to be a feeble, skeletal old man, when accosted proved to be less than forty years of age, and when Somerville later visited his wife and six young children, he found them to be 'skeletons all of them, with skin on the bones and life within the skin'. Of cases similar to those he witnessed at the oat-field, Somerville wrote, 'I might relate twenty such seen within a week'.[12]

By mid-January 1846, less than three months after they had opened, it was decided to close down the public works and to replace them on a temporary basis by an emergency network of soup kitchens. These, it was intended, would tide the surviving poor over for some months until a permanent solution to Irish famine destitution had been found. The decision represented at once an ideological *volte face* on the part of government and a tacit admission of abysmal failure. By the time all works were closed in the summer, £4,850,000 would have been spent on them, and the country's roads wrecked by their abandonment in mid-repair to the elements. Worst of all was that far from having their wants relieved, in the course of the public works programme, thousands of labourers had been effectively worked to death, and the health of tens of thousands more gravely affected.

British cabinet records, however, show that the abandonment of the works for soup kitchens was prompted as much, if not more, by financial and administrative considerations as by humanitarian ones. Trevelyan, indeed, who was close to both parts of the decision, devotes four pages of his *Irish Crisis* to the other reasons before speaking of 'daily instances of starvation in connexion with the Relief Works', this one brief clause being his only reference to what had befallen the labourers.[13] Likewise, the soup kitchen model was adopted largely because recent experience suggested it would be relatively inexpensive. In addition, soup kitchens operated by private charities, especially the Society of Friends, were seen to have been effective as poor relief in certain areas, and to have mitigated in some small measure the horrors of west Cork. By early January, under the encouragement of the relief authorities, many local committees were busy establishing them.[14]

The new relief system was given effect in the legislation known as the Temporary Relief Act, and a series of modifying regulations introduced subsequent to its passing in late February. There were many familiar elements in the system: a Relief Commission, local committees, and an inspectorate featuring a substantial number of individuals transferred from other relief duties, all of which tended to conceal the fact that, temporary though it might have been, the soup kitchen expedient signalled a new direction in relief policy. This was because the system was to be administered through the Poor Law, which for the first time was to take centre stage in relief of distress, an early indication that government intended an even greater role for it in its ultimate solution to famine distress. The district electoral divisions which provided the territorial base for the local committees were essentially Poor Law units, and each committee was overseen by a union-based finance committee. Financial responsibility for the soup kitchen network, in addition, was to be shared, though not equally, between public subscriptions, government funding and the Poor Law rate.

For the labouring poor, the new arrangement had implications that were overwhelmingly negative. Aside from the inadequacies in the size and content of the ration and the conditions under which it was served, which are discussed below, the poor would come to loathe the system because Poor Law control meant their automatic reduction to the abject condition of paupers, with all that implied for their human dignity and self-esteem. Once in place, their ability to reassert these qualities by collective protest was precluded both by their need to access food and by their own gradual internalization of their new degraded condition. Psychologically, this was extremely damaging for them, and as long-term in its effects as the experience of disease and hunger; and few who survived it ever recovered fully.

Closure of the works was to be timed with the progressive introduction of soup kitchens, the Prime Minister, Russell, being adamant that no 'rude dismissal of the people at once' would take place. However, the reality would be entirely different, since the government badly underestimated the extent of bureaucratic delay and overestimated their own ability to impose the new system on committees which were extremely reluctant to abandon the public works. Throughout February and March, in fact, presentment sessions were still being held for further public works, and the number of labourers on them continued to grow, alarming Trevelyan to the extent that, on 10 March, he had formal instructions issued to the Board of Works that twenty per cent of their labourers were to be dismissed by the end of the month. Presentment sessions were ended immediately.[15] A further ten per cent reduction was ordered for the end of April, and all works were to be closed by 1 May, and, although this timetable did not prove practicable, by the end of June only 28,000 labourers were still working, mainly engaged in operations other than those under the Labour Rate Act. The reductions and the final works closure were carried out whether or not soup kitchens were in operation to replace them, and regardless of the consequences when they were not.[16]

These consequences involved a repetition on a much wider scale of the disturbances and social dislocation of the previous autumn.[17] On 12 March, the sudden closure of nine separate works in Swinford, County Mayo, left 860 labourers, 'representing nearly as many families', without any means of subsistence. A few days later, discharged labourers at Ashford, County Wicklow, were 'walking, starving' through the countryside. A few days later again, in Newmarket-on-Fergus, County Clare, a newly appointed relief inspector, a Lieutenant Gardiner Fishbourne, barely escaped with his life when set upon by a crowd of labourers whom he had curtly dismissed from the works before pushing his way through their ranks. In early April, at Glin, County Limerick, another inspector who had been obliging labourers to begin work two hours earlier as a means of forcing them off the works, was attacked in his home. At Kilmacteige, in Sligo, the

Woman at Clonakilty, County Cork, 1847, begging for money to bury her dead child. *Illustrated London News.*

dismissal of 2,000 labourers about the same time aroused 'the greatest consterna-
tion and alarm amongst them'.[18] In none of these locations were soup kitchens
ready to dispense meals to the discharged labourers and their families.

In many areas discharged workers took to marching in force in public, as they
had done the previous autumn, sometimes carrying their loys, at other times
holding their children by the hand. At the end of April, vast crowds of dismissed
labourers assembled at Drone, County Tipperary, clamouring for food and
employment, their 'wretched emaciated children . . . clinging to them for sustenance'. In early May, Galway merchants who had been frightened by rumours
of labourer intentions of plundering their businesses were greatly relieved when
the few hundred marchers who eventually arrived were so weak as to be able
only to march as far as the relief committee office behind a white banner bearing
the legend, 'We are starving: Bread or Employment'. On 3 June, when the soup
kitchen legislation was already three months old, a crowd of discharged labourers
marched in protest into Castlecomer, County Kilkenny, so feeble from hunger
that they were forced to halt at intervals along the road. In some districts of the
Ballinasloe union, where the last soup kitchen was not in place until 16 June,
groups of discharged labourers who failed to obtain relief from the committee
reportedly made a number of attacks on grain stores.[19]

The tribulations endured by labourers and their families at this time were,
however, just one aspect of the greater horror endured by all of Ireland between
January and June of 1847, the first full cyclonic blast of a national famine, during
which mass death from starvation, disease and exposure to the cold occurred
on a truly apocalyptic scale. From its early origins the previous autumn, this
great cycle of mortality had already blanketed regions such as south-west Cork,
west Clare, Conamara and a portion of the midlands by December, spreading so
rapidly beyond them as the year ended that it appeared to sweep in everywhere
with the new year, bringing such total devastation as would leave the mark of
Black Forty Seven forever etched on the Irish psyche. Almost impossible to
comprehend in its totality, even at the remove of more than a century and a half,
the evidence left by this calamitous period, in its vastness and in its minute detail
alike, remains deeply, powerfully shocking.

The immensity of what happened is perhaps best appreciated in the micro-
scopic detail of local experience and if, for instance, one extracts all the relevant
references from a single issue of one local newspaper, what emerges is as stunning
as it is bleak. In the *Clare Journal* for 4 February, for example, straightforward
reportage accounts for two instances of death by starvation, one an elderly
vagrant, of unknown name, who died near Kilkee; the second a sixteen-year-old

wandering beggar from Cork, named David Clifford, in Kilrush. By far the greater body of data relating to starvation in this issue, however, derives from four letters, three of them written by Catholic priests, the fourth by a west Clare physician, Dr. James Hill of Miltown Malbay. From Carrigaholt, in the far west, Fr. Malachy Duggan wrote of fifty deaths in his parish in the previous three weeks. The curate in Kilmurry Ibrickane, Fr. Thomas Moloney, told of seventy people who died of starvation in his parish in the previous three months; in travelling the graveyards he related having found 'fewer green graves than red'. One of them was a young labourer, James Keane, who fell dead in a field on his way home from the public works; another, John Blake, the four-year-old son of another labourer, whose family lay starving in their cabin. Six thousand 'breathing skeletons of men and women' inhabited his parish, he told the *Journal*'s readers, with 'hundreds upon hundreds' more who were 'unable to crawl forth'. From Kilnamona, Fr. Thomas Quinn wrote of 8,000 parishioners in severe want; in the previous six weeks neither he nor his curate had carried out any pastoral service apart from ministering to the sick and the dying.

Dr. Hill's letter begins with a reference to the deaths of seventeen labourers, both male and female, who had been employed up to a few weeks previously on a local works. He goes on to tell of having recently watched the tortured progress of a 'human skeleton' pursuing through a field a crow which had flapped away from a pit with a large potato. Eventually the man retrieved his potato, but the effort cost him so much that he collapsed and died. Hill also tells of a woman in the parish who had eight children, and who kept them in bed by day in order to keep up their strength, bringing them hay to chew on so as to 'extract some nourishment from it'. The last part of his letter relates to a gang of labourers who, when digging out a trench, came across a hoard of what appeared to be gold sovereigns. Trampling on each other in their frenzy to get hold of some of this wealth, their efforts proved futile, since the coins were later found to be seventeenth century Jacobite 'gunmoney'; base and worthless.[20]

Closer focus on individual instances, where this is possible, is equally instructive. To take one example from County Sligo, on 2 March, the county relief inspector, a Captain O'Brien, visited a number of distressed locations in the north of the county along with Sir Robert Gore Booth, landlord of a large estate nearby. Their first call was to what O'Brien called a 'wretched hamlet', occupied by three related families, in all some 32 persons. Formerly prosperous, the occupants were now 'either starving or dead'. In one cabin where a sister and brother had died the previous week, the brother's fever-stricken widow lay immobile on the ground, her children 'bloated in their faces and bodies, their limbs . . . withered to bones and sinews, with rags on them which scarcely preserved decency, and assuredly afforded no protection from the weather'. Earlier that day they had been gnawing the bones of a pig that had died in an outhouse. In another settlement along the shore of Sligo Bay, the two men entered a hut that was so miserable that they had to crawl awkwardly down into it. Inside, the only furniture was a child's cradle and a broken table; on the floor a coffin held the remains of the occupier's wife, who had died of starvation days before. The husband had just returned from the public works in order to see to the burial, and he told the visitors that,

> he was about to depart 'to dig a hole to put her in, and try to get a couple of men from the works to help him carry her there'. A skeleton of a living child was in a cradle, in a corner near the fire. A woman, a neighbour, was sitting by it and rocking the cradle, and said it would be dead before morning, and added (truly!) 'It would be better if we were all dead'.

Death did commonly come to whole families and communities, quietly and anonymously, the survivors and eyewitnesses ransacking their vocabularies in search of similes that might adequately describe their passing. Some comparisons represent the crudity of death, as in the comment made by one of the Carrick-on-Shannon Guardians, at the end of December 1846, that the people were dying 'like rotten sheep'. Most, however, couched references to otherwise unremarked, painful deaths, in poetic language that is especially affecting when the reason for its euphemism is realized. In Belmullet, County Mayo in April, for example, the poor were said to be 'dying as numerous as bees on a harvest day'. A letter from an emigrant in Canada in September refers to those at home having 'melted away ... like snow before the sun'. Of one district in west Clare, a newspaper reporter was told later in the year that the inhabitants had 'died as the birds do when the frost comes, and what we thought we never would see, they were buried without the coffin.'[21]

Much of this imagery is accompanied by remarks on the sadness of burial without coffins, seen by contemporaries as an almost blasphemous departure from Irish funerary traditions. Coffinless burials became widespread everywhere, not just in the cases where there was no money to pay for coffins, but also where no family members were still living who could lead these socio-religious rites. Where neighbours came upon cabins in which all the occupants had died, it became the practice either to bury the dead in the garden and burn the building, or simply to pull it down around the corpses, the ruins furnishing a ready-made tomb. Family members commonly dragged bodies of parents, children or siblings to cemeteries, wrapped in súgáns (straw ropes), or laid on wattles covered in old sackcloth. Dead children were often brought to burial in panniers slung on the backs of donkeys. Such burials took place mostly at night, as families sought to conceal their shame at being unable to provide for members, either in life or in death.

In countless instances, people simply went missing, their bodies lying in fields or by-ways before rotting to skeletal or mummified form, never to be identified or perhaps even to be found. Corpses littered the roads and roadsides, and the Quaker philanthropist, James Hack Tuke, was told by different car and coach drivers in Connacht that they 'rarely drove anywhere without seeing dead bodies strewn along the road side, and that in the dark they had even gone over them'. Because of the numbers of the unclaimed dead, the phenomenon of re-usable coffins emerged, apparently spontaneously, all over the country. These were equipped with sliding or hinged bottoms, or moveable sides, and sometimes given in charge to persons paid to bring corpses to mass burial plots. Only a tiny fraction of starvation deaths were ever subjected to investigation by inquest.[22]

Counties which had so far been relatively unscathed by distress were badly stricken in these months. Of County Down, in February, *The Banner of Ulster* declared that it 'would be impossible to find more distressing cases, short of the horrors of Skibbereen . . . than those narrated by our reporter from the eastern divisions of Down . . . There are many cases of suffering in the immediate neighbourhood of Belfast not less distressing than in any other part of Ireland'. In Armagh, towards the end of January, the poor in Portadown were described as being in a 'most wretched state', while 'extreme deprivation and distress' was reported from Drumcree. In Loughgall at the end of February, one observer wrote of having seen cases where the living lay on straw beside corpses of people who had died three days before.[23]

Incidental to all such descriptions of scenes are the universal references to shrunken faces, sharpened features, tottering steps, feeble and ghastly skeletons and silent, staring, wizened children, on whose faces a light fuzz of hair grew, their heads becoming bald. Visitors unaccustomed to such things sometimes experienced a kind of disorientation in the midst of groups of these spectral figures and, horror-struck by their presence, the odour of decay they exuded and their slow, silent, deliberate bodily movements, became possessed of an overpowering urge to flee.[24]

In the struggle for survival, the poor exhausted all the resources of the land, domesticated and wild, their scavenging veering progressively from the edible to what had previously been considered inedible, repulsive or dangerous to eat. Old horses and donkeys were killed and eaten by their owners, as was carrion and even domestic pets. The starving fed on wild edible plants, such as charlock, nettles, watercress, dandelions and dock-leaves, and where they could find them they gathered berries, nuts and mushrooms. Rabbits and hares were trapped almost to extinction, and even hedgehogs, foxes and badgers were devoured. On the coastline, various kinds of seaweeds and seafoods were eaten regardless of season or safety. Crabs, bairneachs (limpets), mussels and shellfish of all kinds were greedily consumed where found. As they had done in pre-Famine times, but now with total desperation, poor people hung over the edges of sea-cliffs on ropes to scrabble for birds' eggs, often falling to their deaths through physical weakness. Seaweed gatherers, compelled to glean farther and farther out on exposed rocks, were often dashed to their death by freak waves.[25]

Fishing undoubtedly saved many, although the herring fishery on which many coastal fishermen depended failed for most of 1846 and 1847. During this time so many fishermen had pawned or sold their boats and tackle, that they were unable to profit by the return of the herring in 1848; those few who retained or redeemed them and headed out to sea in a physically weakened condition were often unable to haul in their catch, or having done so, too feeble to row ashore. Many drowned within sight of land, their boats filled with fish.

Having no alternative, the poor turned to thievery, stealing from urban stores and shops, and in the countryside from the gardens of their better-off neighbours. As the Famine worsened, farmers began to employ full-time watchers on the growing crops, by day as well as by night. Instances of sheep and cattle stealing rocketed from the negligible activity of a tiny underground of professional criminals to endemic proportions. Cattle and sheep were routinely taken from fields by night and crudely butchered, sometimes on the spot, farmers often finding their mangled carcasses the following day. Sometimes the screaming of animals in the night told of meat being hacked off the backs of living beasts. Landlords' parklands and private fisheries were continuously subjected to poaching of game animals and fish, despite the best efforts of gamekeepers and water bailiffs. Songbirds and wild-birds on these and other lands were trapped and eaten, as the country became denuded of its edible flora and fauna. 'Ní chluintear in áltaibh cárlach is ceiliúr ar chraobh,' lamented one County Meath poet, 'is níl bric an áill mar ghnách in Oileán na Naomh.' [No bird is heard in the valleys, or singing in the trees, and the trout is not seen in the streams as once was common in the Isle of the Saints].[26]

The disappearance of wildlife and domestic creatures accounted for one aspect of Famine in Ireland that was often remarked upon – that is, the eerie silence that hung over the landscape, in this period and later. Pigs and poultry had disappeared from farmyards even earlier; cocks no longer crowed from dunghills, farmyard dogs no longer barked. Some dogs had been eaten by their owners, thousands of others put down when discovered feeding on half-buried corpses in graveyards, or for fear they would do so. When Asenath Nicholson asked a boatman in Arranmore, Donegal, why the dogs there were so 'fat and shining' when there was no food, her interlocutor balked at answering, leaving her in no uncertainty as to the reason. Children no longer played on the roadside or in the fields around cabins, and, in the middle of the year, Nicholson noted that their 'gladsome mirth everywhere ceased'.

It was during this period that the social rituals attached to births, marriages, deaths, processions and fairs came to a halt, resuming gradually only when the Famine was over. When they did resume, they did so at much lesser levels of activity. The rich culture of music, song, story and dance, for which Ireland had been famous and which had so fascinated visitors before 1845, was extinguished in these years, and never recovered its full vitality afterwards. Those not directly vulnerable to starvation became increasingly careful in their socializing, remaining in their homes whenever they could for fear of attracting contagion. The poor no longer went to Mass because their rags would shame them. A general despondency prevailed. 'It is remarkable', wrote one Quaker philanthropist, from Clonmel in Tipperary, at the end of February, 'to observe the total absence of anything bordering on pleasantry or cheerfulness in the countenances of the people, old and young; all seemed to be down-stricken and dejected.'[27]

If all the maddened scavenging that we have been describing was at its most widespread as the emergency relief system came slowly into operation during the late spring and early summer, the soup kitchens did not put an end to it. Indeed, it was probably only by combining the soup kitchen ration with what they could eke from the land that many thousands were able to survive at all. This was because the ration, at one pound of meal daily (soup was rarely dispensed at the kitchens), and half that amount for children under nine, was not enough to maintain health, and its insufficiency is put into context when it is realized that the average pre-Famine adult labourer could comfortably dispose of fourteen pounds of potatoes in a day. The ration was nevertheless approved by the Central Board of Health, which recommended it be dispensed in a cooked form, ironically enough, on the grounds that a raw ration was inadequate nutritionally and would 'predispose to attacks of dysentery and diarrhoea'. When the advice was reiterated in May, the reason given this time was that the poor would otherwise 'dispose of it for money, tea or tobacco'. Trevelyan agreed: 'Undressed meal might be converted into cash by those who did not require it as food', he wrote later, 'and even the most destitute often disposed of it for tea, tobacco, or spirits'. A cooked ration 'which becomes sour by keeping', he concluded, would only attract those intending to consume it.

By early July, some three million persons, substantially over one-third of the country's pre-Famine population, were in daily receipt of soup kitchen rations, representing a level of dependency that was approximately the same as that during the public works programme, if one ignores for a moment the substantial section of the poor who failed to obtain any access to food rations, and those who had died in the meantime. The level of dependency on the soup kitchens is even more striking when viewed at union level. Predictably, this was heaviest in the Connacht and Munster unions, Ballinrobe union, for example, having a massive ninety-four per cent of its population on rations, and Clifden, eighty-seven per cent.[28] Even in the comparatively well-off north-east, where three unions (Antrim, Newtownards and Belfast) did not organize relief committees, the average dependency was of the order of seventeen and a half per cent. Omagh and Clogher unions (Tyrone) both had nearly twenty-one per cent of their populations dependent on rations.

The soup kitchen phase of relief coincided with a huge drop in the international price of grain, which hugely reduced the cost of the overall programme. However, government did not take advantage of this unexpected windfall to improve the rations, and when the kitchens were closed in September, a massive £530,000 of the sum budgeted remained unexpended.[29] Throughout, the bureaucracy remained as fixated by 'imposition' as it had been while the public works were in progress, and among the many expedients devised to counteract it were an insistence on cooked food, the enforcement of a roll call, and the stipulation that all family members should be subjected to daily inspection at the kitchen. All of this led to interminable delays, especially painful for people who had walked miles to be present.

In such circumstances, by the time the ration was received it was spoiled and unpalatable, and where recipients angrily refused the nauseous mess offered them, officials seized on the refusal as an admission of attempted fraud, convincing themselves that 'impostors' were everywhere and that many of those who walked long distances and lined up in humiliation for hours were in reality well-off persons who had dressed in rags in order to claim rations. The Relief Commissioners themselves gave credence to these claims and to equally preposterous ones that relief committee members and Poor Law Guardians were putting themselves on relief lists.[30] To be fair to the relief committees, most were acutely aware of what the poor suffered on the soup kitchen line, and all too often it was the relief inspectors who were behind the acts of particular officiousness that piled further misery upon all their other miseries. Bitter conflict emerged between certain committees and their inspectors, the former resisting regulations they saw as foolish, heartless and damaging, and even when pressurized by the Relief Commissioners, many persisted in opposing them.

For the most part, the poor were too physically weak and psychologically cowed to protest, and certainly in no position to challenge the bureaucracy. Wherever we find them expressing their feelings about the soup kitchens, however, they are remarkably united in identifying the humiliation of the distribution procedure as their principal grievance, along with the repulsiveness of the ration. In mid-May, at Kilbarron, County Tipperary, discharged labourers told one official that they would never submit 'to be placed on the level of the common beggar' by lining up for meal with a can or a bag, while in June, a petition drawn up by Newmarket-on-Fergus labourers protested at their reduction to the level of mere carriers of pots and pans, in a system which they held debased and demoralized them. Similar sentiments lay behind attempts at sabotaging soup kitchens in Counties Wicklow and Meath. In the Meath incident, which took place in Kells in mid-May, a massive crowd prevented the relief committee from opening the soup kitchen for an entire week in a vain attempt to force a reversion to public works relief, soup kitchens being 'an offence to the dignity of the people'.[31]

The phenomenon of soup kitchen disorders, although widely reported from around the country, was most heavily concentrated in the Munster counties of Tipperary, Limerick and Clare, which, as we have seen, shared the old pre-Famine traditions of social protest. Wherever soup kitchen protests emerged, the pattern they followed was strikingly similar. In all cases the disturbance seemed to emerge suddenly; in many instances women rather than men figured as protagonists; during most of the disorders the soup kitchen itself was attacked, participants devoting special attention to overturning tables and tearing up ticket stubs. In almost every case an attempt was made to destroy the soup kitchen boiler.

The concern with the boiler was clearly ritual; the dominant feature of each kitchen, it was large and ugly and obvious; it was the cause of most delay and the source of the unpleasant mush doled out to the people, and therefore powerfully symbolic of the cumulative humiliations inflicted by an uncaring managerial regime. At one kitchen near Littleton, in County Tipperary, the crowd smashed the boilers even before they had been installed, and at Ennistymon, County Clare, police fired on a crowd that was in the act of sacking the kitchen there. At Kilfenora in the same county the people took the boiler outside the village in ceremonial procession before dumping it in a turlough. At Clarecastle, a crowd of women took the vat for steeping the meal and broke it into fragments.

Oral tradition affords us an even stronger sense of the emotions propelling participants in soup kitchen disorders; indeed, the very fact that the soup kitchens, which after all only lasted a few months, left any trace of itself at all in popular consciousness testifies to the strength of community rage. In these stories scorn is poured on persons employed in the distribution of the 'soup' and on landlords perceived to have been involved. Heroic roles are ascribed to certain named individuals in various aspects of the revolt, especially in the smashing of the boiler, which is perhaps best comprehended as a kind of collective consola-tion, necessary to the preservation of community self-esteem. For this reason, these stories look at the soup kitchens from an angle that is entirely different to those of eyewitnesses, as for example, in the memories set down in the late 1870s by the noted journalist and political activist, A.M. Sullivan:[32]

> Around these boilers on the roadside there daily moaned and shrieked and fought and scuffled crowds of gaunt, cadaverous creatures that once had been men and women made

Society of Friends soup kitchen, Cork. Few soup kitchens would have been as orderly as this one. *Illustrated London News.*

in the image of God. The feeding of dogs in a kennel was far more decent and orderly. I once thought . . . that never, never would our people recover the shameful humiliation of that brutal public soup-boiler scheme.

For his part, Charles Trevelyan's account of the soup kitchens is remarkable for its blandness. As a result of the programme, he tells us in the *Irish Crisis*, the Famine 'was stayed'. The 'affecting and heart-rending' crowds were no longer to be seen, the 'cadaverous, hunger-stricken countenances of the people gave place to looks of health; deaths from starvation ceased; and cattle-stealing, plundering provisions, and other crimes prompted by want of food, were diminished by half in the course of a single month'. More than this, Trevelyan informs us, citing Count Strzelecki, one of the great figures of the charitable movement, it was the 'grandest attempt ever made to grapple with famine over a whole country'.

> Organised armies amounting to some hundreds of thousands had been rationed before; but neither ancient nor modern history can furnish a parallel to the fact that upward of three millions of persons were fed every day in the neighbourhood of their own homes by administrative arrangements emanating from and controlled by one central office.

Much of this is true. Deaths from starvation, it is known, abated abruptly in the summer of 1847, and large numbers of people were alive in September who would otherwise have perished; it is also true that the establishment of the kitchens represented a considerable organizational feat.[33] Following the establishment of the kitchens, moreover, many other accounts testify to a much improved physical appearance among the people, and the disappearance of the haunted, hollow-eyed, dying look borne by so many earlier.[34]

However, there are other factors at work here besides the availability of soup kitchen rations, and the diminution in starvation deaths during the summer was as much due to the fact that the first great cycle of famine mortality that had begun in late 1846 had now expended itself, and that those who had been especially vulnerable were now, for the most part, dead. It is this which in many places accounts for the sudden absence of 'walking skeletons' by late summer. It was the socio-economic strata just above those who were now gone, and whose health had not yet broken down, who were able to subsist by combining the soup kitchen with whatever they were able to scavenge from the land. For many, however, it would prove to be a temporary rescue, since another foodless winter loomed beyond the planned closure of the soup kitchens late in the summer.

There are, in addition, many indications that a sizeable proportion of the starving poor failed to obtain access to soup kitchen rations, and that hunger-related

deaths continued through the soup kitchen phase of relief. In June, the parish
priest of Schull, Fr. James Barry, complained that 'the administration of relief
did not embrace all the afflicted community', and that although some 'were
pretty well supported through the eventful visitation – others only for a time,
and then left with the greatest number to struggle out as they best could or perish'. In Clifden, County Galway, where kitchens were in operation, in mid-July,
magistrates informed government that deaths were still 'fearfully numerous', the
chief cause being 'the absolute present want or long spells without sufficient food'.
Also excluded from access to the soup kitchens were those who had abandoned
their cabins, and as wandering vagrants crowded into the streets and poorer
quarters of towns and cities far from their original homes. Not alone were such
individuals, whom the respectable classes perceived as 'infesting' their vicinity,
denied relief, but in cities such as Cork they were rounded up by the authorities
in batches and after a night spent in jail, without food, were released miles into
the countryside, and abandoned.[35]

The concentration of the poor outside soup kitchens had one last, disastrous
outcome, in that the close physical proximity of such enormous numbers, in
circumstances which precluded personal cleanliness or hygiene, created the conditions in which epidemic disease might spread. As starvation mortality abated
in the summer, deaths from fever began to increase. In Dingle, in June, one relief
official described how those queuing at the soup kitchens brought 'home to their
families not only a few quarts of soup, but also a fever contracted in the crowd'.
In Killglass, County Roscommon, in mid-July, fever was reported to have made
its way into every house, their occupants 'wasting away and dying of want'.[36] One
of the greatest pandemics ever to have struck Ireland was now well under way.

Emaciated Frames and Livid Countenances: From Fever Pandemic to Amended Poor Law

Yet the tottering gait, emaciated frames and the livid countenances of the poor creatures but too truly evince the direst destitution. The truth is they are crammed into pest houses in order that they may perish and taxation diminish. Every spare house . . . that could be at all rendered fit for the purpose is taken as an 'auxiliary', even cowsheds are pressed into service.

– FR. MATHIAS MCMAHON, BALLYBUNION, KERRY, APRIL 1850

Historically in Ireland, famines had been accompanied by outbreaks of epidemic disease, and although the link between them had often been remarked upon, its exact nature was not known. On the eve of the Great Famine, there were many differing views on the subject among Irish medical men, who constituted an exceptionally distinguished generation, but few of them would have agreed with one colleague, the eminent Dominick Corrigan, who believed that starvation was the direct cause of disease. The Famine, which might have provided the opportunity for definitive research on the issue, did little to resolve it, if for no other reason than that the great epidemics that came with it overwhelmed medical and public health facilities, making clinical analysis impossible and killing many physicians, among them several prominent specialists in epidemiology.[1]

In later decades, medical and public health investigations would determine that the connection between starvation and disease was an indirect one, arising out of the increased geographical mobility of hungry persons in search of food, and the close concentration of large numbers in relatively confined spaces. This had the effect of bringing disease out of the contained urban and rural pockets where it had lurked between epidemics. The very mechanisms of relief, therefore, the public works and soup kitchens, and much more than either, the workhouses, provided ideal conditions for the spread of the three great killer diseases of Famine Ireland: typhus, relapsing fever and bacillary dysentery. In this broad sense, therefore, the relief programmes were major contributors to mass morbidity and mass death during the Famine.

In the absence of detailed medical knowledge, practitioners throughout Ireland tended to lump all the epidemic diseases associated with hunger in an undifferentiated 'famine fever'. So frequently did typhus and relapsing fever occur together that they were especially liable to be confused, their individual symptoms seen as different manifestations of the same disease. Both are transmitted by body lice, although through different micro-organisms and in different ways. Typhus was accompanied by shivering, prostrating head and bodily aches and by delirium and stupor, plus a spotted rash that appeared some days after the onset. A 'moderate' attack of typhus might last a fortnight, severe cases considerably longer, fatalities occurring where the body was not strong enough to withstand the force of the attack.[2] Its onset was rapid, and the transformation from full health to incapacitating symptoms might take less than a day. Its Irish name, *fiabhras dubh*, or black fever, reflected the mottling of the skin suffered by patients, and during the Famine the mortality rate was often of the order of seventy per cent of those who contracted it.

Relapsing fever was far less frequently fatal to those who contracted it than typhus, although its onset was even more rapid and its symptoms more frightening. Typically, an apparently healthy person was suddenly afflicted by violent rigor, along with the nausea and vomiting that gave the disease the clinical name of 'gastric fever' ascribed it by medical practitioners. After perhaps five days of fever, a crisis occurred, involving heavy sweating and physical exhaustion, following which a few days of relief preceded a major relapse, or indeed several in succession before the victim died, effectively of exhaustion. So often accompanied by jaundice, relapsing fever was often called *fiabhras buí* in Irish, or yellow fever.

It was noted by practitioners during the Famine that persons rescued from starvation were especially susceptible to becoming infected with 'fever', that is, typhus or relapsing fever, or both together. Infected persons, or those incubating the disease while travelling through districts hitherto unaffected by Famine, might bring the infection with them, leading to an outbreak of fever that devastated areas normally seen as comfortable and safe. It was also remarked frequently that the survival rate among persons from more elevated social levels who contracted fever was relatively lower, even though fever seldom ran through their families as it did in the case of poorer sufferers.[3]

Bacillary dysentery, the third great killer among infectious diseases during the Famine, was spread by micro-organisms transmitted by human contact, by flies, or through water polluted with the bacillus. Moderate forms of the disease were often confused with the symptoms of diarrhoea that resulted from a change in the type of food consumed, as in, for example, the changeover from potatoes to meal or turnips. Dysentery was highly infectious, and was frequently fatal to the victims, often killing those who came into contact with them also. It was characterized by 'bowel colic, painful and exhausting straining, violent diarrhoea, with passages of blood'. A fearful and fatal phase of the disease was signalled by stools 'consisting solely of fluid resembling water in which raw meat has been washed,' an indication that intestinal gangrene had set in.

In addition to the fevers, there were also the non-infectious diseases of scurvy and famine dropsy. Scurvy was caused by the absence of vitamin C, and became widespread as a result of the abandonment of the potato for other foods which did not supply that vitamin. Among its symptoms were spongy swellings and ulceration of the gums, loss of teeth, and the presence of haemorrhagic blotches on the skin, and 'massive effusions of blood into the muscles and under the skin, causing tension and great pain'. Because the legs of sufferers sometimes turned black, in Irish it was known as *cos dhubh*.[4] Virtually unknown in Ireland before the Famine, scurvy was often inaccurately diagnosed as part of the typhus infection; it is believed that some proportion of those who dropped dead suddenly on the public works may have been killed by scurvy. Dropsy was caused by protein and Vitamin B complex deficiency; often set off by an attack of fever, it led to gross swelling of the victim's joints and body with fluid, which made the slightest physical movement excruciatingly painful.

Among the assortment of 'lesser' diseases that afflicted the poor during the Great Famine were smallpox and a virulent strain of xerophthalmia that took its toll on hunger-emaciated bodies, blinding rather than killing its victims.[5] The short-lived cholera epidemic of spring and early summer 1849 added its share of horror to the sufferings of the poor. The symptoms of cholera were so dreadful that it generated a level of terror greater that any other disease, transforming the social behaviour of the people, and affecting social classes which had been able to take precautions to avoid the other diseases.

Where they occurred together, these and still other diseases interacted in an intricate manner, impacting on victims of hunger and malnutrition in much more complex ways than by the mere ravaging of weakened immune systems or physically exhausted constitutions. All were extremely painful for the sufferer; relatives who were not stricken themselves had to endure the torment of witnessing loved ones suffer and die, often against a background of poor nursing and indescribably foul conditions. Families and communities were torn apart by the conflicting impulses of caring for ill members and fear of contracting the disease themselves. The emotional responses of families with regard to fever-affected members were often blunted to indifference and apathy by the physiological and

This (later) image of starving crowds surrounding an Irish workhouse powerfully conveys what such scenes might have been like. Wilson, *Life and Times of Queen Victoria*.

psychological effects of their own hunger, a fact that was widely commented on during the Famine, and often seized on by officials to reinforce their own anti-poor prejudices.

For all who had contact with fever patients during the Famine, one of the most difficult things to deal with was the extraordinarily strong smell exuded by their bodies, worsened by the effects of emaciation. There are many descriptions of physicians being almost overpowered by this stench, some of whom had experience of pre-Famine outbreaks. To one Clare physician, the stench of fever had replaced the 'sooty and peat-smoke odour of former times', while another in west Cork called it a 'suffocating odour' which was 'always the forerunner of death'. Fever-ridden crowds waiting for admission outside workhouse walls also gave off this odour, which became almost intolerable in the confined space of the workhouse itself or in the shut-in hovels of the starving.[6]

Bearing in mind that disease usually carried off persons already far advanced in nutritional deprivation, it remains broadly true that during the Famine deaths from disease exceeded those from starvation. Apart from the incomplete and, in any case, unreliable institutional record of fever hospitals, infirmaries, workhouses and jails, we do not have the means of establishing even an approximate ratio between starvation and disease. Thanks, however, to a set of statistics compiled for six west Cork parishes by an unusually active relief inspector, a Colonel Marshall, in the period between September 1846 and September 1847, some inferences are possible. As analysed by Fr. Hickey in his authoritative study of that district, Marshall's figures break down into a fever and dysentery to starvation ratio of 66:34, or slightly less than 2:1, which may have some validity for the country as a whole.

As to the manner in which epidemic exploded outwards from its pre-Famine pockets to the population at large, MacArthur's evocative scenario remains the likely one:[7]

> The neighbours crowded into any cabin where a fire was burning, or where some food had been obtained which might be shared or bartered. The lack of cleanliness, the unchanged clothing and the crowding together, provided conditions ideal for lice to multiply and spread rapidly ... In such circumstances an initial case or two of fever could serve to infect a whole district. In general the worse the famine in any part the more intense the fever, and crowds of starving people forsook their homes and took to the roads, thus carrying disease with them wherever they went.

It does seem, however, that human movement did not reach what might be called a 'critical mass' on a wider scale until the later months of 1846 and the advent of the Labour Rate public works and the soup kitchens. A steady increase in the incidence of fever was noted, it is true, in the months following the first failure of the potato, but this is believed to have been a continuation of a pre-Famine trend relating to the progressive impoverishment of rural society, without any necessary connection with the circumstances of the first potato failure. Sporadic outbreaks occurred in the spring of 1846 and afterwards, but the sources in general feature starvation rather than disease mortality until the autumn of that year. Only at that point, about late October, do the references to fever escalate to levels suggestive of a full-blown epidemic or pandemic.

In Belfast, fever broke out in September; in Roscommon and Sligo, a little later in the year, but as in Belfast, it escalated rapidly, raging widely in these counties by the early days of 1847, just about the time it was first reported in Wicklow, Longford and Louth. In Clare, we first hear of fever 'spreading rapidly' in mid-February 1847; by mid-June people were reportedly 'dying in every direction' in the county from its effects. Relatively remote County Leitrim escaped until well into the summer, while over substantial parts of Wexford there would be no outbreak until 1848. Even in that county, which is generally accepted as having escaped the worst of fever as well as starvation, at the height of the epidemic it was reported that old and young were 'dying as fast as they can bury them,' and that those 'there are in health in the morning knows not but in the evening may have taken the infection.'[8]

The general pattern in the Famine epidemics was that fever outbreaks reached their peak about a year after they first began, thereafter entering a long decline. However, in many areas of the west and south, especially, the decline would be interrupted by recurrences which were sometimes worse than the initial outbreak. In a number of isolated locations, fever would not appear until very late in the Famine; and in the case of the western offshore islands of Inisboffin and Inishark, it did not occur until visitors brought it with them in the course of 1850. Only one district in the entire country is believed to have been spared the epidemic altogether. This was the area comprising Warrenpoint and Rostrevor in County Down, which lay off direct approach routes between towns, and was not subjected therefore to a steady flow of infected poor people, which was central to the spread of contagion elsewhere.[9]

The fever epidemic impacted on inmates of all public institutions; infirmaries, fever hospitals, jails and most of all on the workhouses where the destitute poor were most concentrated and spent the longest periods. Fever morbidity and mortality in these institutions, however, furnish only an approximate guide to the progress of the epidemics in the country as a whole, mainly because of the peculiar concentration of humanity within them and the measures taken by the authorities, which usually involved moving them elsewhere.

At the same time, the trend inside and outside institutions was a broadly similar one, with a rising incidence reported in the last two months of 1845 and into the new year. In Galway workhouse, for example, in early January 1846, fever cases increased markedly in reflection of an outbreak in several parts of the union. These cases were, however, easily contained within the workhouse infirmary. In a similar context, in June, the physician appointed by the Rathdrum Guardians (County Wicklow) to the fever hospital reported that fever was on the increase there also.[10] Even though the rising statistical graph was not yet alarming, the Tory government was sufficiently nervous of what might shortly be expected to pass an anticipatory Temporary Fever Act in March 1846. This Act authorized the appointment of as many medical officers as might be required to deal with an outbreak, under the supervision of a Central Board of Health. The Central Board was empowered to instruct Boards of Guardians to establish, equip and staff temporary fever hospitals on their grounds, which would function for the duration of an outbreak.

However, the anticipated outbreak did not take place, mainly because the population had not yet become sufficiently mobile and concentrated for the spread of disease, or desperate enough to start crowding the workhouses. This being the case, on arrival in office Lord John Russell's new Liberal government decided not to renew the legislation, and the Central Board of Health went out of existence when the Act expired at the end of August, even as news of the second failure of the potatoes made a major outbreak highly likely. At that time, the Board was operational only in four unions, and the task of discharging the additional medical men and the dismantling of precautionary structures was accomplished quickly. Within a matter of weeks of its disbandment, however, public institutions all over Ireland, and especially the workhouses, found themselves in the grip of major outbreaks of fever, reflecting the national pandemic outside their walls.

In the present state of our knowledge, these epidemics can be traced with any accuracy only in the workhouses, and to some extent the fever hospitals to which many patients were transferred. Fever broke out in the workhouses at this point because of a huge increase in admissions, as the prospect of death by hunger or disease finally began to prevail over fear and dread of the Poor Law. At the very end of August, the total inmate population of Irish workhouses stood at just 43,655 inmates, less than half the number they were designed to accommodate, the vast majority of them belonging to non-able-bodied categories. Slowly, and then more rapidly, admissions mounted, and by 17 October, four workhouses – Cork, Granard, Ballina and Skibbereen – were full.[11] As Peter Frogatt graphically puts it, 'reports of fever multiplied as autumn progressed and the great migrations of ravenous, starving hordes of fevered scarecrows flocked to the workhouses and fever hospitals and to the reeking slums of ports and cities'. A major inrush into workhouses was now under way, and by the end of the year most were full or approaching capacity.

At this point, even the Ulster workhouses were heavily affected: by the end of December, twenty-one out of forty-three houses in that province had exceeded their legal limits; seven others were almost full; while a further fifteen reported that they were coping well with the situation.[12] A month later there were few workhouses in Ireland that were not floundering in their attempts to deal with admissions. By the end of February, the inmate population of the workhouse system had reached 116,321, greatly in excess of its original capacity. Outside the workhouses, fever rampaged unchecked in towns and cities and across the countryside. In Killarney, people were dropping dead in the streets with fever; the town of Castlebar was reported to be 'dead with fever', while in Skibbereen, the bodies of fever victims lay unburied for over a week, none daring to approach them or to risk their lives by burying them.

By now many of those seeking admission were so weakened physically, whether by hunger or fever or both together, that their objective was limited to being assured a burial with a coffin; others were possessed of a determination that their children at least should live. Fever hospitals and workhouse infirmaries were overwhelmed. At the end of October 1846, when the total workhouse population was 68,839, a weekly mortality of four per thousand was reported; when it rose to 111,621 at the end of January 1847, the mortality rate had jumped to thirteen per thousand; at the end of February it had risen to twenty per thousand out of a population of 116,321, and twenty-five per thousand in mid-April when the inmate population had fallen back, temporarily, to 104,455. At that point some 2,267 persons were dying each week in the workhouses. Despite a fall-off in admissions, therefore, fever mortality was still on the increase. By now, according to George Nicholls, in his *History of the Irish Poor Law*, every relief applicant admitted to a workhouse was a patient, suffering either from dysentery, fever or extreme exhaustion. Under such circumstances, he wrote, 'separation became impossible, diseases spread, and the whole workhouse was changed into one large hospital without the appliances necessary for rendering it efficient as such'.[13]

A number of factors account for the short-lived fall in inmate numbers, mainly the fact that soup kitchen 'outdoor' relief was now becoming widespread, and was at that time, at least, preferable to workhouse admission. Another contributory factor was the policy pursued by the Poor Law Commissioners of dealing with serious overcrowding simply by closing workhouses. Whenever a house reached capacity, the Commissioners allowed Guardians to increase accommodation by such means as juggling with the interior arrangements, or by building sheds or adding second storeys to one-storey buildings. Heavy overcrowding of a work-house, or a fever hospital under Poor Law control, resulted in the issuing of sealed orders by the Commissioners closing the institution until numbers fell below legal capacity. In the meantime applicants for entry were abandoned outside.

In January, the Cookstown workhouse (County Tyrone) was forced to turn away eighty-nine relief applicants; when the Guardians requested permission to give food to those they had refused admission, they were forbidden to do so. At the end of February, the Commissioners ordered the closure of Omagh workhouse, also in Tyrone, to further admissions: grossly overcrowded as it was, diarrhoea, dysentery and measles were rampant among the child inmates, while fever patients lay so close to each other on the floor of the probationary wards that the 'workhouse physician had to walk over one to see another'. Omagh would remain closed until the end of July. At the end of March, after closing the work-house on several occasions over the previous weeks, the Rathdrum Guardians

(County Wicklow) expelled forty inmates in order to bring down the house to permitted levels of occupation. The workhouse was closed again at the end of April, and at the end of May, a further expulsion of another forty inmates took place, with some of those expelled reported to be still 'lying under the hedges' near the workhouse a week later. In April, sixty-two applicants were turned away from the Banbridge workhouse (County Down) despite the fact that all of them 'exhibited symptoms of starvation and some of death'.[14]

Workhouse staff and Guardians, for all their faults, were usually blameless in the execution of inhumane actions such as these and carried them out, sometimes over their own strongly worded written objections, because they were obliged by law to do so. A substantial minority of Boards of Guardians either resisted the regulations passively (the Banbridge Guardians in the above case without sanction gave the rejected applicants dinner and some bread before sending them home), or openly resisted peremptory orders from the Commissioners by continuing to afford relief illegally to poor people after they had been reprimanded for the same offence previously.[15]

Under the pressure of this influx of the fever-stricken, workhouses went from the grim but orderly institutions they had been previously to even grimmer ones beset by confusion and disorder. When fever began to take a heavy toll of staff, proper management disintegrated altogether, since so many officials became ill or died. Fever first struck Derry workhouse, for example, in January 1847 and by the following May, all the workhouse officers were ill with it – the master, the acting master, the matron and acting matron, the schoolmaster, the porter, the wardsman, assistant-wardsman and the clerk of the union. In the country as a whole, in the first four months of 1847, over 150 workhouse officers went down with fever, some fifty-four of them perishing, including seven clerks, nine masters, seven medical officers and six chaplains.

The fever epidemics of the Famine years represent something far greater than an intensified version of the local and regional outbreaks familiar from previous decades. By their near-universal prevalence and their exceptional virulence they amounted to a national pandemic of proportions never before experienced in Ireland. Remarkably in the circumstances, for months the government insisted that nothing out of the ordinary was taking place, and as late as 25 January 1847, the Chief Secretary for Ireland, Henry Labouchere, made a statement to that effect in the House of Commons. Government denials were embarrassingly contradicted the day after Labouchere's remarks, when Lord Bessborough, the Lord Lieutenant, without consulting Westminster, ordered the reconvening of the Central Board of Health in order to deal with the situation. Resuming operations under the 1846 Act, the Board would serve while a new Fever Bill was drafted and passed, recommencing from scratch the work of erecting fever hospitals and dispensaries and the hiring of medical staff and nurse-tenders.[16]

Under the new fever legislation, passed in April, 373 temporary fever hospitals were to be built and 473 additional doctors hired for fever duty.[17] However, this would take months to carry into effect, and many thousands would die untended before the fever hospitals were set up in the localities, before the marquees, tents, fever sheds and other temporary accommodation had been erected in the grounds of workhouses, or acquired elsewhere. Whether the delay in the provision of this accommodation (or the provision itself) made any difference to the mortality rate is unsure, however, since patients in this temporary accommodation were actually not treated at all, but merely made as comfortable as possible, while those tending to them waited for them either to recover or to die. And no sooner had such facilities been put in place in any given location than they were swamped by fever cases, concentrating the impact of the different fevers and setting off a raft of cross-infections. The vast majority of fever victims were never to receive medical attention at all.

The trajectory of each localized Famine epidemic, from emergence to peak to decline, varied according to a timescale based on the specific conditions in the different districts and regions. An initial onset which threatened to overwhelm medical and public health facilities of each affected area was typically followed by a desperate accommodation crisis which exacerbated the incidence of fever, and led to a soaring mortality rate, the dead including not just the unfortunate patients, but also a swathe of the medical and workhouse staff attending them, all of whom died in appalling conditions and profound suffering. Many tense and dreadful months then followed before the epidemic finally abated. Over much of the country the great epidemics had noticeably receded by mid-1848, although the cholera outbreak of spring and early summer 1849 brought mortality rates up to extremely high levels once again, before they too subsided.

But even then, fever mortality was slow to return to pre-Famine norms, largely because of the emergence of cross-infections, from dysentery, diarrhoea, smallpox, measles and scarlatina, the death rate among children being particularly high. Through 1849 and into 1850 fever would flare again and again, even in workhouses and fever hospitals in more favoured districts, persisting in places even after the legislation was allowed to lapse in August 1850 as no longer necessary. The situation was far worse in the embattled western and southern unions, which, as we shall see, continued to endure major outbreaks inside and outside workhouses each succeeding winter until the end of 1852.

How many died of fever in the Famine epidemics is not known. Between July 1847 and August 1850, some 34,622 persons were recorded as having died in the temporary fever hospitals, out of a total of 332,462 persons treated, a mortality rate of 10.4 per cent. This figure hugely understates the number of those who actually died in these hospitals, not to mention those who perished at any time in infirmaries, jails, convict depots, lunatic asylums and other institutions. It does not provide us with even the crudest basis for estimating the numbers who died in their own homes, in the street, in the fields, on the public works or the soup kitchens, or, indeed, in a desperate headlong flight from the country. And even if we did possess such figures, it would be impossible to separate purely fever deaths from those where sufferers were already far gone in starvation, or affected by hypothermia, both equally lethal conditions on their own. In the end, the exact cause of death for individual Famine victims is neither a simple question, nor perhaps a useful one to pose.[18]

It was the influx of the disease-ridden to the workhouses during the fever pandemic that first saw the Famine impact significantly on the Poor Law. Under the soup kitchen programme, as we have seen, the Poor Law assumed a direct role in relief of distress on a temporary basis, its apparent success in this dissipating any remaining Whig-Liberal aversion at extending the remit of the system beyond ordinary destitution. As plans were drafted early in 1847 that combined solutions to ordinary destitution and Famine distress alike, they were built entirely around the Poor Law, which was to be amended to include a provision for some form of outdoor relief, the only way of catering for a hugely enlarged population of relief recipients.

Outdoor relief had constituted a last great ideological stumbling block for government, but two factors now made it more palatable to those interest groups that comprised Whig-Liberal supporters in Britain. One was the proposed ring-fencing of outdoor relief with such ferocious restrictions so as to make it a resort of extreme emergency, and extremely difficult to access. The second related to the belief that outdoor relief would be required for a very short time only, the assumption being that Famine was now virtually at an end, and that all that was now required in relief terms was to carry the destitute poor safely over to the next, undoubtedly bountiful harvest, when they would again have work and their own cheap potatoes.

In Ireland, public discussion of the relief Bills was muted and criticism of them rare, which might seem strange given that their significance for the country could hardly have been exaggerated. The likely explanation for this was an Irish assumption that the proposed outdoor relief would amount to a continuation of the previous system under a different name (and perhaps not even that since the term 'outdoor relief' was already widely used to denote the soup kitchen system). At any rate, when the core of the new legislation was passed early in June, in what became known as the Poor Law Extension Act, it caused no great stir in Ireland.[19] The first section of the Act (also known as the Poor Law Amendment Act) granted to Boards of Guardians the power to dispense outdoor relief, at their own discretion, to destitute disabled persons and widows with two or more children. The second section permitted the same in the case of destitute able-bodied persons, although in this case it could only be given when a workhouse was full or severely affected by fever; outdoor able-bodied relief was limited to short two-month periods, and might be sanctioned or renewed only by formal sealed orders issued directly by the Commissioners. It could only be given in the form of food, the daily ration laid down by later regulation being identical in composition and quantity with that doled out by the soup kitchens. Regulations imposed later would insist on full eight-hour workdays for able-bodied recipients. Under the tenth section of the Act, no relief, either indoor or outdoor, might be afforded persons holding more than a quarter acre of land. The implications of this section, the notorious Gregory Clause, will be discussed in the next chapter.

Two other enactments completed the legislative package comprising the amended Poor Law. At the end of July, a Vagrant Act was passed, imposing severe punishments for public begging or for seeking relief in different district electoral divisions, and increasing to three months hard labour the penalties for men found to have left their families 'on the rates' while they went abroad in search of employment. Such individuals were deemed deserters, and fears that their 'offence' was one likely to increase under the new dispensation explains the harshness of the penalty imposed. The other Act, which was passed on the same day as the Vagrant Act, hived off the Irish Poor Law from its English parent, and placed it under the authority of three Commissioners sitting in Dublin, providing also for local monitoring of Poor Law unions by a new category of Poor Law Inspector.

The amended Poor Law emerged against a background of charity fatigue in Britain, born of revulsion at the overspill of Irish distress in that country, the anger of both public and politicians being deflected towards Irish landlords whom it was now convenient to blame for the morass of destitution that Ireland was now exporting.[20] A major objective of the Poor Law Amendment Act, therefore, was to punish the landlords, and make them pay for the cost of relief through Poor Law rate payments that were envisaged to increase substantially. Landlords were already liable for the entire rates of all holdings with a valuation less than £4, and fifty per cent liable for holdings on or above that figure, the other fifty being paid by the occupiers. For the moment, the political influence of those prominent Whigs who were absentee owners of vast tracts of Irish land and not at all happy with the new relief legislation, was temporarily outweighed by other considerations. In the satisfaction of having successfully targeted landlords it was forgotten that among those who would also see their rates liability increased massively were those smallholders whose holdings hovered on or above £4 annual valuation, and who were themselves only marginally better off than those whose poverty they would help relieve.

Under the amended Poor Law the financial cost of relief of destitution and distress was transferred almost entirely to Irish resources. While the Famine lasted, further support from the British Treasury would be minimal, and government intervention limited for the most part to monitoring expenditure and redistributing financial liability internally within the Irish Poor Law. In administrative and financial terms, therefore, the British government had used the Poor Law adroitly to disengage itself from direct involvement with Irish destitution and famine relief.

Implicit within the amended Poor Law from the moment of its passing was the potential for major humanitarian disaster. What transpired was calamity on the largest scale yet seen during the Famine. During the summer, Poor Law unions had been instructed repeatedly to acquire extra accommodation to cater for the changeover to the new system, but few of them did so significantly. At the end of August 1847, the total accommodation within the Irish Poor Law, including the fever hospitals, amounted to just short of 117,000 places, all of them occupied. The agricultural work which Trevelyan, now at the peak of his influence, had been once again banking on to lessen the demand for relief in the autumn failed entirely to materialize, since farming families continued last year's practice of doing their own agricultural work. In any case, the collapse of the conacre system meant that labourers in most places had lost access to potato ground; unwilling to risk their seed potatoes in another destroyed harvest, smallholders had eaten them instead, placing all their chances for the survival of their families on the public works. In the event, the harvest proved to be a disaster, not because of blight, which did not materialize at all in 1847, but because so few potatoes were sown during the spring. The acreage under potatoes that year was only about one eighth that of 1845.[21]

All of this had been entirely predictable much earlier in the year. The general neglect of tillage had been lamented universally in the newspapers in the spring, and noted widely in official correspondence; accurate cultivation statistics collected by the constabulary were available at all times, as was an enormous body of supplementary documentation that crossed Trevelyan's desk every day. Long before the potatoes were ready for lifting, it was known that even if the blight did not recur, there would be a huge shortfall in the potato harvest, and that there would be no 'breathing time' of agricultural work to lessen the demand for relief in the autumn any more than there had been the previous year. With the approach of winter, distress would inevitably increase massively, and it was a forgone conclusion that the Poor Law could not remotely hope to deal with it, let alone cater for more than three million people who would be left without food when the kitchens closed.

Trevelyan, however, remained immoveable, impervious to the advice available to him, ignoring, for example, a pointed remark from the new Chief Secretary, William Somerville, in October, that the use of the Poor Law as a conduit of relief during the autumn and winter shortages was a 'terrifying' prospect. Under his direction government policies went ahead according to schedule and without alteration. The grain depots were closed, and, within weeks of the passing of the Poor Law Amendment Act, returned to their owners, the stock in hand sold off. Government supply ships returned to service with the fleet, seconded officers either returning to their former posts or to duties as inspectors under the new Poor Law. From the late summer the soup kitchens were progressively closed down, against the piteous clamour of those depending on them, there being little appetite or energy left for stronger protest. It was a reality that was very far from Trevelyan's anodyne account written later that year, according to which the people were 'again gradually and peaceably' thrown on their own resources 'at the season of harvest, when new and abundant supplies of food became available, and the demand for labour was at its highest amount.'[22] Happy that his labours had been completed, in mid-August Trevelyan departed with his family for holidays in France. In Ireland, after one last issue of meal to 1,136,591 recipients on 12 September, operations under the Temporary Relief Act came to an end.[23]

The impact of the amended Poor Law was immediate, coinciding with a seasonal upsurge in agrarian crime that was indirectly related to it, and involving cattle-stealing, intimidation, threatening notices and raids for arms. Predictably, it was again the western and southern unions that experienced the greatest pressure in what became a great surge in relief applications. Within weeks a huge tidal wave of distress and destitution built up all over the country, as quickly smashing over the walls of the country's workhouses.[24] By October many workhouses were overwhelmed, with crowds assembling outside their gates on board days clamouring for relief, which could not be granted because of the strict limitations on indoor places, and the fact that outdoor relief could not be granted without the sanction of the Poor Law Commissioners. Such crowds were left to fend for themselves where they had assembled, many among them dying where they lay of starvation and disease. The plight of those waiting outside the Nenagh workhouse on a cold, wet day in October was typical of scores of instances:

Ranged by the side of the opposite wall, which afforded some shelter from the wind, were about twenty cars, each with its load of eight or ten human beings, some of them in the most dangerous stages of dysentery and fever, others cripples, and all, from debility, old age, or disease, unable to walk a dozen steps . . . their clothes – if the rags they wore could be so called – were no protection from either the wind or rain; their legs and arms were in many instances completely naked, and their features pallid with disease and want. Not the least sickening part of the picture was the sight of several groups of children squatting under the cars for shelter.

Faced with scenes like this, or in order to avoid them, a number of Boards of Guardians provided outdoor relief without waiting for the Commissioners' sanction, an illegal act which brought down immediate censure. However, even in the face of repeated reprimands, Guardians in unions such as Cahirciveen and Listowel in Munster, and Ballina in Connacht, continued on this course in the belief that the condition of the poor left them with no choice. Probably the most extreme example was that of the Dungarvan Guardians, who provided outdoor relief for months to persons whom even the permanent union inspector, Joseph Burke, who delivered the Commissioners' furious reprimand to the Board, admitted were 'filthy, sickly and starved in appearance'. The disobedience of the Dungarvan Board would be an important factor in its dissolution in March 1848.[25]

Most Boards were compliant, however, and where caught between genuine concern for the starving, and the illegality of providing effective relief, generally accepted the guidance of the union inspectors, either the permanent inspectors with regional responsibilities or the temporary inspectors attached to individual unions. These, for the most part, were men for whom there were no higher principles than those laid out in statute law and bureaucratic regulation, and their dedication to enforcing compliance with both was unshakeable as indeed was their belief in the innate dishonesty of the poor. Much against their inclinations, from October onwards, in union after union, they found themselves obliged to recommend that outdoor relief be sanctioned to able-bodied persons. At the same time, they were careful to groom Boards of Guardians in the use of various administrative devices whose object was the reduction of legal eligibility for relief, the principal target being those very people who were admitted to outdoor relief, the absolutely destitute, famished, barely clad ghosts still classified as able-bodied.

One stratagem was to oblige infirm and disabled persons to accept outdoor relief, thereby creating workhouse space for able-bodied persons, who were considered more likely to feign need, and whose state of need could be 'tested' by offering them indoor places. Another was to expel 'deserted' women from the workhouse along with their children unless they agreed to give evidence against their husbands. Another again involved the posting of the lists of outdoor paupers in each electoral division in public places, mainly the doors of chapels.[26] To modern eyes, all three methods reek of bureaucratic cynicism: disabled and infirm persons were in the workhouse precisely because they were unable to survive outside; desertion was a legal fabrication, and all but a tiny fraction of women so circumstanced were in chronic need, their husbands' supposed acts of desertion a last-ditch anguished attempt at fending for their families. Posting of relief lists was supposedly a means of detecting fraud, but in practice it operated most effectively at the level of inciting social shame among needy people, who, though starving, still retained a strong sense of social pride.

The workhouse test was the most cynical and most effective of all these devices, and it operated by the deliberate maintenance of a substantial number of indoor vacancies, even in very crowded workhouses. These places were then offered to recipients of outdoor relief, refusal of which was expected and taken as an admission of feigned destitution. Refusing persons were deprived of all relief, and the Poor Law thereby absolved of any further responsibility for them. Apart from an almost superstitious dread of its soul-destroying workhouse regime, there were other reasons why poor persons should have refused to accept these 'offers' of indoor places. The two greatest would have been fears that families might be swept to their deaths by workhouse fevers, or that the landlord might destroy the cabin in their absence, leaving family members stranded for life in the condition of paupers.

The evidence for persons consciously opting to die rather than accept workhouse places is plentiful, and in many investigations, especially inquests, we are given the exact words uttered by dying persons to this effect, as told to neighbours, priests or Poor Law officials. Such investigations also reveal instances where persons refusing the workhouse test, or persons who experienced workhouse life for a short time before leaving, return to the familiarity of their cabins (or more often to its ruins), and in the end allow starvation, fever or exposure to cold make the final decision for them. Those rescued from the results of such passive decision-making were often carried to the workhouses in a dying state. Official reports and correspondence do not refer to the physical or emotional state of persons refusing indoor relief, or discuss their motivation in detail, which is understandable given that refusal was the essential factor required by the Poor Law. They do, however, abound with assumptions of thwarted criminality and endless recitation of the threadbare mantras of abuse and imposition.[27] Without the workhouse test, the Irish Poor Law could not have functioned at all in the years after 1847.

To take one example from Donegal, early in February 1848 the inspector in Ballyshannon union, a James D'Arcy, attributed the recent steep rise in relief applications to a belief among the poor that, since the workhouse was now nearly full, outdoor relief might now become available. Outdoor relief being much preferable to inmate status, D'Arcy was no doubt correct in this supposition. However, his sole concern was with the 'imposition' involved. Elsewhere in D'Arcy's reports are references to cases where persons died rather than accept the workhouse regime, one of them a woman called Susan Kerrigan, the other a man named Keenan. In D'Arcy's view, Susan Kerrigan's death, of exposure to the cold in the open in February, was no one's fault but her own since she had left the workhouse of her own free will. Keenan's death had left his five children in 'the most melancholy misery', and his death was to be deplored, certainly, but he had 'fallen a sacrifice' to his stubborn refusal to surrender his two-and-a-half-acre holding, which 'could have been no use or benefit to him or them'. Nowhere does D'Arcy ponder the anguish that lay behind the decisions either of Susan Kerrigan or Keenan to refuse workhouse places, which at some buried level of consciousness he understood, given that the Poor Law exploited it as a means of reducing the outdoor list. A diligent officer, D'Arcy would die of fever contracted in the exercise of his duties in February 1849, at the age of 36.[28]

Rather than sanction outdoor relief, the Irish Poor Law Commissioners encouraged Boards of Guardians to acquire 'auxiliary' workhouses. Most unions acquired several, each assigned a particular function, catering for boys or girls of different ages, for example, or for young married women and their infants. Often located at a distance from the 'parent' workhouse, auxiliaries were usually unsuitable for human habitation, consisting as they did of disused residences, defunct warehouses or breweries, and, in at least one instance, a recently decommissioned slaughter-house. Acquired at profiteering rents from unscrupulous owners, not infrequently the cronies of individual Guardians, the fitting-out of auxiliaries was often shoddily executed by corrupt contractors, leaving inmates in uninhabitable surroundings and at the mercy of hastily engaged, incompetent staff.

The results of all this were soon apparent, nowhere more so than in the Limerick union. Early in January 1848, Alderman Walnutt, one of the few conscientious members of the Limerick Board inspected the new auxiliary at Mountkennett, which housed several hundred children. Before entering the building, an old warehouse with no glass on one entire side, he and the physician who accompanied him had to pick their way through mounds of filth. In the freezing dormitories, the visitors found four dead children lying in bed alongside their living comrades, having perished 'without medicine, without firing, or any other comfort in the place'. Informed of all this, the Chairman of the Board refused to believe the reports produced by the two men or to visit the auxiliary in person, and impatiently ended discussion of the matter by suggesting that someone should 'well, write to the Commissioners'.

Parent workhouses as well as auxiliaries became overcrowded in the influx of this period, some of them, indeed totally overwhelmed. At the end of January 1848, the medical officer in Tullamore union reported that the workhouse was filthy, that the dormitory floors exhaled a 'urinous' odour, and that the inmates were allowed to store their personal possessions behind their beds: bundles of clothes, cooking utensils, crocks of all kinds and other forlorn reminders of their previous lives. The day room was filled with smoke from small turf fires lit on the earthen floor, around which groups of women and children warmed themselves. Some were 'comfortably seated near a small fire preparing tea in their tea-pots', most of them dressed 'in their own private clothes, which were of the dirtiest description'. In one part of the room a child who had died the day before was laid out as if for a wake, and 'permitted to remain exposed to the gaze of all the bystanders'. In the men's day room, a disabled man was found warming himself on a fire he had lit under the metal rungs of his bed. In the fever hospital, many of the beds contained two patients; in one bed four patients lay side by side.

The shortcomings of the Tullamore Board of Guardians led to its dissolution and replacement in early February. It was one of thirty-nine Boards to suffer this fate during the Famine, something short of one-third of the original total number.[29] Although internal disorder and the neglect of the Guardians figure among the reasons given by the Commissioners for dissolving boards, the decisive factors were almost invariably financial: failure to strike or collect a rate commensurate with expenditure, or to control the cost of relief. Boards which had presided over conditions that were as bad if not worse than those in dissolved unions, but which still managed to collect rates and keep outdoor relief to a minimum, were allowed to survive, the Limerick union being a case in point.

Dissolved boards were replaced by Vice-Guardians, two- or three-man teams of paid administrators who managed the unions to which they were appointed in conjunction with the district inspector, and under the close eye of the Commissioners. Although there were exceptions, Vice-Guardian regimes were generally efficient and soon brought order and regularity to unions under their control. In addition to cleaning and properly ventilating the workhouses, they struck new rates and collected them, although in the Poor Law unions designated by the Commissioners as 'distressed' late in 1847, and therefore meriting extra consideration, this usually meant racking up extra levels of debt in order to relieve destitution in accordance with their particular bureaucratic perceptions. Because of their honesty, Vice-Guardians were sometimes seen in a heroic light, but in fact they were as much creatures of the system as the inspectors, with no brief for the mitigation of its harshness. Because of their efficiency, indeed, they were able to operate its pauper-rejecting stratagems with much greater success than elected Boards.[30]

If the stark inhumanity of the Poor Law cannot fail to emerge from the study of almost any union in the first half of 1848, it is more clearly traced in those where a semblance of order still existed rather than in the chaotic, horrendous circum-stances of those in the west and south. One example was the Munster union of Cashel, situated mostly in south Tipperary, where early in February 1848, a newly appointed inspector, Major Archibald Robinson, took upon himself the task of bringing order to the workhouses there. An army engineer since the Peninsular campaign, despite his age, Robinson was zealous and energetic, his particular priorities being to improve the appearance and cleanliness of the workhouses, to ensure that inmates were properly clad in workhouse garb and that the rates were collected with greater efficiency. He was particularly concerned with the subject of outdoor relief to the able-bodied, where the Guardians, he believed, had been lax and unduly liberal. Over succeeding months, although he did continue to recommend renewal of sealed orders, at the same time he strove to choke off outdoor relief over time by consistently enforcing a labour test, by relentless application of the workhouse test, and by the progressive restriction of relievable outdoor categories.

In regard to the labour test, Robinson required all able-bodied recipients of outdoor relief to break stone each day for eight hours in their home electoral division, absence resulting in the immediate stoppage of rations to the recipient and his family. On 3 March he reported that by such means 'improper persons' were being kept off the outdoor lists, citing as an indication of his success the fact that at the end of the previous week over a thousand men's rations remained unconsumed in the different electoral divisions, apart from those of wives and children. Robinson first used the workhouse test to induce 270 men and boys to enter a newly fitted-out auxiliary workhouse in Cashel town in mid-February. Shortly after arriving there, however, the inmates broke out and marched to the main workhouse, occupying some of the wards in protest at the 'unhealthy' state of the auxiliary, and declaring that they would die rather than return there. After listening with apparent sympathy to their complaint, Robinson used the parley to identify four 'ringleaders', whom he promptly had arrested and charged before a magistrate.[31]

In mid-March, Robinson reported that capacity now existed in the auxiliary for some 170 men and their families. That number exactly were then struck off the outdoor lists and offered indoor places. When the vast majority of the men refused, they and their families were immediately deprived of relief, the exercise proving for Robinson 'how much more efficacious the workhouse test is than any other'. Less than a week later, he gave his opinion that the advent of spring agricultural employment and extra indoor capacity that had become available now permitted the testing of all single men, together with married men who had only two children in family. Every one of the 600 single men subsequently offered workhouse places refused and were struck off the lists.

Independently of the inspector, some time earlier the Guardians had administered the test to other able-bodied categories of men, some with very large families. All had refused it and even though they were then struck off the relief lists, the Guardians later relented because of a realization of what would become of the families if they had not done so. Infuriated at the change of mind, Robinson complained to the Commissioners who promptly issued a sharp reprimand to the Board. This in turn led to a confrontation between inspector and Board, at which many revealing comments were passed. One Guardian angrily told Robinson that 'when a man came into the workhouse, his own house was always pulled down, and thus he was made a permanent pauper', and according to another, 'it was a greater expense relieving a person in the house than out of it'. This latter comment was, of course, true, in that the cost of an indoor pauper was as much as three times that of one on the outdoor list, but it missed the point that the workhouse test was aimed at deterring the much greater numbers who would otherwise be eligible for outdoor relief.[32] But Robinson had his way, and following the confrontation, he was able to prevail on the Guardians to refuse outdoor relief to men with 'only' three children 'and so on by degrees either fill the house or strike off the relief lists all those at present relieved under section 2 of the Act'. Throughout March and April he proceeded doggedly with reducing the lists, next excluding men with four in family, followed by those with five.

As in many workhouses 'insubordination' on the part of inmates constituted an ongoing problem at Cashel, and in March 'a slight symptom' arose when two male inmates refused to work at stone breaking. Placed under confinement according to regulations, they were then committed to jail by magistrate's order, charged with refusing to obey the master's instructions, and sentenced, respectively, to a month and three weeks' hard labour. Three weeks later, one hundred outdoor paupers rushed a Guardians' meeting when told they were to be offered workhouse places. After a standoff that lasted some hours, the men were persuaded to leave the boardroom, but dispersed only after the arrival of the resident magistrate and the parish priest. Only four or five of the men accepted indoor places following the incident, allowing Robinson to conclude that the whole thing had been a sham whose object was 'merely to intimidate the Guardians, and force on out-door relief'. In this, as in other incidents, he was greatly irked by the fact that the Guardians blamed him personally for cutting off relief, regardless of the fact that he was merely a servant of the Poor Law and that 'we are all obliged to obey the law, and the different orders we from to time receive'. When he received a threatening letter on 22 April, he seems to have been bothered less by the injunction that 'I might get my coffin ready' than by the accusation of the anonymous writer that it was by his action alone that relief was being restricted.[33]

The mindset of Robinson and D'Arcy was typical of Poor Law inspectors in general, and traces of it can even be detected in such genuinely compassionate figures as Colonel George Vaughan Jackson of Ballina, and Captain A.E. Kennedy, in west Clare. The official communications that passed between officials and the Poor Law Commissioners are notable for the absence of any acknowledgment of the massive human casualty engendered by close adherence to regulations. In the case of the latter two individuals, such an awareness can indeed be discerned, but even here it is in the nature of a subtext that can be deciphered only by close reading across the entire body of their writings.

Despite the most determined efforts of the relief authorities, by January 1848 more than fifty per cent of unions were dispensing outdoor relief to the able-bodied. In the first week of February, over 445,000 persons were in receipt of outdoor rations, of whom about a quarter were designated as able-bodied. By early April, there were over 638,000 on the outdoor lists, one-third of them able-bodied – the able-bodied figure had doubled since February. In May more than a million persons were being sustained on a daily basis by the Poor Law, four-fifths of them through outdoor relief. After July, however, the outdoor lists and workhouse occupancy began to decline at an uneven pace, before rising again in autumn. By the end of the year, only twenty-five unions had been able to avoid outdoor relief altogether.

An unanticipated outgrowth of the administrative battle against outdoor relief during 1848 and 1849 was the gradual transformation of the Poor Law from a simple nexus of union and workhouse to a network of union systems, each nucleated on a much expanded parent workhouse, and each with its satellite auxiliaries and fever hospital. By the time the Famine ended, the number of unions had increased from 130 to 163, the total level of indoor accommodation having increased from the original 100,000 to 150,000 in early 1848, and to 250,000 a year later. In the course of the expansion, the workhouse system became the dominant feature of the union towns in which they were situated – bloated repositories of the deepest human unhappiness. Within these systems, the bureaucracy worked to obliterate the personal, familial and social identity of the inmates. This was done by formal workhouse classification on new admissions; by the separation of families, ages and sexes; by the dreariness of the workhouse uniform; the unpleasant and insufficient diet and the mind-numbing monotony of stone-breaking.[34]

Even in such desolate surroundings, however, it never proved possible to crush the human spirit entirely, and there is considerable evidence to suggest that adaption to long-stay status engendered an interesting dynamic among the inmates of many systems. Little is yet known about this phenomenon, which is currently being investigated by Gerard Moran, but we do know that a level of solidarity emerged in many workhouse populations, in which regulations were subverted and flouted, and in a number of cases sustained resistance was maintained to particularly harsh regimes. Subversion was easiest achieved where management was inefficient and Guardian oversight poor, but it occurs even under relatively closely managed regimes, notably in a number of Leinster workhouses. Wherever it does occur, we find instances of paupers walking about freely in nearby towns; being lent out to Guardians for work on their farms, gardens or businesses and idling at their own pauper work.

Widespread disturbances took place within workhouses, the most noticeable feature of which was the role played by women inmates, either as leaders or participants.[35] The prominent showing of women is partly explained by their numerical superiority as inmates, and it raises the question of a possible continuity with the soup kitchen disturbances. During these years wholesale pilferage of workhouse food was common, as was deliberate damage to workhouse property. There were mass breakouts by youthful inmates, heedless of the punishments inflicted on those who were caught. On at least one occasion in the Callan workhouse, in 1848, inmates took part in an organized fight in rooms from which staff had been locked out; in April 1849, a number of teenage paupers escaped from the Ennis workhouse, killed and butchered a sheep in a field outside the town, and were eating its roasted flesh around a fire when the police arrived. The recklessness of these escapades is surely an important indication that those who took part in them were engaged in conscious acts of assertion of those qualities of dignity and personal sovereignty of which the Poor Law seemed determined to rob them.[36]

The widespread existence of such incidents must not be taken, however, as an indication that workhouses were sociologically stable places, or in any sense islands of human solidarity amidst a surrounding societal turmoil. Conditions outside and inside workhouses were, after all, closely connected, and upheavals outside invariably had seismic effects on the inmate populations, which in most workhouses were continuously shaken up during 1848 and the following years.

Two interrelated factors were responsible for this, the first that the potatoes continued to fail, on a widespread basis in 1848 and a much-reduced regional scale the following year, hastening the mass impoverishment of smallholders and sections of the once comfortable sectors that was now taking place. Those most affected were those who had so far been able to hold on to land and cabins, but were now following in the footsteps of the labourers and poorer smallholders of the previous years, a large proportion of whom were now dead. The second factor was that landlords were taking advantage of tenant vulnerability in order to rid themselves of the occupiers as fast as they could. The principal method by which this was achieved was mass clearance, which took place on a colossal scale in the years following the passing of the Poor Law Amendment Act. More than any other factor it was the clearances of these years that kept the Poor Law supplied with what seemed at times like an inexhaustible quantity of human raw material.

Asylum by the Neighbouring Ditches:
The Famine Clearances

Many have been turned off by process of law to seek asylum by the neighbouring ditches, the high canopy of heaven their shelter, the green sward their couch, the stars in their firmament their watch-light, and the scarecrow and skeleton dogs keeping their vigil close by the dying.

– MAYO TELEGRAPH, *OCTOBER 1847*

The perspective of landlords with regard to evictions was generally pretty clearcut. Theirs was the undoubted right and duty to maintain and improve their properties and to ensure that tenants did not wreck rented farms or smallholdings. However unpleasant it might be, action had to be taken against those who failed to pay their rent, and beyond showing insolvent tenants a reasonable level of humane leeway, the reasons for non-payment were not really the landlord's concern. Those who witnessed evictions, on the other hand, could not fail to see them as great social evils. By their nature they desecrated the sanctuary of hearth and home; they were often accompanied by physical violence and the wanton destruction of personal belongings and by heart-rending emotional scenes. When added to the subsequent fate of the evicted families, onlookers with no immediate interest in the proceedings found evictions profoundly disturbing, and indeed on occasion, so did personnel involved in the eviction act itself.

Pre-Famine evictions took place for a variety of reasons, ranging from defaulting on the rent to a cold managerial calculation of better profit from a new tenant and, not infrequently, the mere whim of the proprietor. It was often fatal for a tenant to excite the hostility of his landlord, whose determination to be rid of him could then lead to extremes of retaliation that outweighed the inconvenience and legal expense involved in the eviction process. In many cases, indeed, legal forms could be ignored entirely, since few tenants were in a position to challenge landlord illegalities. Where tenants lived in the shelter of leasehold – a small minority – there were many circumstances where a lease afforded no protection at all.

Before 1845 critics of landlord behaviour reserved their strongest condemnation for mass clearances, which, though less frequent than individual evictions, caused shocking devastation to entire rural populations where they did occur. Clearances arose mainly where landlords sought to improve and modernize their properties by ridding them of the inefficiency of large numbers of small-holding tenants, and usually formed part of a process of estate improvement and modernization known as consolidation. Consolidation, as we have seen earlier, involved 'squaring the land', that is, reordering farm boundaries within an estate and amalgamating smaller holdings into larger units. In the west it was directed to a great degree at eliminating the age-old Rundale system of common tenancy, which informed agricultural opinion considered to be backward. Ridding the estate of 'surplus' tenants was central to consolidation, whether by emigration schemes represented as voluntary (which were usually nothing of the kind), or by mass eviction. Lands that had been cleared were let to a smaller number of the remaining tenants, to new tenants altogether, or retained by the landlord in his own hands, usually for grazing purposes.

Consolidation-type clearances were often carried out piecemeal wherever the expiration of middlemen farm leases, contracted in different economic circumstances decades earlier, furnished the opportunity of restoring control to the head landlord. Carried out carefully, they might attract little notice, and it was by such means, for example, that the Smiths of Baltiboys, County Wicklow, had been able to 'get rid of all the little tenants and to increase the larger farms' (Elizabeth Smith's own words) and by watching out for 'opportunities' to pursue 'this delicate business without annoying anyone or even causing a murmur'.[1]

Middlemen lessees typically allowed or encouraged subdivision over the period of the lease, crowding the lands with miniscule holdings so as to maximize their profit rent, and the clearing of just one farm after its recovery by the head landlord could result in the expulsion of a great number of individuals and families. These were regarded by the law as squatters for whom the landlord had no legal responsibility. Few landlords felt any moral responsibility for squatters either, and in recognition of the grim fate that faced evicted families, already in pre-Famine times, large-scale clearances were known as 'exterminations'.

In pre-Famine time, landlords were inhibited from carrying out clearances to the extent many would have wished because of an unwillingness to attract adverse public reaction or government censure, but even more so by fear of violent organized tenant opposition, delivered through the ritual violence of the secret societies. The circumstances of the Famine would be such as to liberate them from those fears.

The onset of famine did not lead to any significant immediate increase in the pace of eviction, which may be due in large measure to the strong upsurge in Whiteboy activity that began in the early days of 1846. Two major clearances from this time, however, are of interest for a number of reasons: for their intensity, for the wave of public odium they generated, and for the manner in which they prefigured the enormities that were shortly to come. The first took place in March 1846, in County Galway, when Mrs. Marcella Gerrard evicted over 300 persons from her property at Ballinlass, in the east of the county; the second the following month when some 357 persons were expelled, in two separate episodes, from the estate of the Marquess of Waterford in the vicinity of Kilmacthomas, County Waterford.[2] Both clearances were classic consolidation operations; the tenants in both cases were solvent and up to date with their rents, and in both cases also, the opportunity was furnished by the expiration of old middleman leases.

The Ballinlass clearance was carried out with such brutality as to give rise to the expression, 'to gerrardise', denoting evictions accompanied with particular vindictiveness. In the House of Commons, partisans of Mrs. Gerrard who sought to defend her actions, could not convincingly deny that the evicted families were dragged from their homes with violence, nor that when they took shelter in the ditches of the nearby fields, they were physically beaten out of them also – women and children as well as men. Parliamentary apologists for the Marquess of Waterford, on the other hand, were more effective in presenting their case, arguing that the Kilmacthomas tenants had left their homes peaceably on payment of compensation money, and that many of them had agreed to dismantle their houses as they left. However, as the radical M.P., George Poulett Scrope, and *The Times* newspaper (which unusually for an English print, referred to the episode as an 'extermination') pointed out, this was a false picture. The so-called compensation was a 'miserable pittance' and, far from leaving willingly, the tenants departed only because refusal to do so would have resulted in their immediate ejection in circumstances similar to those visited on the unfortunate Ballinlass occupiers.

But the Ballinlass and Waterford clearances, as well as a number of others that took place at approximately the same time, were still within the norms of pre-Famine consolidation, and it was January 1847 before mass eviction in Ireland had increased to the point where the Quaker philanthropist, William Todhunter, could speak of landlords 'availing themselves of the present calamity to effect a wholesale clearance of their estates.'[3] Although other commentators would make similar statements over succeeding months, only with the arrival of the autumn can it be said that the Famine clearances proper had begun, when the level of evictions in virtually every corner of Ireland underwent a sudden massive acceleration, and thousands of families were expelled summarily from homes that were promptly destroyed.

It is now generally understood why clearances emerged at this point, two years after the first failure of the potato crop. Over the intervening period landlord rental income had been falling steadily, adding to the burden of pre-Famine debts and encumbrances and the first repayments of loans under the Labour Rate Act, which promised hefty increases in the county cess, or occupier tax. In the situation where a substantial proportion of tenants were no longer contributing to estate finances, anticipated changes in the other local tax, the Poor Law rate, threatened to make them a ruinous economic liability.

As things stood, landlords were liable for the entire rate levied on holdings of £4 annual valuation or below. Since occupiers at this level were defaulting wholesale on their rents, and since the rates could now be expected to rise dramatically because of the transfer of all relief to the Poor Law, as landlords saw it the only sure way of avoiding bankruptcy was to eliminate the smallest holdings by the mass eviction of the occupiers and the destruction of their dwellings. Much discussed by landlords among themselves was the appalling vista that would open up if this were not done, the prevailing nightmare scenario being of estates turning to 'pauper warrens' whose shiftless denizens would never again either pay rent or need to work, but would remain burrowed in their hovels, sustained by an outrageously generous outdoor relief, which they, the landlords, would have to fund as principal ratepayers.

Clearances undertaken in these circumstances, therefore, had something of the nature of emergency consolidations, whose immediate reward was the rescue of properties from near-bankruptcy and in the long term, the improvement of estate management and finance. An added reason for carrying out clearances now was that it could be done with impunity, since the collapse of Whiteboy activity after 1847 meant that those who might have resisted or exacted retribution were for the most part dead, in the workhouses, in prison or had departed overseas as emigrants or transported felons. An extra benefit of clearance in these circumstances was the possibility of rooting out forever the remnants of those social elements who had made the lives of landlords so difficult over such a long period, and particularly since the onset of famine, when many proprietors had fled abroad because of fears for their security, most others remaining besieged within their fortified mansions. Clearances, therefore, brought the opportunity for retribution, of which landlords took full advantage.

Another factor which has a bearing on the extraordinarily ruthless and thorough character of Famine clearances relates to the Gregory Clause of the amended Poor Law, which excluded all tenants holding more than a quarter acre from relief. Named after William Gregory, the east Galway Peelite landlord who moved the relevant amendment, and who was personally motivated by fears that his own badly indebted property would be swamped by pauperized tenants, it was acceded to by government as a concession to its free-market and landlord supporters, and for what it might achieve in terms of the long-term goal of most political economists, that of driving smallholders off the land altogether.[4]

Under the Gregory Clause, wherever smallholder applicants for relief sought to hold on to cabin and quarter acre after parting with the overall holding, landlords routinely refused to accept the surrender unless these were included also. In other cases, having surrendered all but cabin and quarter acre, landlords illegally levelled the cabins whenever the occupants departed for any length of time, for the workhouse or even during absences lasting mere hours. So widespread had this practice become in parts of County Meath, that in April 1848, the Kells Guardians threatened prosecution on those interfering with cabins while their occupiers were in Poor Law custody. In Meath, in 1850, one parish priest accused the Navan Board of Guardians of colluding with landlords in admitting applicants to the workhouse and expelling them a few weeks later, the interval being used by the landlords to destroy their cabins and prevent their return. In other cases, landlords' agents or bailiffs lied to local Poor Law officials regarding poor smallholders' circumstances, so that they were refused relief initially, and thereafter strong-armed into parting with everything. Fear of what might happen if they left their cabins for any reason led many destitute smallholders to remain in them until they starved to death.[5]

Compilation of official eviction statistics began only in 1849, when the clearances had been under way for well over a year, and because of this and the fact that the statistics themselves represent a serious undercount, it is not possible to say precisely how many persons suffered permanent expulsion from holdings and homes during the campaigns. However, authoritative recent estimates have put the total numbers evicted from the start of the campaigns in 1846 to their end in 1854 at between 500,000 and 600,000 persons. These include both evictions where legal forms had been complied with and a huge number of 'informal', that is, highly illegal evictions. There is also the issue of the innumerable so-called voluntary surrenders of land that took place over the same period. The gross illegality of so many evictions and the brutality attached to them were 'matters of general knowledge', according to the philanthropist, Rev. Sidney Godolphin Osborne, who visited Ireland in 1849. 'I have never been in any society in

Ireland', he wrote, in his *Gleanings in the West of Ireland* (1850) 'where it was not admitted that a very large proportion of evictions were carried out by fraud or by violence'.[6]

As a rule clearances were carried out most extensively in districts where subdivision had been most chronic and dwellings of £4 valuation or less accordingly more prevalent. On a regional basis, the counties most affected were those of the west and south, with Clare, Tipperary, Mayo, Galway and Kerry suffering proportionately more than others. The level of eviction in Tipperary was some twenty times that of Fermanagh, the county with the lowest incidence of clearance, and in Clare, the county with the highest overall rate of eviction, it has been calculated that one in every ten persons was permanently ejected from holding and home in the years between 1849 and 1854.

The extent of human dislocation represented by the basic statistics of Famine clearances is staggering; the scale of suffering they represent is hardly imaginable. It is conveyed to some extent, however, in many of those accounts that survive from the campaigns. At Ballysaggartmore, in Waterford, for example, at the end of 1847, after the expulsion of 280 persons 'in the severest part of the winter', it was reported that 'whole families' were 'lying on stone benches in small sheds, with a stream of water running through the centre of the horrible abodes'. Most of the evicted were believed to have died of fever and dysentery afterwards. In mid-December, the *Galway Vindicator* reported that during the previous week the city had been 'literally inundated with a tide of rural pauperism' as a result of evictions in Conamara, carried out by Christopher St. George, the county M.P., and owner of 26,000 acres of land in the county. Eleven large boatloads of 'wretched outcasts of landlord despotism' from St. George's island and mainland properties were landed at Galway quays for despatch to the workhouse; failing to gain entry there, these were currently thronging the 'doors of the inhabitants, demanding a morsel of food to save them from perishing'. This 'vast mass of expelled pauperism' was so great, according to the *Vindicator*, that 'it would require another workhouse, nearly as large as the present one, to afford the poor outcasts an asylum'.

During the clearances, urban as well as rural areas were emptied; one-street hamlets, substantial villages and even entire sections of towns. In October 1847 the *Mayo Telegraph* lamented the sight of 'whole villages without smoke issuing from a single cabin, the doors being built up with stone', many of the owners now having been 'turned off by process of law to seek asylum in the neighbouring ditches, the high canopy of heaven their shelter, the green sward their couch, the stars in the firmament their watch light and the scarecrow and skeleton dogs keeping their vigil close by the dying'.[7] The *Illustrated London News* and other pictorial publications provided a certain level of coverage of the clearances, and published evocative illustrations sketched by their artists on site, of ruined villages devoid of inhabitants, amidst the surrounding bleak consolidated landscape. What is striking about these illustrations is that the ruins they depict represent for the most part what had been substantial dwellings, often complete with unroofed outhouses; the furniture and household objects scattered round indications of relative comfort. These were far from the fourth-class cabins of labourers and cottiers, but clear indications that famine destitution was rapidly spreading upwards through rural society. Probably the best-known of these are the illustrations of the villages of Moveen and Tullig, in the remote Loop Head peninsula of west Clare, which have been among the most widely reproduced images of Famine Ireland.[8]

Less well known from that county was the destruction of much of Newmarket-on-Fergus by the grandson of its builder, the otherwise well-regarded Dromoland squire, Sir Lucius O'Brien, brother of the revered patriot, William Smith O'Brien. From Erris, County Mayo, comes the story of the mass clearance of three villages containing over 400 persons by the Dublin solicitor, J.J. Walsh, at Christmas time 1847, the site of which Asenath Nicholson came upon in her wanderings. 'Worse than died', she was told on inquiring of the plight of the evictees, '. . . if they are alive, they are in the sandbanks of the sea-shore, or crowded into some miserable cabin for a night or two, waiting for death, they are lingering out the last hours of suffering'.

Over several days in May 1849, the inhabitants of the north Tipperary village of Toomevara were removed by the owner, Rev. John Massey Dawson, in a consolidation subsequent to the dispossession of three insolvent middlemen. Now reduced to the condition of squatters, without any rights of tenure, the occupying under-tenants and their families were all ejected: some 576 persons in all, 263 adults and 313 children. The clearance was recorded in detail by the journalist and historian, Maurice Lenihan, whose description of parents leading their children by the hand into the pouring rain, and mothers kneeling on the wet street, 'holding their children up to Heaven, beg[ging] relief from the Almighty and strength to endure their afflictions' was widely circulated in Ireland and abroad. The sight of 'bereaved women and men, running half frantic through the streets or cowering from the rain under the shelter of their poor furniture piled confusedly' was one that clearly had a profound effect on Lenihan personally. Another disturbing scene he describes related to the wretched huts built by the evicted in the grounds of the Catholic parish chapel and up against its walls. Inside one of them he encountered 'a group of complete misery', consisting of father, mother, and four children, who 'were literally reduced to skeletons by starvation'. Traces of recently destroyed buildings elsewhere in the village were all that remained of a community whose members 'were now located in the ditches in the adjacent townlands, wherever a dry nook or an overhanging tree afforded a favourable situation for re-erecting a hut'.[9]

The Sack of Toomevara, as it is referred to in some accounts, was one of the most atrocious examples of mass clearance in a county that suffered greatly as a result of them. But even counties close to Dublin, Meath and Wicklow, in particular, experienced mass evictions, which intruded also into the smiling strong farmer lands of south Wexford. Of all the counties that endured clearances, however, Mayo and Clare, which stand at the head of the eviction statistics, merit particular attention. The circumstances underlying clearances in these two counties were very different, yet two common factors stand out. One was that very small holdings proliferated in both: on the eve of the Famine an astonishing 75 per cent of holdings in Mayo were valued at £4 or less; in Clare only about 25 per cent were above fifteen acres.[10] The second was that the chief promoters of clearance were landed magnates, whose enthusiasm for eviction greatly influenced the behaviour of other landlords who looked to them for leadership and example.

Eviction scene, December 1848. As agent and soldiers stand by, wreckers destroy the roof, regardless of pleas of family. *Illustrated London News.*

One of the greatest Mayo evictors was Sir Roger Palmer, absentee owner of a colossal, very badly managed estate of 80,000 acres, situated mostly in the Ballina Union. Despite the fact that he was not at all under financial pressure – he was to purchase at least one property from the Landed Estates Court – Palmer fitfully consolidated parts of his estate in clearances staggered out over a number of years. For the entire night after one clearance, at Islandeady, in July 1848, the evicted families lay exposed in the open fields under heavy and continuous rain, and the following day were seen rooting out the timber of their ruined houses, as they attempted to build shelters that might screen their children from the weather. Another Palmer eviction, in the same district, in September 1849, saw the wrecking gang 'hunting the occupants to seek shelter or death beneath the hedges, clefts of rock and in peat banks'. No mercy was shown these evictees, and one unfortunate man, already 'in the convulsive pangs of death', was physically ejected from his cabin, 'and in an hour or two after . . . death put an end to his miserable existence'.[11] Exactly how many persons were evicted by Palmer is unclear, since most of his evictions were carried out before 1849. Even in that year, however, clearances on the Palmer property were described as being 'without parallel as regards the numbers evicted'.

Best known of all the Mayo exterminators was George Bingham, third earl of Lucan, of later Crimea fame, whose 60,000-acre estate centred substantially around the towns of Castlebar and Ballinrobe. Lord Lieutenant of the county, Lucan, like Palmer, was a major defaulter on his rates, with arrears that amounted to almost £700 by the spring of 1848.[12] A determined consolidator since entering into his inheritance just before the Famine, he famously declared that 'he would not breed paupers to pay priests', and from the end of 1847 embarked on mass eviction on an epic scale. In the parish of Ballinrobe alone his clearances involved the ejection of 2,000 persons.

Aptly labelled a 'gerrardiser' by the *Mayo Telegraph*, Lucan's evictions were pitiless and brutal, and one in particular, carried out in June 1848 at Treenagleragh in Killedan parish, attracted wide publicity and condemnation. For years Lucan had been harassing the occupiers of this townland on minor issues, and now, regardless of the fact that their substantial holdings were well cared for, the lands cropped and the rents for the most part paid, he had 33 families, comprising 145 individuals, ejected and their houses razed, all under the supervision of the county sheriff and a force of police. A week after the clearance, the townland bore 'the appearance of a battlefield', according to one account, with 'nothing to be seen but the shattered ruins of what were so lately the abodes of men'. The evicted, many of them children and elderly grandparents, were now 'stretched along ditches and hedges . . . falling victims to cold and hunger and destitution'.

An investigation ordered by the Lord Lieutenant resulted only in the conclusion that however harsh such evictions were in the long term they would diminish the level of destitution by attracting investment to the district.[13]

Constabulary returns record some 26,000 persons as having been evicted from their holdings in Mayo between 1849 and 1854, which even though certainly an undercount, is more likely to bear a closer relation to the actual numbers than elsewhere, since Mayo clearances began and ended much later than in other counties. Another unusual feature of Mayo evictions is that a great many evicted smallholders were able to retain access to land by renting and reclaiming large areas of scrub and mountain. For this and other reasons, the survival rate for Mayo evictees was probably greater than for other clearance-afflicted counties, and, in addition, it is believed that the level of emigration among evicted families in Mayo was relatively high also.

Things were rather different in County Clare. Here landed properties tended to be smaller, the largest being the 37,000-acre estate of the absentee Colonel Wyndham, the average size varying between 2,000 and 3,000 acres. Their relative poverty may have inspired Clare landlords to go to greater lengths to preserve their revenues than their counterparts elsewhere, and, certainly, it is true that clearances began very early in the county. As in Mayo, the lead given in evictions by prominent figures had a significant influence on their peers. In Clare two individuals exercised this role: Crofton Moore Vandeleur of Kilrush and Marcus Keane of Beech Park, near Ennis.

At just under 17,000 acres, Vandeleur's Kilrush property was modest by comparison with landed magnates elsewhere, but he did have extensive commercial investments in Ireland, and by any standards was extremely wealthy. Much of his considerable energy was devoted to the improvement of the town of Kilrush, which he owned and for which he had great civic ambitions. Despite the drop in rental income incurred by several years of famine, Vandeleur was very secure financially, so much so that he was able to purchase the Duke of Buckingham's Clare property, some 7,000 acres, when it was sold by the courts in 1848.[14] Altogether Vandeleur evicted over one thousand of his tenants, both the smallholders of the hinterland and the poor of Kilrush town, whose broken-down cabins reflected poorly on the fine new houses and business premises with which he was progressively lining its broad streets. Tenants whom Vandeleur spared were warned not to shelter their neighbours and relatives who had been expelled, on pain of sharing their fate, a threat which was carried out rigorously.

Marcus Keane was a substantial landlord in his own right, but it was as land agent that this influence was most felt during the clearances. At the time they began, despite his relative youth (he was still in his early thirties) he already had three large properties on his books as well as a number of smaller ones, and enjoyed a reputation as a 'stringent and successful collector of rents'.[15] It was this reputation, and his efficient and financially competitive services as evictor, that attracted lesser, cash-strapped landlords to his agency in droves. By the end of the Famine he was managing upwards of 100,000 acres of land in Clare, to which county his activities were confined. Combining an unrivalled local knowledge with expertise in ejectment law, Keane was well versed also in the practical difficulties attached to the eviction process. His clients valued him most, however, for the manner in which he assumed entire responsibility for evictions, separating them from the distasteful, guilt-bearing aspects of the process.

Early in his evicting career, Keane learned that it was more cost-effective to take out ejectment decrees in the superior courts in Dublin against whole townlands, rather than become involved in expensive piecemeal actions against tenants on an individual basis in the local courts. He also found that it paid to maintain at his disposal a small army of staff, comprising under-agents, bailiffs, drivers and surveyors, who saw to the details of each clearance and the subsequent consolidation. Rarely appearing in person at evictions, he deployed a gang of 'destructives' or 'wreckers' on each site for the purpose of physically overawing any tenant who might be disposed to offer resistance, to remove those unwilling or unable to vacate their dwellings and afterwards to 'slaughter' these cabins, to use the phrase favoured by one of his under-agents. Before a parliamentary committee in 1850, Keane eventually admitted that altogether his men had destroyed some 500 cabins in the Kilrush union, ejecting in all about 2,800 persons.

Many of Keane's cost-cutting methods were those we have seen elsewhere, or refinements of them. Tenants were persuaded to vacate cabins on the promise of a paltry 'compensation', which as often as not went unpaid; most were actually induced to 'tumble' their own dwellings in exchange for a similar promise. The practice of destroying cabins while their occupants were temporarily absent was as widespread in Keane's domains as it was in other parts of the country; in west Clare, this was done most often by setting them alight. In mid-1850, Rev. Sidney Godolphin Osborne witnessed at first-hand the effects of Keane's activities in this regard when, on a journey from Kilrush to Ennis, he noted the 'roofless gables' that met his eye on both sides of the road, commenting that 'as far every way as I could command with a telescope, there was evidence of this forcible removal of the population'.[16]

Left with the alternative of walking to the Kilrush workhouse, with its horrors of overcrowding and disease, most evicted persons chose to remain on in the vicinity of their former dwellings. Some built crude shelters of branches and turf-sods called 'scalpeens' on nearby commonage, bog or waste ground. Where such waterlogged places did not become their graves, as often happened, the evicted did not long survive removal from them by other parties when in states of incredible filth, emaciation and glaze-eyed fever they were finally admitted to the workhouse. 'There were three cartloads of these creatures, who could not walk, brought for admission yesterday,' Captain Kennedy, the temporary inspector at Kilrush, wrote to the Poor Law Commissioners in March 1848, 'some in fever, some suffering from dysentery, and all from want of food.' On another occasion, he described a group of evictees as 'a tangled mess of poverty, filth and disease . . . Numbers in all stages of fever and small-pox . . . and all clamouring for entry . . . it was really an appalling sight'.

In the Kilrush union alone, exterminating landlords led by Crofton Vandeleur and Marcus Keane evicted approximately 20,000 persons between 1847 and 1854,

Five people inhabited this scalpeen at Kellines, Conamara, in January 1850. *Illustrated London News.*

just short of one-quarter of its pre-Famine population. These were extremely poor persons, and in contrast to the situation in Mayo, only a tiny minority of the evicted families had the resources to emigrate. Since access to relief was severely restricted for much of the period by the Kilrush Guardians – essentially the same landlord clique that was carrying out the evictions – the vast majority of them are believed to have perished.[17] All this took place within a short distance of the Victorian gentility of Kilkee, a favourite landlord watering place, and of Colonel Vandeleur's bustling showcase Kilrush.

Neither the denunciation of philanthropists, political figures or journalists who travelled to Clare to see for themselves what was happening, nor the deliberations of a House of Commons Select Committee established to investigate the clearances made any difference; no legal restraint was placed on evicting landlords. The one significant result of the publicity generated was that Captain Kennedy, who first drew attention to what was happening in the union and confronted the landlords responsible, was quietly discharged from service with the Poor Law some months after the Select Committee investigation closed. In one sense, Kennedy's publicizing efforts had been unfortunate, in that the attention focussed on Kilrush served to distract attention from equally heavy clearances taking place in the other Clare unions, where Marcus Keane's henchmen, led by his brother, Henry, were seemingly omnipresent. In a county where as many as 60,000 persons may have been evicted in all, at the end of the Famine, Clare's Poor Law unions acquired the aura of horror associated with Skibbereen and Schull a few years previously. Small wonder, then, that in November 1849 one despairing journalist should have asked rhetorically if it was the intention of the Whig government 'to make Clare one vast abattoir'.

A characteristic feature of the Famine clearances was that, once begun, the evictors became infected with a sort of panic-haste, an insensate rush to clear properties as fast as possible. There were two main reasons for this, the initial necessity of clearing properties before new and higher levels of Poor Law rate began to bite, and, second, the fear that the eviction option might soon be lost altogether if government introduced some sort of tenant right legislation, as was its rumoured intent. An idea of the breakneck speed with which evictions were carried out is obtained from recollections recorded in July 1880 from a Mayo 'veteran recruit' of a Famine-era wrecking crew.[18] Employed by a Mayo landlord identified only as Lord L (clearly Lord Lucan), the anonymous 'recruit' recalled that each winter and spring in the five years of his employment as wrecker he had worked six-day weeks, beginning at daylight and ending at dusk. During this time he levelled as many as twenty houses per day. His memory of one operation site, an entire townland which he cleared, along with forty other destructives, was particularly vivid. After a breakfast 'feed' of hard-baked bread, he and his gang 'levelled all day until night set in':

> We lodged in the houses, slept on the floors in hay we got in the poor people's haggards, or in the poor people's beds; when we got up in the morning at the dawn we cooked our breakfasts and eat them; threw the houses and went on to the next village. We kept on that work for the greater part of four days, and then started for home without leaving a house standing saving a couple that would suit for herds' houses.

The resemblance to the activities of evicting parties elsewhere in Ireland is very close. Landlords in Cork widely used wrecking gangs like that in which the 'recruit' served, and on the earl of Midleton's estate they were contracted at three shillings per house destroyed. Toomevara was levelled by 'ten or twelve burly ruffians from Nenagh', and in 1850, thirty others returned to the village to destroy the temporary huts erected by the evicted tenants, the wreckers being first plied with quantities of whiskey by the agent, carrying out their duties 'almost in a drunken state'. In Clare, Marcus Keane tells us that he employed about forty wreckers, whom other accounts characterize as youths or young men, furtive, uneasy starvelings taken off the streets of Ennis. Like the Toomevara wreckers, they were supplied with spirits before operations began, and their working day began and was punctuated with heavy drinking, apparently communal, 'from a jar without a handle'.[19]

Because of the frenzied manner of so many clearances, estates were emptied of occupiers to an extent that went far beyond what was originally intended, or indeed what was in the economic interest of their individual proprietors. On some properties the number of tenants left behind after a clearance was insufficient for the redistribution of the land, and there were instances where landlords found it impossible to find tenants for the remainder. Many cleared properties reverted to wilderness, remaining economically unproductive for periods of up to half a decade.

Historians have puzzled over the relative absence of tenant resistance to Famine evictions, especially in districts where secret society activity had been intense before 1845 and had re-emerged strongly the following year.[20] There is, to be sure, a good deal of evidence of retaliation or attempted retaliation against evictors early on in the clearances, when evictors were still faced with an intensified barrage of the old pre-Famine Whiteboy outrages: threatening letters, damage to property and assaults. During this time, numbers of process servers, drivers, bailiffs and the odd landlord were also shot at or murdered.

The best-known incident relates to the assassination of Major Denis Mahon, the owner of the debt-ridden Strokestown estate in Roscommon. In one of the greatest single clearances ever executed, Mahon had earlier ejected 3,000 of his tenants, and 'emigrated' a further thousand, under appalling conditions, to America.[21] His murder in November 1847 caused a sensation throughout Ireland, sent a chill through landlord society and a wave of delight through the ranks of the surviving tenants, expressed in bonfires lit on all the surrounding hills the night of the murder. Tenant glee was shortlived, however, since Mahon's successor at Strokestown, Henry Pakenham Mahon, ordered the immediate eviction of all tenants in the area where he had been shot, before going on to continue his predecessor's clearance policy with equal ruthlessness.[22]

But on the clearance sites themselves there are only a handful of instances where tenants offered physical resistance to wreckers, which is all the more strange given the evidence of strong community resistance to parties distraining for unpaid rates or rent at the same time.[23] The Mayo 'veteran recruit' of 1880 sheds little light on the subject. When asked if the people ever offered resistance, he answered that sometimes they 'would if it were not for the police', adding – not

Often interpreted as a rare instance of resistance to eviction, this scene from January 1847 in fact depicts a family fending off a night-time raiding party. Few tenants were in a position to resist. *Pictorial Times.*

very helpfully – that 'if curses were of avail we got lots of them'. One possible explanation might be that rent and rates militancy was largely confined to social strata that had been secure up to now, leaving neighbourly morale still strong enough to confront the perpetrators of individual evictions. Those who 'stood in the doors with grass pitchforks, sticks and stones' to prevent the wreckers entering Connor Connell's house on the outskirts of Sligo town in August 1848 had clearly been comfortably off, as also the Kinnavane brothers who held off Marcus Keane's 'levellers' at Meelick, near Limerick City, in February 1849. The same it would appear is true of the family of Judy O'Donnell, whose young son kept a wrecking gang at a distance for a time by throwing rocks at them from the roof of the family home, near Doonbeg, west Clare, the following December.[24]

Smallholder communities marked out for clearance, on the other hand, were demoralized by that very fact, and any remaining spark of anger extinguished by the arrival of the wreckers, accompanied by the intimidating state apparatus of sheriff and armed police, against whom even a strong neighbourly solidarity could not prevail. Shattered and leaderless, very few of those still surviving retained the moral force, not to mention the physical ability, to resist the crowbar brigades. In west Clare, relatively early in the clearances, in April 1848, Captain Kennedy explained to the Irish Poor Law Commissioners that occupiers there accepted evictions that were in fact illegal, because 'the great mass are tenants-at-will and dare not resist'. It is this sense of helplessness which best explains the docility of the evicted, their willingness to wreck their own cabins, to take off the thatch and pull down the walls, and accept the pitiful sums offered in compensation which in the circumstances suddenly assumed great importance for their short-term survival.

Helplessness may also explain the apparent gratitude which, some observers remark, was shown by evicted persons when they were allowed to carry away timber or other materials from their wrecked cabins, and the readiness with which they postponed removal and were allowed to remain on in their cabins as 'caretakers', temporary custodians who could be ejected at leisure later on, without further proceedings. It also accounts for the timorous manner in which the evicted constructed shelters inside the ruins when the wreckers had departed, built low in the hope of escaping notice. In most cases, however, wreckers returned and destroyed these also. In Clare, wreckers were particularly thorough in this last exercise, and relentlessly turned over evicted sites to destroy scalpeens and the even flimsier 'scalps'. In December 1850, Rev. Osborne described one truly horrendous instance in *The Times*, where wreckers torched a west Clare scalp in the belief that all the family had left, the result being the incineration of a sleeping infant, whose remains were carried out on a shovel in the presence of her mother.

As we have seen in regard to the pictorial evidence, over the years of the clearances, a progressive impoverishment worked its way upwards through society. Once the cottiers and smallholders below £4 valuation had disappeared, either into the workhouses or the graveyards, those just above this threshold, burdened as they were by rates as well as by rent bills, became vulnerable. Their ruin came about in many areas with the failure of the 1848 potato crop, after which they were sucked downwards into the vortex of distraint, eviction and the machinery of the Poor Law. In May 1849, the temporary inspector at Glenties union in Donegal, Captain O'Neill, commented that many of the small occupiers then being distrained by collectors for non-payment of rates were in fact 'infinitely greater objects of charity than the paupers in the workhouse'. 'As soon as one horde of houseless and all but naked paupers are dead, or provided for in the workhouse,' declared Captain Kennedy the same month in west Clare, 'another wholesale eviction doubles the numbers, who in their turn pass through the same ordeal of wandering from house to house, or burrowing in bogs or behind ditches, till broken down by privation, and exposure to the elements they seek the workhouse or die by the roadside'.[25] In April the following year, a north Kerry priest commented that 'the ratepayer of yesterday is the pauper of today'.

Oddly, perhaps, among the strongest defenders of evicting landlords were their colleagues who did not engage in clearances. Sir Charles Denham Jephson-Norreys, the north Cork landowning magnate, and the marquis of Clanricarde in Galway, neither of them significant evictors, held that the £4 clause in the Poor Law made it almost impossible not to evict. Evictors, on the other hand, tended to place blame elsewhere. In Parliament, the Galway evictor Christopher St. George blamed the middlemen lessees whose reckless greed for profit rent he alleged had brought their farms to the deplorable state which necessitated clearance. He indignantly refuted accusations that he was a bad landlord. After clearing three townlands in County Waterford, Lord Stradbroke laid the onus on the expelled tenants, who had put him 'to the expense of serving ejectments, when I knew they had the means but not the inclination to pay their rents'. They therefore had 'no persons to blame but themselves'.[26]

Some evicting landlords emphasized the anguish caused them by the necessity of eviction. Lord Sligo – whose guilt at having evicted his Mayo tenants was transposed into bitter criticism of his neighbour, Sir Samuel O'Malley, who had refrained from so doing but was now ruined – insisted that he had 'struggled hard not to eject'. Having done so, Sligo held that he had managed to limit the clearance to one-quarter of his tenants, unlike the supposedly humane Sir Samuel, whose

Evicted village in Galway, January 1850. *Illustrated London News*.

stubbornness had eventually seen three-quarters of his tenants face expulsion by the court-appointed managers of his bankrupt estate. Even if Sligo's expressed regret at having to evict his tenants can be taken as genuine, behind it lies the undeniable fact of a thorough subsequent consolidation of his estate, which proved much to his material advantage.

Other landlords preferred to recite their previous record of relief or charitable involvement. In Wexford, where clearances were not as widespread as elsewhere, we find landlords doing this even before they had started evicting, and at the end of 1847, certain proprietors in the county 'who took and received credit for their indulgence to their tenants during the past year', were now 'availing themselves of the helpless condition of those tenants by taking proceedings for eviction'. The veracity of evictors who claimed a previous record of activity in relief operations need not be doubted. We know that Lord Lucan, for example, had come to the rescue of the Castlebar union workhouse in the winter of 1846–1847 by paying for grain supplies out of his own pocket.[27] The charitable credentials of Rev. Frederick Trench, the rector of Cloughjordan, who ministered among the sick and dying of Skibbereen in the winter of 1846–1847, seem impossible to challenge, yet in May 1849 Trench ejected some 200 persons from an estate known as the Forty Acres, halfway between Borrisokane and Cloughjordan, levelled the houses and built a wall around the entire property. Even Marcus Keane, the Clare exterminator, had defenders who could point to his one-time beneficence.[28]

Another way in which evictors, or apologists for clearance evictions, sought to minimize what had been done was to impugn the moral character of the evicted, and suggest that evicted lands were now in more capable and more honest hands. In May 1849, the *Nenagh Guardian*, a landlord organ, justified the destruction of Toomevara on the grounds that the village had become a 'den of midnight thieves and highway robbers' and therefore though apparently cruel, the evictions were 'justifiable and necessary'. Tracts of land formerly dotted with wretched hovels, and occupied by mendicant paupers parasitically dependent on outdoor relief, the *Guardian* held, were now 'cultivated and properly tilled instead of being waste and useless'. The ejected occupiers were now enjoying a 'comfortable and regular diet' in the workhouse.

This self-deluding rhetoric is closely echoed by Marcus Keane's attempts at justifying himself before a parliamentary Select Committee in 1850. Many of those he had evicted, Keane implied, were lazy tenants 'who had lived in listless idleness from year to year', others were 'bad characters' or 'robbers who preyed on their neighbours. Keane felt that the 'painful duty' of evicting was 'an absolute necessity' for the country and for the private interests he represented. The land, he told the select committee, was now 'in the hands of men who were capable of cultivating it and turning it to some advantage'.

The more inhumane their actions became, the more divorced evictors' rationalizations became from the reality of what they had wrought. Many persuaded themselves that the miserable sums given evicted tenants in order to have them destroy their own homes represented, in fact, a generous measure of compensation, that the 'voluntary' surrender of cabins were decisions cheerfully entered into by tenants; even that the evicted were better off than they had been before expulsion. It is difficult not to see the tissue of half-truths, evasions and outright lies that constitute the currency of evictors everywhere as one continuous internal dialogue among themselves, whose aim was to convince themselves that the dreadful crimes they had committed were in some way justifiable. Implicit in much of evictor discourse was the notion that those who had suffered most by the clearances were the perpetrators themselves through having to implement the hard decisions required by their duties.

By the end of the clearances landlords could boast of striking success in consolidating their properties; and as a result of evictions and the other stratagems employed by them, tiny economic holdings had been amalgamated on an immense scale. Between 1845 and 1851, the number of holdings under one acre had been reduced by nearly three-quarters; those between one and five acres by almost a half, and those between five and fifteen acres by some two-fifths. However, Irish landholding had been so microscopically subdivided prior to 1845 that estate improvers elsewhere might not have been so impressed. Irish smallholdings still remained extraordinarily fragmented, and in 1851, there were still 317,665 holdings that were less than fifteen acres, and the proportion of those over fifteen acres had increased by only five per cent.[29]

A more significant adjustment to Irish landholding would take several generations of land agitation, gradual socio-economic evolution and decades of legislation that would become increasingly radical and far-reaching as the century wore on. In the meantime Irish landlords were themselves faced with estate consolidation of a kind. This came with the Incumbered Estates Act of 1849, which was designed to clear away the dead wood of landed property by the enforced sale of bankrupt estates, and the encouragement of capital-rich new owners. In the first decade of its operation, a huge number of hopelessly indebted estates were sold under the Act.

In no sense, however, could the Incumbered Estates Act be interpreted as a form of retribution on an oppressive social class. For one thing, a substantial proportion of the estates which were sold off belonged to that small minority of landlords who had ruined themselves by refusing to evict, bankrupting themselves to keep their tenants alive.[30] These included the Martin estate in Conamara, at 200,000 acres the greatest in Ireland, and the property of the Viscounts Gort, at Lough Cutra, in south Galway. More importantly, so many of those who purchased properties under the Act were Irish landlords who had consolidated their estates through heavy clearances, and were therefore in a position to afford the outlay. Of 7,489 estates sold under the Act between 1849 and 1859, more than 7,000 were bought by Irish landed and commercial interests.[31] Many of these 'new' proprietors then proceeded to evict the sitting tenants.

Nemesis would not overtake the Irish landlord class, in fact, until the end of the century when a series of Land Acts initiated a gradual transfer of ownership to the tenants, a revolution in landholding that took many decades to complete. Even before that time, however, landlord economic, political and social hegemony at local and national level was already on a steeply declining curve. In 1849, however, such a transformation was hardly conceivable, except perhaps in the visionary imagination of the one original thinker thrown up by the Great Famine, James Fintan Lalor, who died at the age of 42 in the year the Act was passed.

For evicting landlords, as well as their apologists, as for the many great men of state whose legislative initiatives had helped precipitate the process clearance of itself did not prove sufficient to address long-term issues of estate improvement and modernization. For such individuals, some form of organized emigration of surplus tenantry was required as a complement to clearance. Spontaneous emigration by tenants, according to this belief, tended to involve the industrious classes rather than those who were unproductive; some kind of sponsored schemes would therefore be needed to spur the departure of the latter.

Certain senior political figures in Britain were among the greatest champions of sponsored emigration and among its most articulate proponents. At the height of the clearance campaign, in November 1848, Charles Wood, the Chancellor of the Exchequer, expressed the belief that farms 'could not be enlarged until the number of holders was diminished'; for this reason he was 'not at all appalled' when told by his parliamentary colleague, Lord Monteagle, that his (Monteagle's) tenants were emigrating. Charles Trevelyan declared in September the same year that he did not know how farms were to be consolidated if small farmers did not emigrate. 'If small farmers go', he wrote, 'and then landlords are induced to sell portions of their estate to persons who will invest capital, we shall at last arrive at something like a satisfactory settlement of the country.'[32] Lord Palmerston, the Foreign Secretary, who believed that without 'a long, continued, and systematic ejectment of small holders and of squatting cottiers' Ireland's agriculture could not be transformed and played his part in the process by clearing his Sligo property, was also a strong believer in sponsored mass emigration schemes.

Few resident landlords, great or small, thought any differently. It was the opinion of Lord Rosse, whose rental from his Birr estate alone amounted to £5,000 per annum, that the emigration of a million and a half people would be necessary to the improvement of the country.[33] As regards the petty gentry, in November 1848 we find Elizabeth Smith confiding to her diary her sense of the extent to which unroofed houses had added to the desolation of the wet and dirty lanes she had just travelled on a drive about the countryside, adding that 'quantities' of the evicted were heading to America, even at that dangerous season of the year. Many of them had 'plenty of money' in their pockets. 'And we miss them not,' she concludes, 'This winter will surely make some room.'[34]

Scalpeen in West Clare, December 1848. *Illustrated London News.*

Leaving this Land of Plagues: The Famine Emigrations

Let the Irish hail with joy the day they land on a foreign shore; leave this
land of plagues, and go where fortune, honour and independence await them
– where their remains will be interred in consecrated ground, surrounded by
their families, relatives and friends, weeping and thanking the Lord that their
corpses are not exposed to the ravages of dogs and swine.

– LIMERICK AND CLARE EXAMINER,
10 JANUARY 1849

The Famine emigrations represent one of the greatest population displacements of modern times, an exodus on a stunning scale that has no other nineteenth-century parallel. Between 1845 and 1855, approximately one-quarter of the inhabitants of an entire European country, amounting to some 2.1 million persons, were permanently removed from their homeland. Over one million left during the Famine years proper, from 1846 to 1852, an outflow which the term 'emigration', with its connotation of deliberate, calm progress from one country to another, describes very poorly, especially during the panic-stricken flight of 1846–1847, when the collective impulse to leave was so strong as to make destinations almost irrelevant.

Mass emigration, of course, was not a new feature of Irish experience, and in one sense the Famine scattering can be seen as a massive spike in a demographic curve originating in historical disasters dating as far back as the end of the sixteenth century. In the seventeenth century the Ulster Plantation and the Cromwellian holocaust had both been attended by heavy population outspill to the European Continent, and the Williamite Wars at the century's end opened up a new stream of mainly military emigration in the same direction. This was to last for much of the next century, proceeding parallel with another stream across the Atlantic, one that largely derived from the Presbyterian north and eventually overtook it in volume.

By about 1800 the emigrant movement to the continent had come to a virtual halt, and, henceforward, the tide would flow for the most part across the Atlantic, to the United States, and Canada. Between 1815 and 1845 alone the transatlantic movement accounted for upwards of 800,000 Irish persons, one-third of the entire emigration from Europe at this time. Diverse in social class and religious affiliation, and two-thirds male in composition, the participants in this great population movement ranged from the political refugees of 1798 and its 1803 sequel, and labouring men who came to build the Erie canal in 1808–1811, to prosperous farmers and tradesmen in search of economic opportunity.[1] In these years also a small emigrant side-stream diverted southwards towards the penal colony of Australia; lesser British colonies would receive some Irish emigrants over the same period, which would also see the beginnings of a small, but intriguing movement towards South America, and, in particular, Argentina.

It was during these decades that state-sponsored emigration of Ireland's 'surplus' population became part of the remedial prescription of social reformers for the country, part of every political economist's confident solution to the evils of its economic backwardness and its supposed disorder. Improving landlords, for their part, saw mass emigration of their tenants as essential to the consolidation

Pre-Famine view of Queenstown (Cobh), County Cork, the point of departure of a great many emigrants. Stirling Coyne, *Scenery and Antiquities.*

and modernization of their estates; many of the consolidators were as enthusiastic about the benefits of mass emigration as they were about those of mass clearance. Inevitably, the promotion of emigration became an article of faith in official thinking also, and the two most important pre-Famine social investigations, the Poor Inquiry of 1835–1836, and the Devon Commission of the mid-1840s, both envisaged state assistance for emigration on a large scale. For financial and political reasons, as well as those of parliamentary apathy, however, no attempt was made by any British government to transform theory into action before 1845. Notwithstanding this, a belief in the efficacy of sponsored emigration was general in political circles, and those few voices expressing contrary opinions and viewing as outrageous any solution to Ireland's problems that involved the wholesale removal of its people, received little hearing.[2]

During the Famine the relationship between 'excess' mortality and emigration was generally an inverse one, and the more afflicted a district was the less likely that some of its population would be rescued by the transatlantic passage. Counties such as Clare and Galway, therefore, along with west Cork, feature as high in the excess mortality statistics as they score low in terms of population outflow. Only 2.3 per cent of those caught up in the charnel house of west Cork in 1847 are believed to have emigrated, while in the Kilrush union of Clare, which suffered huge levels of population loss between 1847 and 1850, flight abroad, contemporaries believed, saved less than one per cent.[3] In midland counties, such as Longford, Leitrim, Roscommon, Laois and Offaly, on the other hand, even evicted smallholders were able to emigrate in substantial numbers. In these areas landlords had employed ejectments selectively as vehicles of estate management, and in contrast to the ruthless exterminations of Clare and Galway, their victims were often left with some small substance.[4] Even for such relatively fortunate tenants, however, the possibility of falling casualty somewhere along the way was high.

Because emigration from Ireland was already of abnormal proportions in the years immediately preceding the Famine, it is difficult to determine exactly at what point the numbers leaving began to reflect the onset of distress and starvation. Although the volume of emigration was greater than ever in the 1845 season, the increase is consistent with the rising trend of the years immediately preceding. Anecdotal evidence does, however, confirm a marked increase from early in 1846, which is well captured in the comments made by one County Offaly bank manager at its very end. Those emigrating at the beginning of the year, the manager identifies as 'farming servants, male and female, steady prudent people who out of their earnings had set aside a fund for the purpose,' their numbers being 'wholly without precedent'. Small farmers, he tells us, had also been making enquiries, their main concern being to emigrate while they still had the means, their great fear being that if they waited until the spring they no long would. Emigration, the manager notes, had not flagged in May as was usually the case, but had continued right through; he himself had never seen so many leaving so late in the season.[5]

The general pattern of emigration from Ireland during 1846 mirrors this local-ized experience, the absence of planning evident in late departures contrasting with the pre-Famine trend whereby emigrants had tended to leave during late spring and early summer, allowing themselves time to settle in their new homes before winter. Towards the end of 1846, we know, the rate of emigration increased rapidly, and accelerated massively throughout the following year, broadly paral-leling the first great cycle of starvation and disease mortality then scything its way across Ireland. From late 1846 also, the earliest reports emerge of a large-scale departure of smallholders who, as we saw above in the case of Offaly, had been merely considering that option up to now.

This development is reflected in comments by landlords that their more industrious tenants were abandoning their holdings without paying their rents, leaving estates bereft of all but the lazy occupiers.[6] Typical of the latter complaint was that made by one west Cork proprietor in the spring of 1847 that some of his best tenants were 'going off with three years rent', and by a Poor Law official in the same area about the same time that others were using their rents for pas-sage money, while leaving the 'dregs' behind. A year and half later, at the end of October 1848, Lord Monteagle was complaining in similar terms to Lord John Russell that 'fraudulent' [defaulting] as well as 'honest' tenants were absconding from his estate. 'We shall be left a pauper warren,' he wrote, '. . . the queen being the matron of the largest union workhouse ever yet founded.'

Allowing for the universal tendency of landlords to exaggerate their woes, the sources do abound with instances where tenants liquidated their remaining assets quietly while giving the impression of normal residence, and then disappearing overnight without paying outstanding rent and rates bills. Defaulting on these payments in the circumstances was likely to have been an important element in a carefully worked out strategy for survival. In this context, also, the extreme tenacity displayed by so many occupiers in resisting parties distraining for unpaid rents and rates can be explained, at least in part, by a determination to retain resources essential to departure. One can speculate, indeed, on the number of tenants who could not emigrate because their livestock was marked out or their crops seized at an inopportune moment by the 'keepers' placed on them, and who subsequently perished as a result.

A further acceleration in the departure of occupiers from all gradations of society resulted when hopes raised by the non-appearance of potato blight in 1847 were dashed in the renewed massive harvest failure of the following year.[7] Public and private commentary from this time, however, emphasizes the emigration of occupiers of relatively high social standing. 'Some of our best, most comfortable farmers have sold out and taken with them anything from £50 to £300,' lamented the parish priest of Cahir, County Tipperary in mid-May 1847, while in a letter to his children in Boston, written at the end of October 1848 James Prendergast of Miltown, County Kerry, speaks of respectable farmers everywhere deserting their farms and 'flying to America as fast as they can'. In March 1850, a letter writer to the *Dublin Evening Mail* complained that the 'respectable class of farmers' was emigrating to America, leaving only the poor behind them.[8]

That contemporaries should have fixated on the departure of the respectable and the industrious is understandable given current assumptions of their worth to society in terms of capital, skill and enterprise and the moral value ascribed these qualities. In reality, however, despite the increased showing over time of well-off farmers fleeing Poor Law rates, the Famine emigrations were predominantly a phenomenon of the lower ranks of the tenantry. As Kerby Miller has established, in addition to being poorer than those of pre-Famine times, Famine emigrants possessed fewer technical skills, and far more of them were illiterate and Irish-speaking. Yet because those leaving under such conditions made the actual decision themselves, historians categorize them as voluntary. Given their attachment to home and community and the hardships they endured in order to remain where they were, as well as their fears of a profoundly alien outside world, this surely stretches the meaning of the word to its semantic limit. Indeed, leaving aside the issue of transported convicts, it is arguable that only those who emigrated under 'assisted' schemes run by the Poor Law after 1847, or those operated by landlords, had less of a say in the matter of their departure than the smallholding Famine emigrants. The absence of any real choice for those leaving Ireland under Poor Law or landlord schemes is underlined by the common use of the verb 'emigrate' in a transitive sense with regard to them.

In regard to the Poor Law schemes, a provision for assisted emigration was part of the original 1838 legislation, although it was only with the amendment of 1847 that these proved workable, allowing unions to share the cost of emigrating workhouse inmates with landlords or inmate relatives living abroad.[9] In subsequent years other Poor Law schemes were inaugurated, whereby different categories of inmates or destitute residents of unions were given financial assistance to emigrate to the United States or Canada; in others again female workhouse orphans were sent out under supervision to Australia, to train as servants in the colony and provide wives for the settlers. All of these schemes were aimed at emptying workhouses of the human freight accumulated during the Famine, and Chris O'Mahony's description of them as 'workhouse clearances' is apt.[10]

Landlord-sponsored emigration was a phenomenon of much greater dimensions and with a longer history, dating to the immediate pre-Famine years when consolidating landlords began to ship their tenants overseas in large numbers. One of the most successful was Francis Spaight, a Limerick merchant and ship-owner who in 1844 purchased a 4,200-acre north Tipperary estate called Derrycastle, which he immediately proceeded to consolidate. He did this by obliging unwanted tenants to emigrate to America on board his own ships and at his cost. It was all done extremely cheaply since the ships were cargo vessels which were empty on each outward voyage in any case. By 1847 Spaight's businesslike approach had rid him of half the Derrycastle tenants, and by the time his consolidation was completed two years later he had removed some 2,000 persons, in an operation which was admired by other landlords for its efficiency and the fact that it was done without arousing any overt protest on the part of the tenants.[11] Even more ambitious than Spaight's programme was that implemented on the great Coolattin estate (80,000 acres) in County Wicklow by its owner, Lord Fitzwilliam, an absentee. As in the case of Spaight, Fitzwilliam had begun to consolidate his property before the Famine, and the process was completed in an enormous emigration scheme undertaken intermittently in the years between 1847 and 1851. Altogether Fitzwilliam emigrated 850 families to Canada, amounting to something more than 4,000 persons.[12]

There were many other landlords who emigrated their tenants in similar fashion, among them Colonel Wyndham, absentee owner of a great estate in Clare; Denis Mahon of Strokestown, Roscommon; Robert Gore Booth of Lisadell in County Sligo; Lord Monteagle in Limerick; and Whig grandees such as Lords Lansdowne and Palmerston.[13] The conditions under which the unwilling and apprehensive tenants of these men travelled varied according to the level of care which they or their appointed agents were prepared to bestow on a task whose execution was of little real interest to them. While no emigrated tenant parties escaped hardship entirely, the most conscientious of the above-mentioned landowners in seeking to minimize it was Colonel Wyndham. Of the remainder, Gore Booth, Fitzwilliam, Lansdowne and Palmerston would be subjected to particular criticism for the wretched condition of their tenants on arrival at ports of disembarkation. The fate of Mahon's Strokestown emigrants, as we shall see, was horrific.[14]

Whether operated by landlords or Poor Law unions, assisted emigration schemes reflected motives that were deeply self-interested, and landlord emigration usually amounted to little more than eviction by another name, and Poor Law schemes were purely cost-cutting exercises that were as dispassionately devised and administered as the workhouse test. Emigrated former tenants or paupers were seen as no more than problems solved, and their subsequent fate a matter of indifference. It is true that among our sources are many letters sent home by sponsored emigrants commenting happily on their circumstances, but for the most part these represent examples carefully selected and retained by landlords or workhouse authorities for future self-justification. Many letters of this kind, in fact, were dictated to the writers, and their glowing descriptions of their new lives often bore no relation to the reality, as we know it, from other sources. Throughout the entire Famine, indeed, the only evidence we have of a genuinely philanthropic impulse in sponsored emigration comes from the schemes inaugurated by Vere Foster in the early 1850s.

But, in any case, assisted emigration schemes represented only a small fraction of the total population movement out of Ireland during the Famine. The total numbers sent out with either state or landlord financial assistance to North America and Australia between 1846 and 1850 amounted to less than 40,000 persons, the overall figure to 1855 (including 5,500 transported convicts) less than 90,000.[15] But for a number of reasons it might have been much greater, among them the fact that proposals for combined landlord- and government-assisted schemes were undermined by landlord insolvency, and that others half-heartedly devised by government foundered on issues of cost and colonial opposition.[16] Ultimately, however, the failure of any serious attempt at state-sponsored emigration during the Famine related to the fact that the 'voluntary' mass exodus from Ireland made it entirely unnecessary. By 1852 all that had emerged were those few schemes we have described above. Moreover, apart from a few ineffectual changes to the Passenger Acts, no significant measures were brought forward to assist emigrants on their passage, to mitigate its hardship, to make it safer or more comfortable or to protect them from exploitation along the way.[17]

A crucial aspect of Famine-era emigration relates to the one enormously significant resource which emigrants were able to avail of; the remittances sent by family members who had already made the journey successfully. Remittances were, of course, not used exclusively to furnish passage money, but also provided regular, sustained and substantial assistance to unknown numbers of beneficiaries in Ireland who would not have survived otherwise. During the Famine these payments (as recorded in post office money orders), rose sharply, from £460,000 in 1848, £957,000 in 1850 and close to £1 million in 1851.[18] During the early 1850s they exceeded the latter figure annually by a considerable amount. Indeed, if it were possible to take account of other means by which remittances were sent, for example, directly through the post or through personal contacts, the totals would be greater still. On the scale on which it occurred, Famine emigration would not have been possible but for remittances.

Remittances were crucial in establishing and continuing a pattern of chain emigration that would become a defining element of the Irish emigration experience over a period of more than a century and a half. Of Lusmagh in County Offaly, in 1848, one smallholder with family in New York wrote that there was 'not a man in the parish that has not a son or a daughter but is sending money home'. Newly arrived in Peekskill, New York, in March the same year, Patrick Garry, now working on the railroad at eight shillings a day, promises to send his 'dear and loving wife and children' their passage money in August. Moneys sent in the meantime, he indicates, are to be used for building up their physical strength, since 'I consider yous would not stand the wracking of the sea till yous had been nourished for a time'.

In September 1850, Margaret McCarthy sent twenty dollars to her father in Kanturk, County Cork, which she hoped 'might be some acquisition to you until you might be clearing away from that place altogether'; later on in her letter she expresses happiness at being 'away from where the county charges man or the poor Rates man or any other rates man would have the satisfaction of once impounding my cow or any other article of mine'.[19] Within four years of being sent out under a Vere Foster-assisted scheme to the United States in 1852, ninety-two female Clare emigrants had sent home over £1,000, and by this means enabled ninety-seven further individuals to subsequently emigrate to that country. And even the Lansdowne emigrants dumped in the unpromising soil of the dangerous Five Points slum of New York City were able to send a total of £2,000 to relatives in Ireland within a decade of arrival in 1851.

The case of the five children of John and Amy Scollard of Ballyhahill, west Limerick, illustrates how remittances and chain migration helped transfer entire families across the globe. In June 1850 sisters Johanna and Mary Scollard left on the *Maria* for Australia, their brother and sister, Daniel and Ellen, following on the *Agincourt* two years later. Fourteen years afterwards, in 1866, the remaining brother, Garrett, his wife and seven children followed on the *White Star*, having surrendered the fifteen-acre homestead to the landlord, Lord Monteagle. The case of Mary Kenna, one of forty pauper girls shipped out from Nenagh workhouse in 1849, exemplifies how extraordinarily far-flung the reach of remittance-aided emigration often was, in her case linking Ireland, the United States and Australia. In a letter written home shortly after arrival in the southern continent, Mary wonders whether her two younger brothers, still in Ireland on her departure, had yet been sent for by uncles in America. 'If my uncles have not sent them any assistance or sent for them,' she wrote, 'I hope I shall soon send them something which may assist them.'[20]

Before examining the mechanics of emigrant departure in detail, the experience of would-be emigrants deserves attention, that is those individuals and families who managed to remove themselves long distances from their homes, yet for various reasons were unable, ultimately, to leave the country.[21] Although this migration partly reflects a movement towards centres where relief and food were most likely to be availed of, the fact that it took place predominantly on a west-to-east basis is a very strong indicator of an intent on the part of participants to leave Ireland altogether. To a degree that has yet to be investigated, it followed the pre-Famine pattern whereby labourers and their families took to the roads during the hungry months of each summer, and very probably also took place along some of the same routes as those traditionally taken by seasonal emigrants to Britain.

The evidence for internal migration during the Famine is all very similar: squalid huts being erected on fair greens, commonages and the outskirts of towns, and angry complaints by respectable townspeople inconvenienced by 'strollers' and 'vagrants' from more westerly counties. In May 1847, the insalubrious suburbs of Taghmon, a pocket of desperate poverty in otherwise prosperous Wexford, were 'thickly studded' with mud cabins, 'where are congregated poor people from all parts of Ireland'. In Kilkenny City two years later, seventy-three beggars arrested under the Vagrant Act gave as their place of origin counties as far away as Tipperary, Cork, Kerry, Galway and Mayo. Asked by magistrates if they would return home if set free, they replied they had no home, that 'there is nothing to be had in the country and we would die along the road'. As late as 1850 migrants were being blamed for the persistence of disease in Dublin City, whose Liberties were reportedly crowded with 'strangers from different parts of the country, especially Mayo, Galway and other western counties', all presenting 'the same listless, stupid care-worn aspect, and the same miserable squalid appearance'.[22]

If in the strict sense these displaced persons do not qualify as emigrants, their experience is important to an understanding of the mechanisms by which Famine emigration proceeded. In so many cases, after all, the difference in circumstances between those who stayed and those who left was often determined by accidents of time and place: the ability to scrape up the price of a ticket to America, or a decision to leave fortuitously pursued or fatally postponed.

Famine emigration was overwhelmingly a transatlantic phenomenon, the United States being the immediate destination of some eighty per cent of emigrants and the long-term destination of the majority of those who could only afford to go to Britain for the moment. If the Canadian emigration is included, then over ninety-five per cent of those leaving Ireland during the Famine travelled across the Atlantic.[23] The vast majority of transatlantic travellers, as we have seen, paid their own way, and except in a fraction of cases removed themselves to their countries of exile with no assistance except that afforded by near relatives. During the blind stampede to the country's ports that took place after late 1846 and throughout most of 1847, they could fairly be said to have clawed their way out. Once established in their host country, remittances sent home helped maintain and accelerate the emigrant outflow from Ireland up to the peak year of 1851, after which the gross numbers remaining to be brought out began to lessen along with the emigrant tide itself. 'This mighty emigration pays for itself', declared *The Times*, with satisfaction in April 1852, 'It seeks no aid from the public purse.'

The years after 1848 brought one strange development in Famine emigration, whereby entire communities seemed to become possessed of a sudden urge to leave, a kind of mania gripping localities for months at a time. This too may be remittance-related. In late November 1848, the *Limerick Chronicle* reported that the impetus for emigration from the adjoining districts was actually increasing as the season ended, and 'not alone were the passenger ships which sail from this port eagerly availed of, but the railway trains to Dublin are filled by emigrants, en route to Liverpool, where they embark'. In April 1850, Elizabeth Smith remarks in her diary that in her own part of Wicklow men were suddenly 'pouring on in shoals to America'. 'Crowds upon crowds swarm along the roads, the bye roads' she writes, 'following carts with their trunks and other property'.[24] The connection here may lie in the fact that emigrants from certain parts of certain counties tended to leave together, tended to settle together, and therefore were in a position to send money back at the same time to their relatives.

Departing emigrants did not have the leisure to marvel at such things or at the unprecedented social phenomenon they collectively represented; regardless of social class or financial means, their minds were too full of heartbreak, loneliness and anxiety for the future to ponder much else. In these years social ritual did not much soften the grief of parting, since fear of contagion had ended traditional familial and neighbourly gatherings of the kind that would re-emerge in post-Famine years as the American Wake. The palliative ceremonial of departure was now limited to family members accompanying the emigrants to the quayside, often over long distances. These quayside partings were very emotional occasions, involving as they did the splintering of families and the acute awareness of all present that there was little likelihood of being reunited ever again. In accordance with the demonstrativeness of their culture, there was a great deal of weeping, with women kneeling and praying, somewhat theatrically, and even the

Emigrants at quayside in Cork, 1851, surrounded by their baggage. Judging by their appearance, they were not of the poorest class. *Illustrated London News.*

adult males embracing and crying. 'The parting scene between these hardy men and their relatives was most affecting,' wrote a Limerick journalist in February 1849 of a departing group of young men on a steamer bound for Liverpool. 'Many wept aloud, men kissed each other as they parted, and when the steamer left the quay, a wailing cry arose from those remaining as if they wept for the dead.'

In 1852, the travel writer John Forbes encountered another emigrant party at the quayside in Killaloe. 'With that utter unconsciousness and disregard of being the observed of all observers which characterizes true sorrow,' he wrote, 'these warm-hearted and simple-minded people demeaned themselves entirely ... clinging to and kissing and embracing each other with the utmost ardour, calling out aloud, in broken tones, the endeared names of brother, sister, mother, sobbing and crying as if the very heart would burst, while the unheeded tears ran down from the red swollen eyes literally in streams.' A young English surveyor, Thomas Colville Scott, watching a similar scene in Galway the following year, was less sympathetic, and generalized that such leave-takings, with their 'boisterous grief and wailings' were 'ludicrous', instancing as proof the sight of two 'unshaven greybearded men' embracing each other 'until as much friction is produced by the contact of their chins, as would result from that of two friendly New Zealanders' noses'.[25]

Where distances were too long to permit quayside partings, relatives travelled some portion of the way with the emigrants, stopping usually at an accustomed crossroads to watch them out of sight. Nowhere is this more poignantly recorded than in the recollections of Jeremiah O'Donovan Rossa, of Skibbereen, whose teenage experience of parting from his mother, sister and brother in 1848 remained etched in his memory, furnishing the emotional fuel also for his later activism in the Fenian Brotherhood. The only member of his family to find employment after his father's death on the public works had been followed by eviction, Jeremiah was to stay in Ireland, the others rescued by remittances from relatives who had reached Philadelphia. On the day of departure he walked with his mother, brother and sister as far as Renascreena Cross:

> Five or six families were going away, and there were five or six cars to carry them and all they could carry with them to the Cove of Cork. The cry of the weeping and wailing of that day rings in my ears still. That time it was a cry heard every day at every cross-road in Ireland. I stood at that Renascreena Cross till this cry of the emigrant party went beyond my hearing. Then I kept walking backward towards Skibbereen, looking at them till they sank from my view over Mauleyregan hill.

When he next met his mother, at this brother's house in Philadelphia, in 1863, neither of them recognized the other.

The ships that carried Famine emigrants from Ireland in these years comprised a vast fleet, ranging from the great passenger 'packets', ships of a thousand tons or more that plied regular routes between major ports on both sides of the Atlantic to the small cargo vessels which in pre-Famine times carried varied cargoes, mainly timber from North America. Typical of these were the six small ships owned by the enterprising Francis Spaight of Limerick, whom we last saw clearing his Tipperary estate. During the Famine, Spaight's ships, *Bryan Abbs*, *Borneo*, *Governor*, *Jane Black* and *Jessy*, carried emigrants on the outward voyage and timber from Canada back to Limerick, and in the 1847 season transported a quarter of all emigrants leaving through Limerick port. Spaight was one of many small-time Irish ship-owners heavily involved in the direct emigrant trade from Ireland, attracted by the large profits to be made by replacing the ballast of the outward journey with paying emigrants. The full extent of this trade is illustrated by the fact that, during 1847, some 85,000 persons were recorded as having emigrated in this fashion, of whom only 9,000 and 4,000 respectively sailed from the larger ports of Dublin and Waterford.[26]

Relatively few emigrant-carrying ships, whether great packets or small, locally owned vessels, conform to the pattern of the coffin ships of contemporary description and later folk memory. However, the condition of the *Vista*, a small brig making ready to sail across the Atlantic from Castletown Berehaven in Cork, in May 1846, certainly qualifies her as a coffin ship, in that as well as overcrowding, inspection revealed rotten rigging, uncaulked timbers, a leaking hull and a foul and filthy steerage (the quarters assigned poorer passengers). The *Elizabeth and Sara*, a tiny vessel of just 230 tons burden which left Killala, County Mayo, for Quebec in the same month, also qualifies; she sailed with neither facilities nor provisions for the 276 emigrants crammed aboard, over 120 more than she was legally entitled to carry. The small brig *St. John*, which sailed from Galway for Canada in the autumn of 1849, could also be said to be a coffin ship; she too was grossly overcrowded, and when she was wrecked on the American coast, close examination of her hull revealed timbers so rotten that one witness believed it almost possible to poke an umbrella through them.[27]

The term 'coffin ship' did not, apply exclusively to these smaller vessels sailing from Irish ports (many others of which were eminently seaworthy and captained by competent masters). Conditions aboard some of the larger custom-built packets were often equally atrocious. It is true, however, that a disproportionate number of the worst vessels were owned and fitted out by the merchants of small Irish city and town ports, who with great inhumanity and ruthlessness exploited the commercial opportunities thrown their way by the booming Famine emigrant trade.[28]

From the time that the rush began across the Atlantic directly to America, refugee emigrants in their tens of thousands were also pouring across the Irish Sea into ports all along the west coast of Britain, from northern Scotland down to south-western Wales. In each port, and especially during the plague season of 1846–1847, their arrival was greeted with appalled hostility, and frequently, as in the case of one group arriving in Newport in Wales, they were angrily accused of 'bringing pestilence on their backs'. The greatest magnet for the Irish fleeing to Britain was Liverpool, the port of embarkation for North America, and a city whose population was already one-tenth Irish-born even before the Famine. Those arriving at the port during the Famine came by a variety of routes, usually as deck passengers on ships from Irish ports, where no shelter was provided from the elements. On the busy shipping routes from Dublin, some ship-owners did afford shelter, but only to cattle, pigs or horses, whose welfare was more important to their owners than the unhappy hundreds of human beings who lay miserable, drenched or frozen on the deck just down from them.[29]

At Liverpool, those whose resources were exhausted crowded into the filthy and damp cellars for which the city was notorious, spreading disease as they went. In April 1847, when the number of 'passengers of the lower orders' travelling to the city from Dublin port had already reached a daily average of between 600 and 1,000, government had received 'urgent representations' from the city authorities 'of the alarming spread of fever in that town owing to the continued influx of large numbers of Irish paupers'. Most of those arriving in Liverpool eventually continued their journey to America, the remainder settling in the city or drifting out to the towns of the Merseyside and Lancashire hinterland. Permanent settlement in Britain was the resort of the very poor, whose options in respect of further movement were almost as limited as those facing internal migrants in Ireland. About 250,000 Famine emigrants, it is estimated, remained in Britain in the six years following 1845.[30]

Where emigrants applied to local English Poor Law authorities for relief they were promptly deported back to Ireland. The extent of this practice may be gauged from the fact that in 1847 alone, Liverpool City deported over 15,000 Irish paupers, and that between 1845 and 1849 the authorities in England and Wales processed some 52,000 orders for removal to Ireland.[31] Irish paupers were routinely deported from Scotland also, and the ultimate fate of many is suggested by the case of the Kilroy family, originally from Leitrim, but who were removed by the Glasgow Poor Law authorities to Derry in August 1847. Refused admission to the Derry city workhouse, they were turned away also at Strabane, a grinding fourteen-mile walk away. Our knowledge of the family derives from an inquest

Emigrants preparing to depart from quay at Liverpool docks, 1850, their luggage unceremoniously being dragged on board. *Illustrated London News.*

report on the body of the father, Thomas, and the eldest son, who were recorded as having died of starvation in a small roadside cabin outside Strabane some months later.

If a great many routes led from Ireland to America during the Famine years, the vast bulk of transatlantic emigrants ultimately travelled via Liverpool. For the poorest emigrants who sailed from that port, or indeed any other in Ireland or Britain, travel options were limited to Canada, largely because American passenger legislation made the passage to the United States much more expensive.[32] However, the great majority of emigrants to Canada subsequently crossed the border to the United States, often taking the greatest pains to do so rather than remain in a British-ruled country, one whose demographic base was, in any case, far too small to absorb them. Ultimately, about seventy per cent of all Famine emigrants settled in seven northerly states of the United States: New York, Connecticut, New Jersey, Pennsylvania, Ohio, Illinois and Massachussetts, and in cities over 100,000 in size.

All stages of the transatlantic voyages and subsequent journeys inland were accompanied by severe, unrelenting hardship, and in so many cases ended in fever and premature death. Among the travails faced by passengers were unpredictable sea conditions, the absence of even the most basic facilities or privacy; poor or non-existent provisioning; brutal treatment by ships' captains and crews, and sickness and shipwreck. For those who survived these perils, many further dangers awaited upon landfall. The tragedies were innumerable: from the fever-beset vessels that shed corpses overboard as the crossing proceeded; to those that disembarked their passengers only to have them die in large numbers from typhus as they lay in quarantine, and those ships that sank as they approached their destination. Sixty or so registered ships carrying emigrants from Britain and Ireland across the Atlantic in the years between 1847 and 1853 are recorded as having failed to reach that landfall at all, most of these wrecked vessels having at least some Irish emigrants on board.[33] The actual figure was certainly much greater.

No definitive figures exist for the total mortality among emigrants en route or after landfall during the Famine, and historians, understandably, have been rather conservative in their estimates. However, if one acknowledges that the numbers who died on the voyage to Britain, the United States and Canada, or shortly after landfall during 1847 exceeded 50,000, and that the cumulative loss of life from the much lesser individual tragedies of the following years – shipwrecks, onboard fever epidemics, and the cholera epidemic of 1853, when ten per cent of transatlantic Irish emigrants perished – was very high also, then it is clear that the overall mortality may easily exceed 80,000 persons.[34]

The following is a random listing of ships which suffered disaster at sea or sank on the Atlantic voyage. At the very end of 1845, the *Robert Isaac*, outward bound from Liverpool for New York, was wrecked hundreds of miles from her destination, stranding her 133 Irish emigrants on an isolated shore. In April 1847, the *Exmouth*, out of Derry and bound for Quebec, was wrecked off the Scottish island of Islay, with the loss of 248 lives.[35] In March 1848, the brig *Barbara* capsized off Petty Harbour, Newfoundland, with the loss of some 115 emigrants, many of them survivors of an earlier wreck. In August the same year, the *Ocean Monarch*, 1,000 tons burden, one of the proudest and most modern of the Boston packets, hardly a year old, caught fire and sank in the Mersey, just after leaving Liverpool docks. Some 176 lives were lost, most of them Irish steerage passengers, while among the saved was a young Leitrim girl, who was thrown overboard by a woman passenger in order to save her from the flames.[36]

In February 1849, the *Jane Black* of Limerick, one of Francis Spaight's ships, bound for Quebec, lost forty-three passengers through cholera and dysentery between Kerry Head and Newfoundland. She then struck an iceberg and barely made landfall at Quebec. In the summer of 1849, the 287-ton, Quebec-bound brig, *Hannah*, of Newry, struck an iceberg as she neared her destination, losing sixty of her 129 passengers to the ice. In mid-July, the *Maria*, of Limerick, also bound for Quebec, lost all but nine of her 111 passengers when she too struck an iceberg. In autumn the same year, the Boston-bound brig, *St. John*, mentioned earlier, which sailed from Galway with 100 passengers, most of them from Leitir Mealláin, was wrecked off Cohasset, Cape Cod; ninety-two emigrants drowned. It was the well-known writer, Henry David Thoreau, then resident in the district, who saw the wrecked vessel and speculated on the permeability of its rotten timbers to his umbrella point. Much closer to home, the 900-ton *Edmond*, chartered by a Limerick merchant in order to carry emigrants from that city to New York in November 1850, did not even clear Irish waters before disaster struck; she foundered in a ferocious Atlantic storm on the Duggarna Rocks at the mouth of Kilkee harbour, in County Clare. Ninety-nine passengers died.[37]

If the loss of life through maritime disaster was extraordinarily high, many more deaths on the Atlantic routes occurred through the more mundane agency of fever. This was hardly surprising given the state of most emigrants when they embarked, and the crowded, filthy, impossible conditions aboard the vessels on which they sailed. For a number of obvious reasons, authentic descriptions written by passengers of their experience are not known to exist, and historians have had to rely on the account left by Stephen de Vere, son of a County Limerick landlord, who travelled steerage to Quebec in October 1847, in company with some of his father's tenants in order to see for himself what they endured. De Vere's outrage at what he witnessed was expressed in a letter written shortly after his voyage ended. In their hundreds, he wrote, passengers were 'huddled together without light, without air, wallowing in filth and breathing a fetid atmosphere'. They were:

> sick in body, dispirited in heart, the fevered patients lying between the sound, in sleeping places so narrow as almost to deny them the power of indulging by a change of position, the natural restlessness of the disease; by their agonised ravings disturbing those around . . . living without food, or medicine except as administered by the hand of casual charity, dying without the voice of spiritual consolation, and buried in the deep without the rites of the Church.

In fact, de Vere and his fellow passengers were probably better off than most of those travelling steerage during the Famine, since captains and crews on the London to Quebec route which they travelled were regarded as being much more humane than those on any other transatlantic routes.[38]

De Vere's widely circulated letter led to a tightening of the British Passenger Acts, but because no serious attempt was made to enforce them by regular ship inspections, three years later when Vere Foster, another Irish gentleman, again travelled steerage, this time to New York, little seemed to have changed. In contrast to de Vere, Foster (despite the similarity of name and the peculiar similarities in their lives, the two men were neither related nor acquainted) embarked on a luxurious American packet, the *Washington*, plying between Liverpool and New York. On the *Washington*, steerage passengers were, literally, dragged on board by the crew, and roughly deposited to the deck; they were refused provisions, beaten by crewmembers; and on several occasions had the ship's water hoses turned on them. Foster's remonstrations with the ship's officers over the treatment of passengers resulted in a violent physical assault by the first mate, and a tirade of foul verbal abuse from the captain.

Landing as he did in New York and very late in the Famine, Foster was at least spared the full awfulness of the quarantine station, which had been fraught with mass disease mortality in the previous seasons, especially during 1847. Of these the most notorious was the Canadian station for Quebec, situated picturesquely on the St. Lawrence River, at Grosse Île, thirty miles downriver from the city.[39] Because so many of the poorest emigrants chose Canada as the point of entry to North America, fever, suffering and mass death became concentrated on this one island to a degree unique in the Famine exodus.

Throughout 1846 the workload of the authorities at Grosse Île increased steadily, and by the year's end, some 33,000 persons from Ireland had already arrived there, twice as many persons being treated in the station hospital as in the previous year. For the first half of the year ships arriving from Ireland had been largely free of disease, many containing comfortable farmers, others being shiploads of smallholding tenants emigrated by their landlords. Passengers in general were well-provided with 'sea-store' (provisions) and the level of sickness was in general manageable.[40]

The arrival of the *Elizabeth and Sara*, the small brig which we have already seen leaving Killala, signalled an abrupt change, anticipating on a small scale the chaotic scenes of fever and death that would reign the following season. Docking 'in a most horrible state of disease, filth and destitution', conditions on board the 230-ton brig were reported to be closer to those aboard an African slaver than a vessel coming from a part of the United Kingdom. Instead of the advertised 155 passengers, the *Elizabeth and Sara* carried 276; insufficient water had been brought on board; the casks had leaked, and no food provision at all had been made for the passengers. The vessel was 'horrible and disgusting beyond the power of language to describe'. Twenty-two of the passengers died on the voyage and were tossed into the sea; when the captain died, the deranged first mate lashed the corpse to the deck, where it befouled the vessel for nearly a fortnight until the passengers were eventually rescued.[41]

Emigrants arriving at Grosse Île during September and early October in the last weeks before ice closed the Canadian ports were for the most part in a similar condition to the passengers of the *Elizabeth and Sara*; like them they were comprised of refugees produced by the second potato failure in Ireland, their desperation evident in the risks they took travelling so late in the season. What they saw of these emigrants and their knowledge of conditions in Ireland caused the Grosse Île medical authorities to brace themselves for a major crisis when the ice would break in the late spring. Nothing, however, could have prepared them for its extent.

The first ship to arrive, on 15 May 1847, was the *Syria*, from Liverpool, with 243 passengers, fifty-two of whom were ill with fever, nine having already died of it on the voyage.[42] The same day, four-year-old Ellen Kane from Kilmore parish in County Mayo died in the hospital; she would be the first of thousands of emigrants to perish in the station that year. The *Syria* was followed four days later by the *Wandsworth* from Dublin, crowded with dead and dying passengers, some forty-five others having already died en route. A succession of emigrant-carrying vessels followed until, by 28 May, thirty-six ships lay moored at the quarantine station. At that point, 13,000 passengers awaited inspection, and medical staff were treating some 856 cases of fever and dysentery in the hospital, while 470 further cases still remained on board the moored vessels.

Throughout the 1847 season, ship after ship landing at the quarantine station disgorged their cargoes of sick, dying and dead. On 5 June, the station medical superintendent, Dr. Douglas, was writing that all the Cork and Liverpool passengers were already 'half dead from starvation and want' when they embarked, and that 'the least bowel complaint . . . finishes them without a struggle'. Dead passengers had to be dragged out of the narrow berths they shared with living ones, by seamen using boathooks. By the end of August nearly 4,000 emigrant passengers had perished of fever, the death toll continuing to spiral upwards with each succeeding week. A noteworthy arrival in August was the *Virginius*, which had set out from Liverpool weeks earlier with 476 tenants emigrated from his Strokestown estate by Denis Mahon. The *Virginius* passengers were in a dreadful state. Already 158 had died of 'ship fever' (typhus) at sea, the master, first mate and nine of the crew along with them. A further 109 died subsequently on Grosse Île; the survivors were described by Dr. Douglas as 'the most wretched, sickly, miserable beings' he had ever witnessed.

By October, of the 100,000 persons who travelled to Quebec so far that year, over one-sixth had died of diseases, either on board the emigrant vessels, in the quarantine hospital, or the general vicinity of the station; in all the death toll was close to 17,000.[43] Overwhelmed by their workload, medical staff too succumbed to fever, with four attending physicians dying at Grosse Île in 1847. The first of them, a Dr. Benson, had arrived as a passenger on the *Wandsworth*. Four Catholic chaplains, two Anglican clergymen and thirty-four other staff also perished before the season was out.[44] As for the emigrant families, so many were broken up by fever deaths that hundreds of orphans were left behind; these were adopted by French Canadians residing nearby, in an act of extraordinary kindness that still resounds in the number of French Canadians in the Quebec area who bear Irish names.[45]

During the same year the quarantine station at Point St. Charles, near Montréal, experienced similar conditions, with over 3,500 dying in the fever sheds there alone. Quarantine stations in the United States were not as badly affected, but because the wintertime closure of the Canadian ports saw as many as 35,000 refugee-emigrants flood into American ports between October 1846 and February 1847 alone, the disease mortality was fearsome in some of them. Something of the order of sixteen to twenty per cent of those entering the New York quarantine station at Staten Island were reported to have died in 1847, a figure which does not take into account fatalities at the sub-station at Ward's Island, which was also high. On the other hand, Boston, otherwise a major destination for Irish emigrants, escaped virtually unscathed largely because the city operated a rigorous quarantine regime at its Deer Island station.

Even though the carnage of voyage and quarantine was at its worst during the 1847 season, throughout the Famine emigrations, all those taking to the sea faced very real possibilities of death through shipwreck and ship fever. It is true, certainly, that the vast majority did arrive at their destinations, but it is also true that comparatively few of them did so in good physical or mental health, or with the security of knowing that their travails were at an end. For most, indeed, arrival signalled the opening of a whole galaxy of new miseries.

The story of the Famine emigrants represents an unparalleled human experience, one that brought about an enormous shift in the demographic balance of both Ireland and the host countries that received them.[46] Paradoxically, the enormity of the overall numbers removing themselves from Ireland, whether across the Atlantic or across the world to the unimaginable distance of Australia, tends to obscure the fact that each individual journey was itself an extraordinary odyssey, each literally the journey of a lifetime. For those to whom journey memories were narrated later on, indeed, they were the stuff of legend.

Two relatively well-known instances preserve this sense of epic endeavour with particular strength, perhaps because in both cases the voyage was unclouded by the threat of starvation or fever. The first relates to the several hundred families brought by Fr. Thomas Hore, of Kilavenny, in south County Wicklow, to the American midwest in 1850–1851. Far from belonging to the destitute classes, Fr. Hore's emigrants came rather from the 'snug' farmer stock of Counties Wicklow and Wexford, the future yet promising them so little in Ireland that as many as 400 families initially signed up for the journey, in all 1,200 persons. Although Hore's project went awry almost from the beginning, its various elements make it by any standards an astonishing undertaking, punctuated by episodes of great human drama. These moments began with Fr. Hore's unveiling of his intentions to his Sunday congregation in June 1850, followed by the chartering of three ships in Liverpool; the hardships of the voyage; the reunion on the other side; and the picaresque detail of the trek across the United States of the different parties into which the original families eventually broke up. Even the manner in which the project disintegrated in the American interior makes a compelling narrative, as these parties went in separate directions before journey's end was reached in settlements in Iowa, Missouri, Arkansas, Louisiana and Texas.[47]

The second great emigration epic, which was of a very different nature, concerns a group of nearly 200 destitute workhouse girls orphaned by the deaths of their parents who were sent out to Australia under a government scheme in 1849–1850 aboard the vessel *Thomas Arbuthnot*. Coming mainly from Galway, Kerry and Clare Poor Law unions, which were anxious to rid themselves of the cost of their upkeep, the girls' journey abounds with incident and fascinating detail: from the careful manner in which they were selected; their kitting-out at workhouse expense and the supervised journey taken by different groups to Plymouth, the main emigrant depot for Australia; the long months spent at sea amidst the vastness of the southern ocean; and the circumstances in which most of them finished their great journey in the settlements of New South Wales. Unlike most emigrants these girls experienced kindness at the hands of their guardians, most outstandingly in the case of Charles Strutt, the surgeon-superintendent appointed to accompany them. Strutt's pride in his young charges is evident at many points in his reports and journals, and one journal entry where he speaks with satisfaction of 'the fatness of my girls' reveals – movingly in view of their recent experiences – how he measured his success as their protector.

But only a handful of emigrant journeys were recorded in this kind of detail, and a great number of similar experiences lie hidden behind the antecedents of millions among the later generations of Americans, Canadians and Australians. This is as true of ordinary citizens as it is of those who would become outstanding historical figures in their own right in these countries. In the American context, the most significant of all in numerical terms, the variety of those sharing Famine emigrant ancestry in modern times is well illustrated in the cases of individuals from Henry Ford to John F. Kennedy and, if recent research is to be credited, Muhammad Ali and Barack Obama.

The Irish who travelled to Britain and America in the mid-nineteenth century were among the most innocent and fearful of all emigrants and the least prepared for exile. Reared for the most part in a pre-industrial countryside, most would have lived out their lives within a twenty-mile radius of their birthplace but for the calamity that overwhelmed them. Many spoke no English, and the idiom and accent of those who did were often incomprehensible to English or American ears. In Ireland, in addition to their actual existences, most lived also in the imagined alternative cosmos of fairies and spirits, ancestral inventions designed to humanize the rural landscape, and which did not accommodate at all to harsh urban environments in Britain and America. On the voyage, emigrant innocence was manifested in swift mood changes, from despair to elation and vice versa, engendered by the slightest changes in circumstances, and more strikingly in the manner in which refuge was sought from misery in the comfort of music and dance. Contemporary diaries, letters and pictorial illustrations plentifully feature dancers on or below decks, twisting to jigs, reels and hornpipes to the accompaniment of pipe- and fiddle-music, testimony to a merriment consciously fabricated to ward off the fears of fever and shipwreck.[48]

Roll-call on quarter deck of American-bound emigrant ship, July 1850. *Illustrated London News.*

On disembarkation, these gullible, timid people were overwhelmed by their new surroundings, terrified by the great blaring, roaring cities in which they found themselves. This bewilderment is evident in some of contemporary prints which show them huddled on the quayside, baggage piled up protectively about them. As they stood on the quayside in their quaint dress – men in comical claw-hammer, high-collared frieze coats and felt hats, women in strange black hooded cloaks and shapeless dresses – they were the perfect marks for those willing to exploit them. Whether in Liverpool or New York, they fell easily into the hands of runners, crimps and dishonest lodging housekeepers, who swindled them out of their money and belongings. Many of the predators, indeed, were themselves Irish, whose soothing familiar tones in either language lulled the newcomers into a foolhardy trustfulness.

Once swept out into the wider society of the host country, the emigrants immediately felt the full arctic blast of racial hostility. Anti-Irish prejudice long predated the Famine emigrations, but the influx of sickly and ragged Irish who flooded into American and British cities from late 1846, and placed enormous strain on official and private charities, confirmed and reinforced it. A despised, pariah race in the Anglo-Saxon world even before 1845, for decades after the Famine emigrations the Irish would continue to be so.

As Miller has remarked of the emigrants to America, very few of the Famine

Irish were able to raise themselves very far above the condition in which they arrived. Those who did succeed, in professional occupations and in business, almost invariably possessed the ingredients for that success before leaving Ireland.[49] These ingredients eluded every other emigrant: financial resources; education or even rudimentary schooling; opportunity; the goodwill of their new countrymen, and the confidence to confront challenge and adversity. For all but a lucky few the lot of the Famine immigrants was grinding poverty, unemployment or backbreaking, dangerous work for little pay. Immigrants' lives were shortened by work-slavery, psychological alienation and the alcohol with which many sought to obtain relief from both. The brand of their Irishness and therefore their inferiority, was perhaps hardest of all the burdens they had to bear, compounding all other disabilities under which they and their British- or American-born children laboured.

Since so many of them established themselves in the footprint of their pre-Famine predecessors who had faced similar problems, the Famine Irish were able to shelter themselves to some extent from nativist hostility by congregating in Irish neighbourhoods, where they retrenched within the protective arms of the Catholic Church, Irish cultural societies and major political organizations. Although the 'Little Irelands' that emerged over the decades would exhibit wide variations imposed by the different circumstances of the countries and cities where they settled, the general phenomenon of which they were all a part would remain unmistakeably the same in each. These communities would serve the Famine Irish and those who followed them extraordinarily well for a number of generations, before demography, democracy and economic success gradually propelled them outwards again towards a slow, painful acceptance and assimilation within the majority society.

Exiled from Humanity: The Later Years of the Famine

Is there no mercy for the doomed people? Are we exiled from humanity?
Or rather is it exiled from us?

– LIMERICK AND CLARE EXAMINER, *15 JUNE 1850*

In the course of 1847 the sympathy of the British public for the sufferings of Ireland diminished rapidly, and by the end of the year it had evaporated completely. Public opinion, shaped by and reflected in the newspapers, became incensed by the endless calls on its charity and what was seen as rank Irish ingratitude towards a kindly British state which had done so much to succour them. In January, a 'queen's letter' calling for donations for Ireland had netted (for the entire British empire) the sum of £171,000. A second 'letter' at the end of the year, however, raised a paltry £30,000, and it was accompanied by an outburst of anti-Irish vituperation in the British media. Anti-Irish prejudice revived and intensified, violent language filled the public prints regarding Irish laziness, squalor and incorrigibility, and British attitudes towards everything Irish become permeated more than ever by what Peter Gray has called a 'moralistic outrage'.[1]

This general mood was due in large measure to a barely suppressed hysteria in regard to the Irish pauper influx, and few would have disagreed with the picture painted by the *The Times*, 'of England positively invaded, overrun, devoured, infected, poisoned, and desolated by Irish pauperdom'. British newspapers stoked popular fears and prejudices regarding disorder in Ireland, and did not let up even when Irish outrage figures began to decline steadily during 1848 and ensuing years. Following the example of its government, and having convinced itself that the 'good' harvest of 1847 marked the end of Irish distress, the British public set its face firmly against further assistance for Ireland, and recoiled from further engagement with the never-ending drear of the neighbouring island.

No development reinforced this trend more than the attempt at a national uprising made in the summer of 1848 by elements of the Young Ireland group,

until recently a strong supporting wing of Daniel O'Connell's Repeal movement. Motivated by a lofty romantic patriotism that consciously embraced both
Protestant and Catholic traditions, by 1846 the middle-class journalist-poets
of Young Ireland had become disillusioned with O'Connellite politics. Having
formally quit the Repeal Association in July, the following January they formed
themselves into the Irish Confederation, a body that took some time to define
itself philosophically, largely because of fundamental differences between socially
conservative leaders such as William Smith O'Brien and physical force separatists
such as John Mitchel. By the autumn, however, the Confederation membership
became radicalized by what they had witnessed of the impact of the Poor Law
Amendment Act, and by early 1848, the political clubs into which they had
organized themselves were gripped by a new determination to resort to arms
in a national insurgency. Buoyed by the success of the French revolutionaries of
February 1848, whom they saw as kindred spirits, they were filled with optimism
that something similar could be achieved in Ireland, and as new Confederate
clubs sprang up across the country in the spring, their young, middle-class supporters became infused with a militant nationalism what was as romantic as it
was impractical.

By March the Confederate leaders were envisaging a spontaneous uprising
all over Ireland, in which freedom would be achieved by means of a national
guard raised from the Confederate clubs, with the possible assistance of the
French republicans, and perhaps some input from the British Chartists. But this
was all vague scenario-making, far removed from the strategic planning that the
situation called for, and with the French declining any move that might affect
relations with Britain, and most of Ireland lying prostrate in famine, prospects for
even a respectable military showing were dim; the possibility of success remote
beyond contemplation. Over succeeding months the Confederates allowed
matters to drift, even after the end of May, when the arrest and trial of William
Smith O'Brien, Thomas Francis Meagher and John Mitchel for sedition (O'Brien
was shortly released) finally forced them to commit to a rising. Only when the
government suspended Habeas Corpus in July did those leaders remaining at
liberty make any attempt at raising the country.[2]

Concentrating their efforts in the south-east, particularly that general region
where the counties of Tipperary, Waterford and Kilkenny meet, the insurgent
leaders were often greeted with scenes of jubilant enthusiasm as they travelled, but
they were also repeatedly told that the people were in no condition for a rising,
and obliged to move on in search of more fertile revolutionary soil. As they went,
priests who circulated among the crowds that followed them persuaded the people
to return home, and by the time the rising reached its inglorious denouement in

Ballingarry, south Tipperary, on 29 July, a few hundred at most remained, hardly any of them with weapons or provisions to sustain themselves on the march.

Many risible incidents attended the Ballingarry episode, as, for example, when Smith O'Brien, the *de facto* commander, refused to allow the felling of trees for barricades for fear of damaging private property; or where he solemnly gave instructions from the wall of the parish church to men close to starvation that they should go home and provide themselves with food for four days; or again where an officer of hussars, on a mission unconnected with the disturbances, engaged his word as a gentleman that if allowed through insurgent barricades, he and his men would proceed on their way without attacking them.[3] The active part of the insurrection lasted a matter of hours, and consisted of a standoff with a body of police who had taken shelter in the house of a widow, a Mrs. McCormack, before the arrival of constabulary and military reinforcements scattered the besieging insurgents. The leaders either fled or were arrested.

Fortified with anecdotal ammunition of this kind, contemporaries were not slow in heaping scorn on the rising. *The Times* led the charge of the British newspapers, with its denunciation of 'the contemptible figure of Smith O'Brien crouching amidst Widow McCormack's cabbages'. On the nationalist side, John Mitchel, who was en route to penal exile in Tasmania when the rising occurred and learned of it in only in October, spoke of it – most unkindly – as a 'poor extemporised abortion of a rising'.[4] Since that time most commentators have been equally disparaging, and among the phrases employed by modern historians, the adjectives 'ridiculous', 'pathetic' and 'ludicrous' have figured.

Because so much that occurred during the rising justified such epithets, amidst the general derision aspects favourable to the insurgents have tended to be overlooked. For one thing, the semi-farcical conduct of the 'war-house' siege was determined by the fact that the police, who may have outnumbered the insurgents and were certainly much better armed than them, quite deliberately held the McCormack children as shields, thereby limiting any possible action against them.[5] There is also the evidence of courage and self-sacrifice on the part of the insurgents, not just the educated young romantic republicans, but equally the half-starved miners from the nearby Castlecomer collieries who sheltered from police fire side by side with them outside the wall of the McCormack house. The common cause made by these two very different insurgent elements is underlined by the fact that one of two men killed by police at Ballingarry was an outdoor pauper who had come directly from a stone-breaking depot to be present, and that another who was jailed afterwards had just been appointed to the position of union rate collector, and from his prison cell went to the trouble of formally resigning the position.

Siege of the Widow McCormack's house at Ballingarry. *Illustrated London News.*

On the other hand, despite the barrage of ridicule and criticism in the British media, even at the time there were those who evinced sympathy with the insurgents while disavowing any support for their actions. Before the rising Smith O'Brien had been much respected across the political and denominational spectrum, and after it was over even in England was widely seen as more Don Quixote than demon, someone who had behaved honourably, if not very wisely throughout. Even the waspish Elizabeth Smith could mingle pity with outrage in his regard. 'Poor Smith O'Brien must be mad,' she commented in a diary entry early in August, the first of several references to him in such terms. Other observers were impressed by the idealism of the leaders. Asenath Nicholson, the American evangelist, spoke for many when she wrote that the rising was not an 'ungrateful affair' as had been represented in the British press, but one that originated 'among the higher classes' of Irish nationalists who were 'too enlightened not to know the causes of their country's sufferings, and too humane to look on with indifference'.[6] For these reasons, and the inspiration it would afford future generations of Irish separatists, the rising of 1848, fiasco though it undoubtedly was, would continue to resonate in Irish history.

The events of the rising took place in wet, humid weather that added considerably to the outdoor discomforts endured by the Ballingarry insurgents and their opponents. It was also ideal for the incubation of *Phytophthora infestans*, whose spores had lain dormant in the soil during the previous dry summer, patiently awaiting the return of conditions favourable to its dissemination. The heartbreaking news of its recurrence coincided broadly with the excitement associated with the rising, which many became aware of as the blight once again ravaged the potato fields around them. In the renewed visitation, the long-suffering counties of the west and south were again devastated; those of the north and east were affected in large pockets, and the midland counties on a much more localized, patchy basis.

Wherever it struck, the blight ravaged the potatoes as wantonly as it had two years previously. Already, by 15 July, not a garden for nine miles around Bantry, County Cork, had escaped, while on the twenty-fourth, at Miltown Malbay, County Clare, black blotches appeared on the growing stalks, 'just as if the flame of a burning candle had played upon the parts for a time'. In early September potato fields in the vicinity of Ennistymon were reported to be 'nearly unapproachable' because of the stench emanating from them. In Clifden, County Galway, on 11 August, after a ten-day inspection of the union, the temporary inspector, John Deane, reported that every field of potatoes he had seen 'was black'. Some time later, the agricultural instructor for the Wexford union failed to find a single farm where the potatoes had survived.[7]

But even in counties where the blight did not recur with such virulence, or did not recur at all, growing grain and other crops were extensively damaged by endless weeks of rain, which also prevented smallholders from harvesting turf, leaving them to face a winter without any fuel for their fires. From Macroom, County Cork, in late August, it was reported that in the previous fortnight there had been only two days without rain, and in the continuing downpour, 'every heart seems sinking at the unhappy prospect for the harvest'. On her return from a holiday to her Wicklow demesne about the same time, Elizabeth Smith listened to news of this kind, and noted despondently in her diary that the potatoes were 'gone' as a crop, that much of the corn was mildewed, the hay 'partly uncut and partly lying in the swathe under all these heavy showers'.[8]

The effects of the 1848 harvest failure were most apparent among smallholding tenants, who had been encouraged by the blight-free interval of the previous year to make one last-ditch attempt at extracting a subsistence from the land. Their prospects now utterly destroyed, they were no longer in a position to pay current rents or Poor Law rates, and soon began to sink under the weight of arrears. Where smallholders still retained some capital they were able to join the ongoing trek towards the country's exit ports, in the company of many of their better-off neighbours whose circumstances left them with no future in Ireland either. For the most part, however, their capital was exhausted, placing them in much the same position as those who had preceded them in ruin over the previous few years. In some respects their plight was worse, due both to the collapse of private charity and the refusal of the British government to introduce special measures to deal with the new crisis. The funds of the Society of Friends and the British

Relief Association, which had helped rescue many, became depleted, and by the summer of 1849 neither society was still operating in Ireland.

Ruined smallholders who clung to their homesteads were not long left thus, and were soon uprooted brutally by the clearance machinery deployed by consolidating landlords and agents whose campaigns widened and deepened after the harvest of 1848. This in turn brought a further wave of destitution crashing over the workhouse system, which the Poor Law bureaucracy dealt with by redoubling recourse to regulations aimed at lessening eligibility. As before, those accepted by the Poor Law were subjected to the daily humiliation of workhouse routine intended to reshape them into tractable paupers; those who could not bring themselves to apply to the Poor Law, as well as those it rejected, would together die in another cycle of mass starvation and epidemic disease that surged again from late 1848, continuing for much of the following year.

Over a great part of the country, in fact, 1849 proved to be even worse than the year already referred to as Black Forty Seven. Although the distressed regions of Munster and Connacht were again worst affected, suffering in a surprising number of areas far from that famine zone was widespread also. This emerges strongly in a number of recent detailed local studies dealing with Leinster counties such as Wicklow, Offaly, Meath and Westmeath, or smaller districts within them. For such areas parish birth and marriage data reveal a sudden drastic and sustained decline during 1849 and afterwards,while Poor Law and other records show a peak in fever and starvation mortality comparable to that of 1847. In institutional terms, worsening conditions were most strongly reflected in the fact that it was only in 1849 that in a good many of these Leinster unions auxiliary workhouses were acquired for the first time.[9] In Westmeath, one particularly grim reflection of current conditions was that between January and September, over 600 coffins were manufactured in the carpenter's shop at Mullingar workhouse.

The unions in many of these counties also experienced heavy emigration, afftecting smallholding and comfortable tenants who a few years previously had been letting out land to the now vanished cottiers and labourers. In these unions as elsewhere, a major contributing factor to disease and starvation deaths was the fact that so many workhouses were badly and even chaotically managed. Wicklow unions seem to have been particularly beset by confusion at this time, and the Rathdrum, Loughlinstown and Naas workhouses particularly disordered. Many Ulster unions experienced similar conditions, the worst examples being Newry and Lurgan. In early April the workhouse physician at Newry, a Dr. Davis, warned his Board that inmates, especially women and children, did not have enough clothing or food, and strongly hinted that they were actually suffering from starvation.[10]

But it was the distressed unions of the south and west and many others in these regions that had not been so designated that bore the brunt of the suffering of 1849. It is salutary to recall that the general mortality in the workhouse at Ennistymon, in Clare, one of the worst afflicted in the country, at this time was four times that of Rathdrum, one of the worst of the Leinster workhouses.[11] As Christine Kinealy reminds us, conditions within western unions such as Gort, Ballina and Kilrush remained so bad that the Poor Law Commissioners consciously decided not to include material relating to them in the Blue Books for fear of creating a public outcry.

The chronic problems of the local Poor Law were compounded by the indebtedness that crippled so many unions, debts which they had no hope of clearing. Union contractors in consequence either threatened to cut off all supplies, or made good such threats, thereby endangering the lives of inmates. In many instances, too, matters were worsened when unions under Vice-Guardian management were returned to the control of Boards of Guardians: in March, twenty-three of the thirty-nine Boards dissolved earlier were restored (the Commissioners recognized that it would be unsafe for the inmates if the remaining sixteen were to be handed back to Guardians). In most cases, restored Boards reverted promptly to the practices which had led to dissolution in the first place: the striking of rates insufficient to the relief of poverty; disastrous workhouse management; corrupt collusion between Guardians and suppliers over contracts; and a marked deterioration in the diet and health of inmates.

But whether under Guardian or Vice-Guardian regimes, all unions with financial difficulties resorted to ever-more extreme use of mechanisms for reducing eligibility, in the course of which justifications of the workhouse test, the labour test for outdoor paupers and the public revisions of outdoor lists, plumbed new depths of unreality and self-deception on the part of those implementing them. In this period, list revisions figure especially prominently in the arsenal of relief officials. At one revision, at Castlebar, in January 1849, the supervising official, vexed at his failure to detect any cases of fraud among the pitiful collection of human wrecks brought before him, reported that attempts 'at imposition and simulated circumstances of distress' were so 'cleverly contrived' that relieving officers 'cannot in all cases discover them.'[12]

Another list revision, at Louisburgh, in the same county at the end of March, had consequences so appalling that they were seared permanently into popular consciousness in the locality. This was when about 500 starving smallholders and their families who had assembled for inspection outside Louisburgh village were told instead to report to the auxiliary at Delphi Lodge, Bundorragha, twenty miles away. On arrival at Delphi after a painful overnight march, they were refused relief or admission. The relieving officers present informed them of this only after leisurely consumption of their own breakfasts, according to one account. On the return journey to Louisburgh, across a landscape of the most surreal, desolate beauty to be found anywhere in Ireland, scores, including persons of both sexes and all ages, died of hunger-related exhaustion or hypothermia or by drowning in the Glankeen River and Stroppabue Lake.[13]

By this time, the term 'able-bodied' had ceased to have any meaning detectable to anyone but Poor Law administrators, since so many of the surviving poor manifested an extreme emaciation similar to that of the 'unfortunate living skeletons' who comprised the Delphi victims. In February, in Castlebar, investigation of reports of a starving family living near the workhouse revealed two children and their mother lying in an advanced state of starvation in a squalid cabin. The father told of having eaten nothing for the previous three days apart from some raw turnips, and of being repeatedly refused relief by the Vice-Guardians, he 'being an able-bodied man'. In April, the stone-breaking depots of the Ennistymon Union were described as 'loathsome musters of moving skeletons', and at about the same time we find Asenath Nicholson tramping through the Killary mountains, where

Pre-Famine drawing of Delphi Lodge, by 1849 an auxiliary workhouse, set in stunning scenery, and location of the 1849 tragedy. Stirling Coyne, *Scenery and Antiquities.*

she came across group after group of outdoor paupers, 'pale, meagre-looking men', on their way downwards 'to break stones and pile them mountain-high for the paltry compensation of a pound of meal a day'.[14]

Through all this, government maintained its political and financial distance from Ireland, its only response being a proposed increase in the number of Poor Law unions and the levying of a special tax on all Irish unions, which would be used to pay for the extra relief required, it insisted, only in the unions which had earlier been accorded the official designation, 'distressed'. This tax, or rate-in-aid, combined with a small, final grant from the Treasury, was intended to end any remaining dependency of the Irish Poor Law on the Imperial purse. The other unions, understandably, protested vigorously, the most worried being those that were only marginally better off than the distressed ones. Paradoxically, however, opposition to the rate-in-aid was led by the Ulster unions, those which had the lightest relief burden to bear, their views expressed forcefully by the County Down M.P.s, William Sharman Crawford and Lord Castlereagh. Although Crawford and Castlereagh clothed their argument in constitutional garb, i.e. that relief of destitution should be an imperial rather than a national charge, other Ulster unions were more direct.[15] The Lisnaskea union (County Fermanagh), for one, sent a memorial to the Poor Law commissioners expressing 'indignation' at proposals 'to impose a rate-in-aid on the peaceable and industrious inhabitants of the north of Ireland for the support of the lazy, vicious and indolent population of the south and west of the kingdom who fear neither God, honour the Queen nor respect the laws of the land'. It was a cry that found echoes in not a few other unions in the province.

The imposition of the rate-in-aid was such a cynical move that it aroused outrage even in senior Poor Law bureaucrats, and precipitated the resignation of the Chief Commissioner, Edward Twistleton, who of late was becoming increasingly restive over Treasury interference. However, Twistleon's stand on principle, extraordinary in such a doctrinaire, hardnosed promoter of the amended Poor Law, made no difference, and the rate-in-aid went ahead, as did a second rate-in-aid the following year.[16] Pretty soon, in any case, the rate-in-aid controversy would be lost as a source of grievance when another crisis arose, caused by the outbreak of cholera, whose rapid spread through the country in the spring and early summer left a trail of horror and death that was shocking even to sensitivities blunted by the enormities of what had so far been witnessed.

Although the ravages of cholera were greatest among the physically weakened and starving, it brought mass death also to districts and social classes that up to now had remained largely unaffected by the Famine calamity. Its symptoms were more horrific than other Famine-era diseases, and of them all it was the source of a unique dread and terror. Alone of Famine diseases, cholera could cause parents or siblings to shrink in revulsion from stricken family members, and not uncommonly it led to the expulsion of victims from their own homes. These were not necessarily callous acts, however, but more often than not desperate attempts at preventing the disease from striking down an entire family.

Wherever the outbreak occurred and while it lasted, it put an abrupt halt to public occasions, social activities, fairs and markets, and the meetings of all manner of bodies and organizations. Commercial activity came to a standstill; schools and public institutions remained closed; the superior and local courts were poorly attended, and in many counties, quarter sessions failed to find enough magistrates to form grand juries. In addition, the outbreak led to a headlong flight from many workhouses whose inmates preferred to risk starvation outside than certain death within. Although the worst of the epidemic was over by the end of May, the disease was still causing havoc in certain counties as late as September. In its passing over Ireland, cholera was later estimated (by the 1851 Census Commissioners) to have brought sudden, violent and painful death to more than 30,000 persons.[17]

Almost unnoticed amidst the turmoil of the first half of 1849 was a dramatic falling off in the level of serious and insurrectionary crime. This trend had first emerged the previous year, but had been disguised by the fact that assize and quarter sessions calendars remained laden with cases postponed from previous years and with relatively trivial offences. The major reason for the decline, of course, was that those turbulent spirits who had been responsible for outrages had been removed from the scene by death, emigration, imprisonment or transportation to Australia, and that communities no longer had sufficient leadership or collective strength to engage in organized protest or retaliation. Henceforward wreckers met even less resistance at evictions and few attacks would take place on landlords. The last category of outrage with significant community involvement, physical resistance to the collection or distraint for Poor Law rates, died away also in the course of 1849.

In this situation, crime was largely reduced to the fatalistic stealing of food, the perpetrators being usually indifferent to imprisonment, which would at least result in their being fed. In innumerable instances, indeed, imprisonment was welcomed for this reason, and crimes were routinely committed deliberately so that the perpetrators would be sent to jail. At the north Tipperary quarter sessions held in Nenagh in January, for example, the offences dealt with by the assistant barrister related overwhelmingly to food pilfering. In April, the *Tipperary Vindicator* described prisoners committed for trial in the county jail

Domestic animals being distrained for unpaid rent, December 1849.
Illustrated London News.

as 'principally poor wretches whom hunger and sickness have made fit inmates for a hospital and who commit petty crimes for the sole purpose of gaining the shelter and food of a prison'. On reaching the jail many of them were 'scarcely able to crawl.'[18] In Clare, although the calendar for the spring assizes was 'unusually heavy', the vast majority of cases heard were old ones, or were so trivial as to be hardly worth prosecuting. Significantly, during the assizes, the County Grand Jury formally requested the Lord Lieutenant to withdraw the 100 extra police sent to the county two years earlier during the troubles of that time.

At the Limerick quarter sessions in Newcastle West, in April, it took three days to try some those accused of petty crimes, all of whom pleaded guilty in the hope of receiving prison sentences. The following day some of those who were freed tried to break into the jail, and were arraigned for causing a riot, which resulted in at least some of them achieving their objective of incarceration. In Wicklow, at the summer quarter sessions, one magistrate described the calendar as 'fearful', yet he ascribed nine out of ten crimes to robberies committed either by workhouse inmates or those refused workhouse relief with the intent of being sent to jail for the benefit of its food rations. Throughout 1849, Mullingar jail functioned almost as an auxiliary workhouse such were the numbers who had committed petty larcenies and crimes with the intent of taking advantage of the prison dietary. By the time the summer assizes came around in 1851, there were few counties where the judges of assizes would not have agreed with their colleague in County Galway whose address to the Grand Jury viewed the county as being in a state of 'perfect peace'.[19]

One important indicator of the return of peaceful conditions was a government decision that the security situation was now so improved as to permit a visit to Ireland by Queen Victoria, postponed since the previous year, to go ahead in August. The idea was conceived largely by the Lord Lieutenant, Lord Clarendon, and although the purpose of the queen's visit was never quite defined, somewhere enshrined in it was the vague hope that it might act as a stimulus to trade and manufacture, and somehow demonstrate the existence of some kind of unity among Her Majesty's subjects.

Given the state of the country there was little appetite anywhere in Ireland for a royal visit, and public figures across the religious and political divide seethed with anticipatory resentment that the Famine and its realities would be swept under the carpet for its duration, and that the Queen's itinerary would be so structured as to prevent her from coming into contact with any of the prevailing misery. In this situation, the Catholic Archbishop of Tuam, John McHale, found himself in the highly unusual position of being in total agreement with the Tory *Dublin Evening Mail*. MacHale had refused to sign a proposed address of welcome drafted by his primate on behalf of the Catholic hierarchy because it contained no reference at all to the sufferings of the people. For its part, the *Mail* editorialized strongly against the visit, and gave wide scope to hostile correspondence, and to one letter writer in particular, who asked if it was possible that the Queen could be gratified by such a 'wretched display of wealth' as would certainly be involved in a visit 'when thousands of her subjects' were starving. The Whig landed magnates, Lords Monteagle and Fitzwilliam, refused to participate in the ceremonies. In one letter Fitzwilliam referred to the visit as a 'huge lie', given that the royal itinerary would not take the Queen anywhere near the distressed districts of Killarney, Conamara or Castlebar.[20]

At local level, eagerness for the visit was lacking also, as is evident from the lacklustre address to the Queen drafted by a number of Ennis loyalists. The only speaker at a thinly attended meeting called for this purpose, the Repealer Charles O'Connell, a cousin of the fallen Liberator, subverted its purpose by expressing to his mainly Tory audience the hope that the visit might help remove 'all those prejudices and misrepresentations . . . formerly instilled into her mind by evil councillors', and that Her Majesty 'would not allow any minsters, whether Whig or Tory, to prevent her in future from relieving their wants or redressing their grievances'. In proceedings that took just a quarter of an hour, a proposal to illuminate the town for the occasion was quickly voted down.

Despite the absence of enthusiasm, however, Victoria was received well enough on her arrival. Protestant Ireland, garrison Ireland, turned out to greet her along with those few remaining Repealers still content to muster the old operatic O'Connellite devotion to the 'little queen', all in sufficient strength to satisfy Clarendon, the royal circle and the British newspapers. It was expedient to ignore the abundant signs of widespread indifference, and the great gaps in public attendance and adulation. For the ceremonial entry to Dublin, for example, the trains from the city to Kingstown (Dún Laoghaire) brought few passengers to greet the royal party; the fifteen-minute procession was 'scant, formal, cold', containing relatively few horsemen or carriages, and no crowds followed behind. The queen's journals, on the other hand, reveal a conviction that her reception had been rapturous.[21] Although, on her instructions, the more elaborate aspects of royal ceremony were pared back for the visit – she and Albert had taken the less-expensive sea route to Ireland, and Clarendon had been solemnly informed by London that the royal couple 'did not desire State Beds' – the itinerary still abounded with expensive public occasions. The overall cost came to £2,000, almost exactly the amount of the queen's personal donation to Irish famine relief.

To smallholders clinging to their homesteads, evictees shivering in scalpeens, the emigrant multitudes or the pauper legions confined disconsolately in workhouses, the visit of Victoria and Albert was an irrelevancy that might have seemed grotesque and insulting had their circumstances been such as to allow them any real awareness of it. And although Asenath Nicholson could comment at the time that 'the age of Black Bread and pulling down houses certainly has fallen peculiarly on the reign of the Queen and her agent, John Russell', and although the visit gave rise to the once well-known derisive jingle, 'Arise, ye dead of Skibbereen/And come to Cork to see the Queen', Victoria would not be anathematized as the 'Famine Queen' until a later generation.[22]

The months following the departure of the royal couple brought the first unmistakeable signs that famine was at last waning across large parts of Ireland. In certain districts of Ulster, indeed, recovery had begun the previous autumn with the revival of the linen-weaving manufacture. Over the country at large, however, it was the potato harvest of 1849 – a good one in most places – that ensured the winter would not again be fraught with hunger. Hyper-responsive to opportunities for cost reduction, the Poor Law was the first agency in Ireland to react to these signs of improvement. Many unions embarked immediately on the wholesale discharge of supposedly able-bodied paupers, and in unions which had recently fitted out auxiliary workhouses these were closed with alacrity. To take one, perhaps extreme, example during August, over 1,000 inmates were discharged from Mullingar workhouse and by the end of September all its auxiliaries had been closed. Faced with suddenly improving circumstances, the Poor Law Commissioners were able to scrap plans for the formation of many planned new unions, and ultimately only thirty-three out of the projected fifty would be 'declared'.[23] The Commissioners, in addition, placed ever-tighter restrictions on outdoor relief and in the months following the successful harvest refused to issue any further two-month sealed orders sanctioning relief to the able-bodied.

The gradual ending of famine in many districts where these measures were taken has been charted in recent studies, including those for Leinster mentioned earlier. However, such measures were embarked on also in many other districts of the west and south, where no improvement at all took place and where inhabitants could at most hope passively that they had to be 'on the eve of better times', to use the words of Clare newspaper proprietor, John B. Knox, in [March 1850.][24] Unfortunately for such hopes, one last devastating stage of the Famine had yet to be run in these western counties – in Knox's county, recovery was more than a cruel year away. For it was overwhelmingly in these areas that the potato failed again in 1849, and that localized and partial failures would take place the following year.[25] It was in these distressed counties also that the Poor Law had been most murderous in its treatment of those entrusted to its care, and that eleven of the remaining sixteen dissolved unions had their Boards of Guardians restored in November. And it was here also that the Poor Law Commissioners' policy of choking off outdoor relief, no matter that it was later relented upon, had its most excruciating results.

Certain of the restored Boards expressed gratitude to their Vice-Guardian predecessors for the efficient conduct of union business; some indeed requested that the Vice-Guardians be continued in office. Most, however, reverted to the practices that had led to dissolution, in the same manner as those restored in March. Failure to strike adequate rates, postponement of the striking of any rate and laxity in the collection of existing rates compounded already chronic indebtedness, leading to financial crisis in union after union. In Kenmare, contractors agreed to supply meal to the workhouse only when the chairman of the Board of Guardians took personal responsibility for payment. In the Ballina and Clifden unions, as contractors refused supplies, applicants for admission to the workhouses were left outside, and in both cases, the sheriffs finally entered the workhouse premises, seizing certain union property which was auctioned off to pay off debts.[26]

In many Munster towns, the failure of the relief system was reflected in a continuation of street scenes familiar since 1846, all of them strikingly similar. They are exemplified in a description from May 1850 of Newcastle West, County Limerick, which was at that time filled with 'the most emaciated-looking beings'. Private houses and shops were 'besieged' by 'poor creatures and their children crying for the smallest morsel of food or something to purchase it'. Many were sleeping on the streets and 'frequently, at the hour of midnight, their heartrending cries are heard ...' Some had travelled from ten miles to apply for entry to the workhouse, and, having been refused, were 'unable with sheer hunger to go home'. Newcastle West, it should be added, was not one of the unions officially designated as distressed.

Such scenes did, however, become less frequent during the second half of 1850, when a definite improvement was visible almost everywhere. Notable exceptions were parts of south Tipperary, and almost the entire county of Clare. We know most about Clare largely because of the voluminous documentation left behind by the last phase of its extraordinarily prolonged agony. This began in November 1849 when three of its unions, Ennistymon, Kilrush and Scariff, were returned to the control of particularly corrupt and inept Guardian cliques. So intractable and incompetent did the Ennistymon Board prove that the Commissioners dissolved it again a year later.[27] Throughout the winter of 1849–1850, intermittent food supply crises occurred in each of these unions, as well as in the other three unions with responsibility for the county: Ennis, Gort and Limerick.

At the end of November, in Kilrush, over 11,500 outdoor paupers were left without any food at all for eleven days, the workhouse inmates living solely on turnips grown on the union farm when contractors refused to supply the workhouse. At Ennistymon, in the first week of December, a supply crisis left large crowds of relief applicants clamouring weakly outside the workhouse gates, most of them hardly able to walk. 'There they congregated in rags and tatters,' according to one witness, 'a miserable group of God's creatures, assembling with blanched cheeks, feeble limbs, sepulchral tones, and attenuated forms ... I heard one poor woman, that [clutched] with maternal affection one of her dying offspring to her bosom, pray that God would terminate her existence and let her die'. Similar episodes took place at Ennis and Scariff, and in all cases significant starvation mortality occurred in their course.

Throughout the winter and spring relief stoppages continued at intervals in the Clare unions, and individual and mass tragedies directly relating to them became commonplace. The greatest collective tragedy came at the end of December 1849, when a party of about forty starving persons from the Loop Head peninsula, returning home to the west after being refused relief at Kilrush, drowned when the ferry taking them across Poulnasherry Bay capsized. When recovered, the bodies were found to be in a pitiable state – skeletal and nude. Only one corpse was clothed, that of a young girl, which was still clad in a charity dress given her some time previously by the daughter of Captain Kennedy, the union inspector.

Individual tragedies are reflected in the surviving records of inquests post mortem, where the testimony of families and other eyewitnesses brings us about as close as it is possible to get to the experience and the state of mind of starvation victims. Their evidence is delivered very simply, yet it is charged with the unselfconscious intimacy of lost familial existences, and it is made especially poignant by the realization that the speakers will soon, in all probability, be dead themselves. Thus, the last moments of John Flanagan, who was repeatedly refused entry to the Ennis workhouse for being able-bodied, are conveyed in the words of his widow in January 1850:

> I wanted him to get up on that morning, and he desired me to get him a bed. He said he was gone, and then a weakness came on him, and he leaned his head on my lap, and desired me to get something to stretch himself on for that he could not go to Ennis. I said he must come, and was trying to bring him along with me. When we went a short distance I asked a woman for some milk. She said she had none but gave me a few halfpence . . .

Captain Kennedy's eleven-year-old daughter, distributing relief clothing in West Clare, December 1849. *Illustrated London News.*

The death of James Breene at Kilmurry McMahon is described by a Mrs. Stretton, into whose cabin the dying young man was carried one morning at the end of January. Mrs. Stretton was utterly destitute herself, and on the point of leaving her cabin for the workhouse:[28]

> My son Patt Stretton asked the deceased if he was hungry. He replied that he was hungry enough. I then gave him some bread. He took one mouthful, which he was unable to swallow; I then attempted to give him some milk with a spoon, which he was also unable to take . . . he died about four hours after bringing him in. He never spoke more words than his name and that he 'was hungry enough'.

The death of Martin Clancy in Kildysart in May is described by his sister:

> I went out and borrowed a small quantity of meal from one of my neighbours and made a small cake of it for him; he eat it and went to bed . . . on the next morning . . . he told me he did not know what to do, that he would not live with the hunger; he eat a little for breakfast on Thursday morning, and a little of supper on Friday night; My sister got a pound of meal at Kildysert on Friday, and made gruel of it mixed with nettles . . . I put some of the gruel in his mouth with a spoon. It stopped in his throat, he was not able to swallow it; he died in a short time after, before he lost his speech he told me he was weak.

What is striking in all this evidence is the kindness displayed towards the dying by family members, neighbours or even total strangers, persons who were themselves starving; an extraordinary gentleness infuses their care of the dying also. It is true that the presence of fever might well have made a difference to such behaviour, but this is something of which we can know very little since deaths from fever were considered to be from natural causes, and were not subject to investigation by inquest. In any case, such accounts furnish an important corrective to instances of callousness that official sources tend to favour for reasons of self-exculpation. In a great many cases, the inquest evidence reveals deceased persons as having recently been deprived of indoor or outdoor relief, and as having spent the intervening period travelling, either to and fro between the cabins of relatives or merely wandering in the countryside.[29] Such movements seem to reflect a wider, haphazard, disturbed perambulation of starving people and survivors through the landscape. Clearances, which were still ongoing, form part of this phenomenon also, with consequent repeated journeying in fruitless search of relief from a Poor Law system that was indifferent to suffering, and itself in a state of partial collapse.

Yet another aspect of this geographical movement of starving persons relates to the formation of new unions, four of which were declared in Clare during 1850. This involved a realignment of all union boundaries in the county, and led to a scramble on the part of individual Boards of Guardians to divest themselves of responsibility for as many paupers as possible. Inmate exchanges between principal workhouses were organized, and frequently those discharged from one house were refused admission to the one to which they were sent. In mid-April, 200 paupers who had been marched from Ennis to Ennistymon were left outside the workhouse in heavy rain for hours before being admitted for the night; early the following morning 'they were driven out without food', and effectively abandoned. Several weeks later these rejected paupers were found scattered widely over the countryside; some of the women had taken to prostitution to survive; others were rescued by the Society of St. Vincent de Paul, others again feature in inquest reports from a slightly later date.

In September, the new Corofin Board ordered the expulsion of 300 paupers from the Ennis, Ennistymon and Gort workhouses, where they had been lodged pending the completion of the Corofin workhouse. Of those expelled from Gort – forcibly, by police – eleven adult females were found a few days later by a local priest, Fr. Vaughan, moving slowly and painfully towards Corofin in the driving rain along with their children. 'I found some of them yesterday without chemises,' wrote Vaughan in an angry letter to a local newspaper, 'the little children (four of them orphans) who left with them I found . . . in almost a state of nudity; some fell on the way from exhaustion; others were taken into the cabins along the road by the wretchedly poor.'[30]

During the winter of 1850–1851, suffering in the Clare unions was aggravated by yet another localized potato failure, the entrenched misbehaviour of the various Boards of Guardians and a new savagery unleashed by exterminators in the dying throes of their clearances. Starvation mortality was again reported from all parts of the county, and fever once again swept through the workhouses, with death rates in Ennis and Kilrush workhouses reaching new heights. In Kilrush, in April 1851, the corpses of the fever dead were commonly left in the wards along with the living, and sick children were crammed four or five into a single bed, and fed on rations that were rotten. Outside the main workhouse, priests anointed the dying, sometimes 'seven at a time' in damp sheds where rainwater flowed down the warped wooden walls.

In Britain during these same months, public excitement was at fever pitch in anticipation of the opening of the Great Exhibition, a gigantic trade fair celebrating British technology and material progress, which was to be held at the purpose-built and wonderfully futuristic Crystal Palace in London. Into this atmosphere of national pride and exultation, the aristocratic English clergyman, Reverend Sidney Godolphin Osborne, intruded the realities of Irish famine in a series of letters written to *The Times*. 'When, the other day, I looked on the Crystal Palace,' he wrote in March, 'and thought of Kilrush Workhouse as I have seen it, I felt as a Christian and a subject of a Christian government, utter disgust.'[31]

Throughout 1851, the Poor Law in Clare was paralyzed by the indebtedness of all the unions operating in the county. In June creditors forced the sale of the assets of the Limerick union, thereby affecting indoor and outdoor paupers from a large stretch of southeast Clare; in November the sheriff sold off the entire contents of the Scariff workhouse (the second time this had happened), 'down to the last slop bucket'. During the auction, even the beds on which between thirty and sixty paupers lay, suffering from a variety of ailments from dysentery to xerophthalmia, were sold together with their bed clothing.[32]

In any previous year, these episodes would have presaged another winter of disease, death and human misery. That this did not happen on this occasion was something that initially went unremarked by local commentators, who perhaps had unconsciously come to accept famine as a given feature of society. But the potatoes were good in 1851 in Clare; landlord consolidations and clearances were slowly grinding to their end in the county, and these things combined with a surging emigration ensured that workhouses would not again be deluged by autumn and winter avalanches of the destitute and dying. Over the rest of Ireland, as we have seen, starvation and disease mortality had already abated, and in the course of 1850 even the distressed counties of Mayo and Galway, and much of Tipperary, finally became free of excess mortality. The Poor Law systems in these counties were again able to support themselves from the rates, as the numbers dependent on relief dropped radically; in some of the Mayo unions they declined by as much as eighty per cent.

Starvation verdicts, however, were still being recorded by inquest juries in the spring of 1851 in south Tipperary and Clare.[33] Indeed, the last starvation death of the Great Famine that it has been possible to trace in the sources comes from Ennis in the latter county at the very end of April. The victim was a stranger to the town, his name unknown to the owners of the poor lodging house in Mill Street at which he arrived on the evening of the twenty-fifth. Before descending to his bed in the cellar, the man consumed a bowl of stirabout and paid his landlady one-and-a-halfpence for his keep. The following morning, a Saturday, he again took some stirabout, and as he was leaving the landlady told him not to return, 'as she did not wish to have him in the house, since he appeared to be a very delicate man'. But when he returned in the evening she relented. As he paid her for this night's lodging with money given him by a priest, she handed him back a penny to buy milk. The following morning the man was found to be dead. Buried hurriedly the next day his body was later exhumed for the purpose of an inquest, the examining physician finding it 'very much worn and emaciated'. A starvation verdict was recorded by the inquest jury.

If the lonely death of the unknown man in the Ennis cellar brings starvation deaths in Ireland to at least a symbolic end, the Great Famine itself cannot be said to be over while Irish workhouses were still crammed with paupers – when the census was taken in March 1851, the number of inmates stood at 249,877, virtually the full indoor capacity achieved two years earlier.[34] Nor could it be said to be at an end while further tens of thousands depended entirely on meagre outdoor rations, or while fever was still likely to flame suddenly in workhouse outbreaks that were extremely expensive in human lives. Above all, Famine could not be said to be over while hundreds of thousands continued to leave Ireland each year on emigrant ships, as they did in record numbers in 1851, when a quarter of a million persons left the country. And while starvation and fever deaths had ceased by the beginning of 1852, the haemorrhage of Ireland's people would continue for many years to come.

The Murdered Sleeping Silently: Aftermath

Sad, sad is my fate in this dreary exile
Dark, dark is the night-cloud o'er lone Shanakyle
Where the murdered sleep silently, pile upon pile
In the coffinless graves of poor Erin.

– 'LONE SHANAKYLE'

As famine retreated for the last time, and people's minds were liberated from its many preoccupations, they became aware with something like shock how deserted the countryside had become. 'Good God! Where are the people gone to?', wondered one east Clare priest, gazing over his sparse Sunday congregation in November 1851. 'The first day I ever celebrated Mass here, sixteen years ago, the chapel and the yard were full to overflowing . . .' 'You could not light your pipe from Daly's Hill to Eden Street,' an Offaly smallholder wrote to a relative in the United States two years later, his literal and metaphorical way of describing an environment so emptied of people that no houses remained to afford passersby the casual customary facility of lighting their pipes from the turf fire. Also in 1853, a prosperous south Tipperary tenant sought to convey to a recently emigrated neighbour some idea of 'how lonely every place is here', with everyone leaving 'that can go to ye [in Australia] and to America'. 'I rode by your little cottage a few days ago,' he wrote sadly, 'and the thistles were growing in the middle of the road.'[1]

Years of starvation and disease, state relief, land clearance, the ministrations of the Poor Law and mass emigration had brought the country to this condition. According to the census taken in 1851, just 6,552,385 persons were now living in Ireland as compared to the 8,175,124 recorded for 1841. Estimating that the population would have topped nine million if no famine had taken place, the Census Commissioners calculated the total loss between censuses at nearly 2.5 million. Modern scholarship has calculated the numbers who died of starvation, disease and exposure during the Famine at 1.1 million, or 1.5 million if account is taken of averted births.[2] Emigration, as we have seen, accounted for over a million more, all figures necessarily being approximations which do not take account of excess mortality after March 1851, or the absence of reliable emigration figures for much of that year as a whole.

Landlord clearances and consolidations are reflected in a massive seventy-two per cent decline in the number of fourth-class houses between the censuses, with some localized variations that exceeded that average considerably. Throughout 1851 and for some years after, clearances and consolidations were still ongoing, with many evicted properties reverting to untenanted wilderness. Clearances would also continue to increase the numbers of uninhabited houses past the figure recorded in 1851, especially in urban areas where the census had returned them in some cases at ten per cent of the total stock. In the countryside, even though the very worst dwellings were no more, despite the efforts of the wreckers uninhabited buildings were still common in the early 1850s. In 1853, the young English land surveyor, Thomas Colville Scott, who had been despatched from London to value the gigantic, bankrupt Martin estate in Conamara, constantly encountered ruined dwellings on his travels. In many grisly cases the remains of their former inhabitants still lay inside the broken walls:

> Saw some hundreds of forsaken cabins on the Estate today – *sepulchres* of those who had tenanted them while living: the fallen thatched roofs were in many cases their only covering, in others the walls had also fallen in upon them, but all this did not hide from our view the whitened bones of many of the old and young who had huddled together, in these lone spots to wait for death.

The Martin estate had been extensively cleared but not consolidated properly; much of it had effectively been abandoned after the property failed to attract a buyer, and this, together with its wild remoteness, is what accounts for the ruins with which it was still littered.[3] Much of its squatter population, as Colville Scott refers to them, still lingered in the vicinity of their former homes, uncertain as to what lay in store for them under a new owner.

Fully consolidated properties were much neater than those that were merely cleared, since the houses were made uninhabitable as soon as emptied of occupiers, their stones removed to the walls enclosing the new squared-off fields. Roadside cabins had their side walls incorporated wholesale into the new boundaries, to be pointed out for generations. We know that local people followed these minutiae of the consolidation process closely from the detail with which their descendants were able to describe them nearly 100 years later. Of one Donegal townland, a collector was told:

> Bhí ballógaí a gcuid toighthe ann gur rannadh na talta agus scriosadh amach iad annsin agus rinneadh claidheacha leis na clocha agus níl lorg ar bith le fáil ortha anois. [The walls of their houses were there until the lands were divided and they were rooted out then and fences made with the stones, and there is no trace of them now.]

Hunger still lurked in these post-Famine landscapes, and on one trek through Conamara, Colville Scott's guide, a young man named Maude, was struck down by what the people of the district referred to as 'mountain famine', a condition Colville Scott found to be 'not infrequent amongst the people in these wilds' and which arose 'from a weak enervated system, and too long abstinence from food'. Three years later, when Friedrich Engels travelled from Dublin to Galway, he clearly believed that a famine was still in progress: 'I had never imagined famine could be so tangibly real,' he wrote. 'Whole villages are deserted; in between, the splendid parks of the smaller landlords [who are] virtually the only people still living there, lawyers mostly.'

In this aftermath period, in many places the silence of the Famine years still reigned, troubling to all classes, including – it appears – those landlords who bore significant responsibility for it. In 1855, when the artist and antiquarian, George Petrie, travelled the country, recording what was left of its ancient music, he was much affected by the 'awful, unwonted silence' which 'struck more fearfully upon their imaginations, as many Irish gentlemen informed me ... than any other circumstance which had been forced upon their attention'. It was a source of great disappointment to Petrie to find that the music for which he was searching was largely gone, and that the 'land of song' was 'no longer tuneful'.[4]

Petrie's account of a countryside still traumatized by the effects of famine is echoed in A.M. Sullivan's later reminiscences, where he describes the Famine as having struck 'a fatal blow at some of the most beautiful traits of Irish rural life':[5]

> It destroyed the simple confidence that bolted no door; it banished forever a custom which throughout the island was of almost universal obligation – the housing for the night, with cheerful welcome, of any poor wayfarer who claimed hospitality ... A thousand kindly usages and neighbourly courtesies were swept away ... The open-handed, open-hearted ways of the rural population have been visibly affected by the 'Forty Seven' ordeal. Their ancient sports and pastimes everywhere disappeared, and in many parts of the have never returned. The outdoor games, the hurling-match and the village dance are seen no more.

A hundred years after the blight first appeared, community recollection of these aspects of the Famine was still strong in many parts of Ireland:

> D'imthigh an spóirt agus an caitheamh aimsire. Stad an fhilidheacht agus an ceol agus an damhsa. Chaill siad agus rinne siad dearmad de iomlán, agus nuair a bhisigh an saoghal ar dhoigheannaí eile ní tháinig na rudaí seo ariamh arais mar a bhí siad. Mharbh an gorta achan rud. [Sports and pastimes went. Poetry and music and dancing stopped. They lost them all, and they forgot them entirely, and when life improved in some other ways, these things never came back as they had been. The Famine killed everything.]

Life did indeed return to normal 'in some other ways', but the pre-Famine richness of culture and community did not, and what was left was leached out with each succeeding generation as the people continued to emigrate, in a steady outpouring that bespoke the sundering of a once legendary attachment to home and parish. The emigration of the Famine years had been so extensive as to dismantle portions of entire communities and re-establish them substantially intact on the other side of the Atlantic; ever afterwards remittances sent from the new communities irresistibly lured the young with the bright prospects of a far country that yet promised much of the familiarity of home. Each successive

As the Famine ends, the social gulf remains unchanged. Here landlords prepare to ride off, watched by resentful townsfolk, 1851. Steuart Trench, *Realities of Irish Life*.

ten-year census would see the human drain from Ireland continue, until by 1901, the country's population stood at just short of 4.5 million, slightly over half the pre-Famine figure.[6] As the landscape of Ireland became ever emptier, the decline in the Irish language and its associated culture and customs continued at a rapid pace through the first half of the twentieth century. It was little wonder that in the 1940s custodians of collective memory should have abided by the judgement of their immediate ancestors that the Famine had 'killed everything'.

Those who died during the Famine came from a broad section of the lowermost strata of Irish society, the greater part of them consisting of the cottiers and labourers who perished first, and who were virtually annihilated as distinct social groups in its course. However, a large proportion of the Famine dead also came from strata that were higher up on the social scale, those for whom the Famine experience was one of progressive impoverishment over several years before they followed a similar painful path to their graves. Among them were smallholders and their families, tradesmen, shopkeepers and even elements from within the comfortable farmer sector. Relatively few of the walking skeletons of the later years of the Famine were cottiers or labourers, although a higher proportion of the gaunt denizens of workhouse systems may have been. There is no clear disjunction between Famine victims from different social strata, either those who died or those who survived, and it is from the consciousness of surviving victims, as recorded from their descendants, that the collective folk memory of the Famine derives.

Whether in Ireland or abroad, Famine survivors suffered from a variety of physical and psychological disabilities relating to their experiences, which often marked them for life, and which are all the more important for their relative invisibility to historians. Among them are 'physical and behavioural scars' carried by children as a result of starvation suffered in infancy and childhood; the trauma inflicted on those witnessing horrific events such as the deaths of family members, the brutalities of eviction, and all that went with the *via dolorosa* of emigration. To these may be added the psychological anxieties attached to participation in landlord consolidations, or the humiliation endured by those who wore the hated pauper uniform for any length of time and acquired with the garb a self-loathing that was internalized and transmitted culturally across generations. The damage inflicted by famine could be extended, indeed, to all those who were tormented by an unshakeable hatred of Britain (emigrant hatred was something of which the British government was highly conscious during and after the Famine), and who squandered the substance of their lives in hopeless attempts at revenge.

Secret society activity persists at a low level after the Famine. Artist's impression of a
'Ribbon' meeting from 1851. Steuart Trench, *Realities of Irish Life.*

For many the pain of Famine-era experiences and the shame that went with
them was so grievous that they were not among the recollections that could be
passed on to children, something that has left the oral tradition substantially
deficient in many respects in this regard. There are remarkably few instances
where elderly people remember grandparents admitting to having been workhouse inmates, for example, or to have benefited from land consolidations, to
have committed crimes against their neighbours in order to survive or to have
converted to Protestantism in order to obtain food.

What we do have are insightful stories recounting the experience of public
works and soup kitchens, the behaviour of neighbours, exemplary or dishonest,
the misconduct of landlords and land-grabbers, as well as soothing fables telling of miraculous occurrences that rescued starving families. Among the most
poignant of all are the memories related by middle-aged and elderly people
during the 1940s of their survivor grandparents rebuking them in childhood
with disproportionate anger for wasting food, or digging out potato gardens
repeatedly each autumn in obsessive search of the smallest potatoes, or bursting
into tears whenever they sat down before a smiling bowl of floury potatoes.[7]

After the Famine, Ireland would never again enjoy the social intimacy and cohesiveness for which its people had once been famous. Communal interdependence was replaced by a new familial nuclearity, and a distancing in societal relationships that brought with it a deep personal loneliness and alienation to those reared otherwise. Emigration perpetuated a spiritual and cultural weakening that, when added to continuing hunger and material deprivation, left those remaining on the land confused and demoralized. Nowhere is this more evident than in their vulnerability to the efforts made by evangelical organizations to convert them en masse to Protestantism.

The evangelical campaign was a renewal of a failed pre-Famine effort, and it was dominated, as before, by pre-millenialists, those whose objective was the eradication of popery in anticipation of the millennium which was firmly believed to be at hand, its imminence signalled by the divine visitation represented by the Famine. Although mainstream Anglicans (including most British politicians) shared the basic assumptions of the pre-millenialists, the majority balked at the morality of suborning conversion in circumstances of want. Many clergy were, however, tantalized by the prospects opened up by the Famine of finally making a breach in the devotion of the Irish to Catholicism, none more so than Rev. Frederick Trench of Skibbereen fame. In the course of his ministrations there, Trench had been struck by the fact that the lives of the poor seemed 'to be marvellously given into our hands', and while he deprecated 'in the strongest possible manner the holding out of any carnal inducements to the reception of spiritual good', he was prepared to play with its temptations, at least verbally, since 'who can tell what a blessed influence our charity may have upon their spiritual welfare!'[8]

Hard-line evangelicals headquartered at Exeter Hall in London had none of Trench's scruples, especially those associated with the Society for Irish Church Missions. Acting in concert with local Church of Ireland clergy and laity, and with older 'colonies' established in Dingle, County Kerry and Achill Island in Mayo, the Irish Church Missions aggressively pursued the objectives of the 'second reformation' from the late 1840s until the middle of the following decade. Armed with a war-chest contributed by wealthy donors in Britain, they opened or subsidized schools where the children of the poor received a basic education, along with food, clothing and, most importantly, a thorough scriptural indoctrination. Funds were allocated to self-contained convert 'colonies', and they also covered the living expenses of 'scripture readers', converts charged with a more solitary mission in urban and rural communities. Evangelical operations were extraordinarily widespread, and although they were most heavily concentrated in the west and south of the country, they had a presence also as far east as the impoverished parishes of Kilkenny and Carlow.[9]

The initial progress made by the evangelicals was remarkable, their most successful figure being the Irish Church Missions founder, Rev. Alexander Dallas, former incumbent of Wonston, Hampshire. Over a period of years, Dallas established a string of 'feeding schools' and mission stations throughout Conamara, in which the scriptural message was spread effectively through use of the Irish language. Dallas's missions, in fact, accounted for the bulk of evangelical converts, who at the height of the evangelical mission numbered somewhere in the low thousands.

If the number of converts does not seem particularly impressive, it must be remembered that the evangelicals did not at first realize that a pinnacle had been reached, and they rejoiced instead at what they saw as a beginning, a critical breakthrough that would swiftly result in mass conversions everywhere. What happened, in the event, was that over a very short time in the mid-1850s, their entire campaign faltered and died away completely. There were many reasons for this: failure to capitalize on the early gains, and the disaffection engendered among local Protestants by unscrupulous and inflammatory evangelical methods, compounded by the drying up of financial contributions from Britain, which diverted to humanitarian projects in Crimea and at the end of the decade, to the new evangelical opportunities presented by post-Mutiny India.[10] More than any of these things, however, the evangelicals were defeated by a massive counter-insurgency campaign mounted by the Catholic Church. As a result of all these factors, one after another, feeding schools and mission stations closed, most of the converts returned to the fold, and many others emigrated, until, by the early 1860s, all that remained of the 'second reformation' was Rev. Nangle's stubborn Achill colony, and a few other rump congregations where converts lived in semi-outcast status from the wider society.

While they lasted, however, evangelical operations caused great damage among the communities where they were active, causing a bitter internal conflict that was greatly disproportionate to the actual level of conversion, and that was all the more intense for the monolithic Catholicism that had obtained hitherto. For these communities, any level of conversion represented something deeply unnatural, a breach in nature as well as a breach of community solidarity. Since so many conversions had been prompted by the dictates of survival, and because of the community hatred of converts, who suffered the anguish of their own betrayal, one can only speculate as to the psychological burden carried by them. Those who conformed, regardless of whether or not they re-converted later, had to endure the opprobrium of having at one period been 'soupers' or 'jumpers', terms of deadly insult that followed their targets unrelentingly, as they did their descendants over several generations.

Two of the most valuable weapons in the arsenal of the Catholic Church in its battles against the evangelicals consisted of parochial 'missions' and teaching orders of nuns and brothers, both of which were systematically introduced to the localities. Far from retiring from the field afterwards, however, missions and orders were deployed to even greater effect in the imposition of a new devotional orthodoxy emanating from Rome in the wake of the Synod of Thurles (1850), and in ensuring that the intensified religious feeling that emerged after the Famine was maintained at a high level in the ensuing decades. Known to historians under the collective description of the Devotional Revolution, these developments were embraced by the laity with an enthusiasm that was startling even to their promoters. In parish after parish missions became the occasion of great celebration, and membership of the new devotional vehicles of confraternity and sodality enormously valued. This is best explained in terms of the spiritual yearning of a people whose culture and sense of community had been torn asunder by the discontinuities of the Famine years, their uncertainties deepened by mass emigration. Culturally, the major casualty of the process was the ancient indigenous devotional tradition of Ireland, with its rich panoply of popular practices, prayer forms, patterns and pilgrimages, which was swept away within decades, in a transformation that was in its way as radical as anything the evangelicals had aspired to.[11] Because so much of this tradition was an Irish-language one, or one heavily influenced by the language, the ultimate result was a further linguistic and cultural impoverishment.

Not surprisingly, in the immediate post-Famine period, the influence of the Catholic Church rose to unprecedented levels, the respect accorded its clergy increasing to little short of veneration. By now, indeed, the Church represented the only leadership available to the people: in politics, the Repeal movement had collapsed after O'Connell's death, and the political promise of the Young Irelanders dissolved in the aftermath of the 1848 debacle, the political talents of many insurgent leaders displayed not in Ireland, but in the different countries to which they emigrated. The resulting leadership vacuum was one the Church could fill only indirectly, and it did so during the 1850s by lending its support to the one political agitation to emerge at that time, the Tenant Right campaign, whose aim was the achievement of some kind of statutory protection for occupiers against the depredations of landlords.

Although as a concept Tenant Right pre-dated the Famine, and occasioned some limited activism early in 1847, it was only in the early 1850s that it became the focus of a political agitation. Briefly, the movement constituted the uniting principle of a reorganized Irish party in Westminster, before petering out a few years later in division and minor scandal. Division and scandal might have been the triggering factors, but the major underlying reason for the collapse was that as an objective Tenant Right was too limited to form the basis of a national project, and its potential beneficiaries too narrowly confined to the large farmers who formed its only real support base, at least in the south of the country. The Presbyterian Tenant Righters in the northern counties, who were for a time their uneasy allies in the so-called League of North and South, represented another quantity altogether. To this extent, therefore, the Tenant Right movement can be seen as an early attempt at political assertion by large farmers, a group which was to have an important influence on Irish life over the next century.

Historically, the attitudes and behaviour of larger farmers have lent them an especially unattractive profile, especially at the more elevated levels where they shaded into middlemen. Before the Famine, larger farmers were notably harsh in their dealings with bound and unbound labourers, whose violent reaction is reflected in a sizeable proportion of reported outrage at that time. During 1846 and 1847 this harshness was displayed in the summary termination of conacre agreements, and the merciless expulsion of labourers that followed, in at least a proportion of instances. Many large farmers, we know, shared the landlord tendency of having their own sub-tenants placed on public works, and as elected Poor Law Guardians, many wholeheartedly approved the most heartless restrictions on relief in order to minimize their own tax liabilities.

On the other hand, attempts to present the large farmers as subsidiary villains of the Famine piece fall short on a number of counts. Apart from the difficulties attached to identifying such a widely diverse grouping as a single societal entity to which set characteristics can be attached, there is also the strange absence of any consistent evidence that large farmers evicted their conacre tenants on the same systematic, ruthless basis the landlords did. On the other hand, there is quite an amount of testimony that at all stages of the Famine a great number of those referred to in the sources as large farmers afforded charity to the starving in very significant, unpublicized amounts.

But however we define them, large farmers certainly advanced their position greatly in the post-Famine period. Apart from those who prospered on improved livestock and grain prices towards the end of the Famine (Wexford farmers seem to have done particularly well here), there were others who benefited from landlord consolidations, and others so advantageously placed as to be able to purchase their holdings under the Incumbered Estates Acts. It was the large farmers who led the general shift from tillage to pastoral agriculture, which had begun before the Famine and accelerated in its course and afterwards, and who gained most advantage from it. No longer tied to primitive barter relationships with bound and unbound labourers, they lodged the profits of livestock sales complacently in the provincial banks that flourished during the 1850s.

Into their lower ranks were assimilated prospering gombeen men and the under-agents and drivers whose service with evicting landlords was rewarded by the granting of comfortable farms. From the younger sons of the large farmer class emerged the Catholic professional classes of the later century who established lasting dynasties in towns and villages throughout Ireland. To the large farmers it is possible to ascribe much of the new conservatism of Irish society, and theirs certainly were the dominating values relating to the acquisition, management and transmission of land by inheritance. Other values noted by A.M. Sullivan as charac-teristic of the post-Famine period were also theirs, including a 'greater seriousness of character', as well as 'providence, forethought, economy', and a greater 'method, strictness and punctuality in business transactions' than had existed before.

Large farmers were among the most shining upholders of the new Catholic devotional orthodoxy which transformed Irish society in the second half of the nineteenth century, ingesting (as did all Irish Catholics) the most suffocating norms of Victorian respectability and moral prudery. That they did so was hardly accidental since it was from among the large farmer class, after all, that the Irish Church recruited the greater part of its clerical personnel.[12]

If post-Famine Ireland was a smaller, more conservative, less differentiated, and in most respects a less interesting place than pre-Famine Ireland, this is in some measure due to the fact that it was no longer the only Ireland. The Famine emigrations meant that Ireland could now be said to exist on three continents and even more jurisdictions; continuing heavy emigration would see a constant enriching of overseas Ireland at the expense of the mother country. From now on the history of Ireland and the destination countries of its emigrants would be heavily intertwined, and despite the fact that emigration was almost exclusively a one-way process, the economic backwash, in the form of emigrant remittances, would be significant in sustaining the fortunes of a declining country for well over a hundred years more.

The cultural backwash from emigration would also be significant, and as regards purely Irish emigrant communities, it is tellingly illustrated in the vast body of emigrant songs composed abroad, but sung mostly in Ireland. That these compositions served the function of comforting the exile is evident from the fact that most carry an idealized view of Ireland; relatively few contain either Famine themes or the sentiments of hatred towards Britain which we know most emigrants carried with them. (Most of those that do are music-hall or political productions written much later.) *Lone Shanakyle*, the well-known west Clare song, composed by a Famine emigrant named Thomas Madigan, is an exception,

Although clearly derivative, these images from a French-language newspaper (1854) show an interesting international perception of continuing Irish misery after the Famine. *L'Illustration Journal Universel.*

but even in this song, only one stanza, that which begins this chapter, is Famine-referential. This is where Madigan evokes the huge grave-pits of Shanakyle graveyard outside Kilrush where thousands of the victims of Colonel Vandeleur, Marcus Keane and other exterminators lie 'sleeping silently'.

Documentary sources for the demoralized and dull Ireland of the 1850s and 1860s yield very few retrospective references to the Great Famine. A topic too well known to require rehearsal, it was also too recent and painful to be a subject for discussion. Not until a full generation had passed was the Famine dealt with in a historical work – Canon John O'Rourke's, *History of the Great Irish Famine of 1847* (1874) – and not until the advent of a new agrarian-political agitation a few years later were bitter Famine memories reviewed extensively in public for the first time.[13]

The two men whose partnership in the leadership of the new movement accounts largely for the success it achieved, Michael Davitt and Charles Stewart Parnell, were both born during the Famine, both in 1846. Davitt was born in a smallholder's cabin in County Mayo, Parnell, a few months later in the comparative luxury of a County Wicklow landlord mansion. Whether anything is to be made of the time of their birth is unsure, but as in the case of a third Famine-born individual, Michael Cusack (born in north Clare in 1847), destined for national leadership in the very different area of athletics and field games, the significant fact is probably their distance from the Famine generation, in that they came to adulthood unaffected directly by it, yet with sufficient imparted knowledge of its horrors, injustices and outcomes to impassion their own engagement.

Davitt, Parnell and Cusack each represent separate strands of what might broadly be called the great national rehabilitation that took place in Ireland at the end of the nineteenth century. What was involved here was a series of discrete but interacting movements involving culture, language revival, literature, politics, sport, agricultural co-operation, trade unionism, and many other areas that together raised the self-esteem of the Irish people after decades of demoralization. One of the most intriguing aspects of this national revival relates to the role played in it by individuals belonging broadly to what was still known as the Protestant ascendancy, the social elite many would have seen as responsible for much of the misery of the Famine. Although active in many areas, it was in cultural matters that their contribution achieved particular brilliance, including as it did the achievements of literary figures such as W.B. Yeats and Lady Augusta Gregory, scholars such as Douglas Hyde, antiquarians such as Thomas Johnson Westropp, and many more. Again it is uncertain what significance can be attached to all this; if there is any it is likely to be endlessly complex and difficult to pin down. However, there is something very strange about the fact that three of the four mentioned above, who are among the most beloved figures of modern Irish history, have uncomfortably close connections with the Famine: Lady Gregory of Coole, widow of Sir William Gregory of Gregory Clause notoriety; Douglas Hyde, first President of Ireland, son of a Famine-era evangelical clergyman, and T.J. Westropp, son of a County Limerick landlord heavily involved in evictions.

Broadly speaking, two great failures lie at the heart of Ireland's Great Famine, that of private charity and of state relief, and an examination of each helps explain why the astonishing medieval anachronism of a colossal famine took place in a country ruled by its neighbour, the richest, most powerful, most advanced nation on earth, even as that nation was preparing to celebrate its achievements in the Great Exhibition of 1851. Of the two, private charity has received less attention from historians, and we are still not in a position to say exactly how much money was contributed, if we ever will. Private charity, after all, was a wide and diverse phenomenon, ranging from innumerable individual private acts, to local contributions to relief committees, and the major international attempts at collecting money and food for dispatch to Ireland.

The international effort, which we are most concerned with here, began late in 1846 when news of the second failure of the potato led to a great surge in sympathy for the Irish poor. All over Europe and beyond, money was solicited, pledged and collected in small and large sums, led by contributions from world personalities including the president of the United States, the papacy, the British monarch, and the Sultan of Turkey. In many countries, whole cities and towns became engaged in collecting sums which were then forwarded to Ireland through various organizations. To the fore in this great endeavour were the United States, and some 118 relief shiploads of food sailed from American ports across the Atlantic to Ireland – two of the vessels, *Macedonian* and *Jamestown*, warships lent for the purpose by the U.S. government.[14] At the other end of the scale there were the contributions made by ordinary citizens, as well as from exiled Irish communities, and remittances sent by relatives in Britain, the United States and Australia, remittances constituting the greatest single form of non-state relief during the Famine. Among the most moving of all the contributions in this international effort, perhaps, were the small amounts contributed by former slaves in the West Indies, and the £170 sent by the Choctaw tribe of native Americans who were stirred to compassion by the similarities between Irish suffering and their own 'Trail of Tears', a forced population transfer from Mississippi to Oklahoma in 1831 in which thousands had died.

A number of factors, however, lessened the impact of private charity, in its organized and individual forms. One was that it was at its greatest extent during

1847, when international food prices were at an unprecedentedly high level, and the purchasing power of donations proportionately less than would have been the case at other times. Another was that relief often did not get to the remotest, most stricken areas and the manner in which much aid was distributed, in piecemeal donations of barrels of rice or wheat, which were often not renewed in the same locations, did no more than prolong the agony for many of the starving.

Another again, as we have seen, was that organized private charity originating in Britain slowed rapidly during 1847, largely as a reaction to the influx of destitute Irish refugees to British cities, with contributions drying up entirely in the wake of the July uprising of 1848. In the United States, the arrival of multitudes of starving immigrants had a similar effect on public attitudes towards relief, reinforcing an already strong anti-Irish nativism; remaining resources tended to be applied to the relief of the immigrants rather than sent to Ireland. As for the international relief campaign mounted by the Catholic Church, one of the most extensive of all, this came adrift when the papacy fell foul of the international revolutions of 1848, and was no longer in a position to maintain its international collections. Despite this, however, by 1850, the Catholic Church campaign was the only one still in being. By that time, the only major organization still actively organizing relief collections was the Society of St. Vincent de Paul, its personnel in many countries still channelling donations through individual 'conferences' in Ireland towards the starving. Modest and indefatigable, St. Vincent de Paul workers laboured inconspicuously to the end of the Famine and in its aftermath, avoiding any publicity or recognition more than was necessary for the solicitation of further donations.[15]

The failure of private charity at a time when the British state had withdrawn from relief is one of the reasons why a second peak in disease and famine mortality was reached in 1849 – in many parts of the country, one that was worse than in 1847. It was largely for this reason that the hundreds of thousands expelled from their homes by landlords at the end of the Famine were not reached by organized relief of any kind, no more than those legions of others rejected by the Poor Law as not being worthy objects of relief.

In regard to state relief, what is immediately striking is that proportionate to the resources of the United Kingdom, of which Ireland had technically been an integral part since 1801, it was abysmally small in volume. Altogether, the Treasury spent some £8,000,000 on relief programmes in Ireland, most of it consisting of advances on loans that it was intended should be repaid, and on which instalment payments amounting to something less than £1,000,000 were paid before the remainder was written off in 1853 as uncollectible. This expenditure did not stretch the financial resources of the British state to any degree, let alone the immeasurably greater ones of the empire, and it is put into perspective by comparison with the £20,000,000 compensation paid to former West Indian slave-owners in 1833, and the £69,000,000 cost of the Crimean War of 1854–1856. A large proportion of the sums spent by the state in relief, in addition, was swallowed up in administrative costs, which soared with the proliferation of generously paid officials, whose functions revolved around the restricting of relief rather than making it available. The results of this policy have been amply illustrated throughout this book.

Explanations of the general behaviour of the British state in regard to the Famine under two successive governments have centred on their adherence to political economy, with its emphasis on non-interference with the free market. Contemporaries well understood the impact of government ideological obsession, and the most common accusation made by critics of the Whig-Liberal regime, in particular, was that the Irish poor were being killed by political economy. It has taken modern historians, however, and especially Peter Gray, to demonstrate that the ideological framework was part of a wider set of beliefs shared across the British political spectrum, including the conviction that the Famine had been sent by providence, and that it furnished the British state with both the opportunity and the moral responsibility to reform Ireland thoroughly. Political economy, therefore, combined with 'providentialist' and 'moralist' views, furnished the assumptions underlying the decision-making of the small London-based political elite whose views translated into legislation for Ireland, and none of whom ever witnessed its effects at first hand.

The analyses of Gray and other historians help us understand the extent to which Tory and Whig-Liberal relief policies were qualitatively the same, the differences between them relating not to the question of what should be done, but to the size of the challenge faced by each, and the accident of being in office at a particular time to face it.[16] Whig-Liberal policies, indeed, could not have been implemented without the support of the Peelite Tories in the years following Peel's fall from office. If the ideological commitment of the Whig-Liberals was stronger to begin with, it was enhanced even further by the closeness of their relationship with Charles Trevelyan, the most entrenched ideologue of them all. Whig-Liberal determination to act accordingly, as Gray has shown, is evident in a series of didactic letters sent to the Dublin administration by Charles Wood, the Chancellor of the Exchequer, immediately on coming to office, in which he declared the Irish crisis to be 'neither accidental nor temporary', but rather the 'necessary harbinger of a "social revolution" in Ireland', and that the 'present habit of dependence on Government' found among landlords in Ireland as among occupiers would have to be ended forthwith.

Arguing on much the same lines, Christine Kinealy takes the idea of the 'moral revolution' back to pre-Famine Whig-Liberal notions of social engineering, particularly as they underlay the original Poor Law of 1838. The purpose of the Poor Law was two-fold, that of relieving destitution and of 'playing a vital role in the transition of the Irish economy from a subsistence-based one to one based on wages and capitalised agriculture'. The amended Poor Law of 1847, Kinealy has shown, represented the implementation of the second of these objectives, under which advantage was taken of the opportunity presented by famine to take the first step of driving occupiers off the land. Kinealy's analysis, indeed, could usefully be extended to official policy on emigration, and the very inaction of government on the issue perhaps interpreted as one enormous passive act of social engineering.[17]

Two further points have an important bearing on British government behaviour in relation to the Great Famine. One is that the social engineering of Ireland's population by the British state, and before that its English predecessor, already had a long history by 1845. That history extends as far back at least as those early modern writers whose schemes for the reconstruction of Irish society take up so many sixteenth and seventeenth-century State Papers. The assumptions of barbarousness and backwardness that underlie these early schemes are not that far removed from those of moralizing nineteenth-century political economists, and the demographic catastrophes that followed attempts at implementation in the great Tudor and Stewart plantations prefigure interestingly what happened in the nineteenth.

Above all, the indifference of the promoters of these early modern schemes to the human consequences that arose out of them strikes a familiar tone, as does the belief expressed by military officers in 1652 during the Commonwealth cataclysm that Ireland was to be likened to a blank sheet, 'ready to have anything writt in it that the state shall think fit'.[18] It is hardly stretching the evidence to see the ultimate outcome of these previous experiments in social engineering as the very structure of nineteenth century Irish society, whose condition so exercised the minds of moralizing political economists.

The other point relates to the extent to which government adherence to ideological prescriptions during the Famine served as a mere mask for the deep-seated anti-Irish racism that pervaded British society at all levels, a phenomenon as complex in its nature and historical causation as the anti-African American racism that lay at the heart of society in the United States. It was Trevelyan's belief, for example, that the 'great evil' in Ireland was not the Famine, but the 'selfish, perverse and turbulent character of the people', a view shared by cabinet members such as Palmerston, Lansdowne, and Stanley, great absentee magnates who were currently expressing it in more practical fashion on their Irish properties. The Prime Minister, Lord John Russell, was of a similar mind, and in November 1847 told Clarendon that 'starvation has arisen from the misconduct of the Irish ... on the spot, not from any neglect on the part of government'. His reaction to a proposal made two years later that occupiers should be compensated in some fashion for eviction, that 'you might as well propose that a landlord compensate the rabbits for the burrows they have made', fairly reeks of racist contempt.[19]

The views of the political establishment reflected that of the public at large, and by the autumn of 1848, according to Gray, 'a broad swathe of British opinion was convinced that mass starvation was inevitable in Ireland, and should not be prevented'.[20] Remarks made by those few individuals who were close to the seat of power and who disagreed with these views are all the more persuasive as to their effect on policy. Thus, Lord Clarendon, who as Lord Lieutenant of Ireland was technically a member of government and in many senses a reactionary (his solution to distress was to 'sweep Connacht clean' through emigration), by the end of the Famine violently opposed government policies, which he held meant only that 'the right thing to do was to do nothing', and that Ireland was being sacrificed to a belief in 'natural causes'. 'I cannot get rid of a very strong impression I entertain,' wrote the well-connected philanthropic aristocrat, Rev. Sidney Godolphin Osborne, about the same time, 'that there has been a disposition to look at the difficulty of the crisis in these respects as so great, that there was a sort of tacit determination to let things take their course, at any cost.'

Was it this 'tacit determination' in political and administrative circles that ensured that the mass death of the Irish poor was acceptable as the price of reform? Is it this tacit determination that lies behind the strange equanimity of the Census Commissioners of 1851 in assessing the results of the Famine? Following their conclusion that the population of Ireland had been diminished 'in so remarkable a manner by famine, disease and emigration between 1841 and 1851, and has been since decreasing', the Commissioners are yet able to state, blandly, that 'the results of the Irish Census of 1851 are, on the whole, so satisfactory, demonstrating as they do the general advancement of the country'.[21]

Whether or not British government behaviour during the Famine can be described as genocide is something that hangs largely on definitions. Since the mid-twentieth century, the term 'genocide' has attached itself so completely to the holocaust perpetrated by the Nazis as to change and confine the meaning of the term; and if genocide is taken to signify the deliberate, systematic annihilation of an entire ethnic or religious group by mass murder, there is no nineteenth-century equivalent that applies anywhere. However, if it is defined as the deliberate, systematic use of an environmental catastrophe to destroy a people under the pretext of engineering social reform, then there is certainly a case to be answered.

At the very least, a uniquely hideous humanitarian crime was committed upon a defenceless people. During the Great Famine, the 'emerging people' of Elizabeth Smith's description were shattered by a succession of mortal blows that began with the failure of their potatoes, and continued subsequently in the actions and omissions of the British state charged with their relief. By 1852 the Irish population had been thinned to a tractable remnant, and all Britain's irrational fears regarding the country reduced to a manageable level; never again would a brimming Irish population pose the sociological and political threat that it had before 1845. In the circumstances in which they found themselves in 1852, the survivors of the Great Famine, in Ireland and overseas, could be forgiven for failing to observe fine semantic distinctions as to the exact meaning of the term 'genocide', and it is in terms of their state of mind that John Mitchel's comment, that 'the Almighty, indeed, sent the potato blight, but the English sent the Famine', should be understood. Perhaps it is only Mitchel's notoriously intemperate nature that continues to obscure the fact that only the first part of this famous remark can now be said to be demonstrably inaccurate.[22]

Source Notes

PROLOGUE

Source is based on Ciarán Ó Murchadha, 'The Ballycoree Monster Meeting', in *The Other Clare*, vol. xxxii (2008).

CHAPTER ONE

We must always remember that these are but an *emerging* people, civilising a little too rapidly to improve *equally* as they proceed.

Extract from diary of landlord's wife, Elizabeth Smith, Baltiboys, County Wicklow, 12 July 1846. Source: Pelly, Patricia and Tod, Andrew (eds.), *The Highland Lady in Ireland: Elizabeth Grant of Rothiemurchus: The Highland Lady in Ireland, Journals 1840–1850* (Edinburgh, 1990), p. 235.

CHAPTER TWO

Mo mhíle slán do na fataí bána
Ba subhach an áit a bheith in aice leo
Ba fáilí soineannta iad ag tíocht chun láithreach,
Agus iad ag gáirí linn ar cheann an bhoird
[A long farewell to the white potatoes
How great the happiness they could afford
How glad they made us when they came before us
With faces smiling at us from the board]

Lines from song/poem, *Na Fataí Bána*, by Galway smallholder-poet, Peatsaí Ó Callanáin of Craughwell (1791–1465). Source: Seán Ó Ceallaigh, (eag.), *Filíocht na gCallanán: Peatsaí Ó Callanáin, 1791–1865 agus Marcas Ó Callanáin, 1789–1846* (Baile Atha Cliath, 1967), p. 67; contemporary translation by Thomas Chapman, cited in Cormac Ó Gráda, *An Drochshaol: Béaloideas agus Amhráin* (Baile Atha Cliath, 1994), p. 52.

CHAPTER THREE

I passed from Cork to Dublin, and this doomed plant bloomed in all the luxuriance of an abundant harvest. Returning on the third instant, I beheld with sorrow one wide waste of putrefying vegetation. In many places the wretched people were seated on the fences of their decaying gardens, wringing their hands and wailing bitterly the destruction that had left them foodless.

Extract from letter by Fr. Theobald Mathew to Charles Trevelyan, Assistant Secretary of the Treasury, 7 August 1846. Source: *Correspondence from July 1846 to January 1847, Relating to the Measures Adopted for the Relief of the Distress in Ireland*, Commissariat Series (London, 1847), p. 4.

CHAPTER FOUR

On yesterday, all without exception were dismissed from the public works . . . the new committee has not as yet . . . distributed a single ration to the starved multitude who have been for weeks waiting on them. This district will be one vast graveyard and afford a most beautiful illustration of the blessed effects of political economy.

From the 'death census' compiled in his locality by Fr. Philip Fitzgerald, Catholic Curate of Callan, read out at a meeting of the Repeal Association in Conciliation Hall, Dublin, on 3 May. Source: William Nolan, 'The Famine in Slieveardagh', in Michael O'Dwyer, (ed.), *The Famine in the Kilkenny/Tipperary Region: A History of the Callan Workhouse and Poor Law Union, 1845–1852* (Kilkenny, 1998), p. 84.

CHAPTER FIVE

Yet the tottering gait, emaciated frames and the livid countenances of the poor creatures but too truly evince the direst destitution. The truth is they are crammed into pest houses in order that they may perish and taxation diminish. Every spare house . . . that could be at all rendered fit for the purpose is taken as an 'auxiliary', even cowsheds are pressed into service.

Extract from a letter written by Fr. Mathias McMahon, Catholic Curate, Ballybunion, to the *Nation* newspaper, dated 28 April 1850, referring specifically to workhouses and auxiliaries. Cited in Micheál Ó Ciosáin, *Cnoc an Fhomhair* (Magh Nuad, 1988), p. 184.

CHAPTER SIX

Many have been turned off by process of law to seek asylum by the neighbouring ditches, the high canopy of heaven their shelter, the green sward their couch, the stars in their firmament their watch-light, and the scarecrow and skeleton dogs keeping their vigil close by the dying.

Extract from editorial in Mayo newspaper, *The Telegraph*, 6 October 1847. Cited in Ivor Hamrock, *The Famine in Mayo, 1845–1850: A Portrait from Contemporary Sources* (Castlebar, 2004), p. 117.

CHAPTER SEVEN

Let the Irish hail with joy the day they land on a foreign shore; leave this land of plagues, and go where fortune, honour and independence await them – where their remains will be interred in consecrated ground, surrounded by their families, relatives and friends, weeping and thanking the Lord that their corpses are not exposed to the ravages of dogs and swine.

Extract from letter written to the editor of the *Limerick and Clare Examiner* by 'An Observer', dated Miltown Malbay, 6 January 1849, published 10 January 1849.

CHAPTER EIGHT

Is there no mercy for the doomed people? Are we exiled from humanity? Or rather is it exiled from us?

Extract from a letter to the editor of the *Limerick and Clare Examiner* by 'A Resident', Kilrush, dated 11 June 1850, published 15 June 1850.

CHAPTER NINE

Sad, sad is my fate in this dreary exile
Dark, dark is the night-cloud o'er lone Shanakyle
Where the murdered sleep silently, pile upon pile
In the coffinless graves of poor Erin.

Lines from 'Lone Shanakyle', a song still sung in west Clare. Source is the version found in Mick Moloney, *Far from the Shamrock Shore: The Story of Irish-American Emigration Through Song* (New York, 2002), p. 10.

Notes

References are grouped together under each number in the order of the textual superscripts. A full stop indicates the end of a separate reference; a semi-colon a separate part of same reference. Repetition of a source note shortly after a first one, with the same or a different page number, indicates referencing of a separate point. In each case a recognizable abbreviation is used. Full references will be found in the bibliography.

Notes to Chapter One: An Emerging People: The Pre-Famine Irish

1 De Beaumont, *Ireland*, p. 128, cited in Woodham-Smith, *Great Hunger*, p. 19. Cited in Quinn, *Father Mathew's Crusade*, p. 126.
2 Inglis, *Journey through Ireland* (1836), pp. 4–5; Nicholson, *Ireland's Welcome*, p. 25; Thackeray, *Irish Sketchbook*, p. 138; Clare, *Young Irishman's Diary*, p. 56. Coleman, *Roscommon*, p. 11.
3 Donnelly, *Great Irish Potato Famine*, p. 7. De Beaumont, *Ireland*, pp. 128–129; see also Quinn, *Fr. Mathew's Crusade*, p. 126. Marnane, 'South Tipperary on the Eve of the Great Famine', in *Tipperary Historical Journal*, vol. viii, p. 27. Crawford, 'Cavan', in Gillespie, *Cavan*, p. 142. *Belfast Penny Journal*, 19 July 1845, cited in Killen, *Famine Decade*, p. 32.
4 Killen, *Famine Decade*, p. 22; Nicholson, *Ireland's Welcome*, p. 296. Ó Gráda, *Ireland Before and After the Famine*, p. 15. Niall Ó Ciosáin, 'Boccoughs and God's Poor', in Foley and Rider, *Ideology and Ireland*, p. 93.
5 Woodham-Smith, *Great Hunger*, p. 31; Bourke, *Visitation*, pp. 111–113.
6 Ó Grada, *Black '47*, p. 55; Bourke, *Visitation*, pp. 98–99.
7 Larkin, *Alexis de Tocqueville's Journey*, p. 7. Donnelly, *Captain Rock*, p. 12. *Devon Commission, Digest of Evidence*, vol. i, p. 364; Griffith to Jones, 19 December 1846, *Correspondence, Board of Works Series*, p. 400.

8   Reader, *Propitious Esculent*, pp. 21–22.

9   Crawford, 'Cavan', in Gillespie, *Cavan*, p. 147. Ó Gráda, *Ireland Before and After the Famine*, p. 18; Woodham-Smith, *Great Hunger*, pp. 24–25. Ó Gráda, *Ireland Before and After the Famine*, p. 10; Bourke, *Visitation*, p.100.

10 Ó Gráda, *Ireland Before and After the Famine*, p. 10. Hannigan, 'Wicklow', in Hannigan and Nolan, *Wicklow*, p. 791.

11 McCabe, *Mayo*, p. 94. *Devon Commission, Digest of Evidence*, vol. ii, pp. 753–756. Hannigan, 'Wicklow, in Hannigan and Nolan, *Wicklow*, p. 806; Grace, *Nenagh*, pp. 6–7.

12 Bourke, *Visitation*, pp. 65–67. Donnelly, *Captain Rock*, p. 12. Donnelly, *Landlord and Tenant*, p. 5. Bourke, *Visitation*, p. 98. McCabe, *Mayo*, p. 109; Killen, *Famine Decade*, p. 27.

13 Larkin, *Alexis de Tocqueville's Journey*, p. 73. McCabe, *Mayo*, pp. 100–102. *Devon Commission, Digest of Evidence*, vol. i, p. 2. Larkin, *Alexis de Tocqueville's Journey*, pp. 26–31.

14 Donnelly, 'Whiteboy Movement', in *Irish Historical Studies*, vol. xxi, pp. 20–54; Bartlett, *Fall and Rise of the Irish Nation*, pp. 53–54, 69–70.

15 Clare, *Young Irishman's Diary*, p. 32. *Devon Commission, Digest of Evidence*, vol. i, pp. 324–329. Grace, *Nenagh*, pp. 184–185; Marnane, 'South Tipperary on the Eve of the Great Famine', in *Tipperary Historical Journal*, vol viii. vol. viii, pp. 7, 35–40.

16 McMahon, 'Homicide Rates in Ireland, 1831–1850', in *Irish Economic and Social History*, vol. xxxvi, p. 19. Murphy (ed.) and Nicholson, *Annals*, p. 118; Clare, *Young Irishman's Diary*, p. 33. Inglis, *Journey*, p. 225.

17 Scott (ed.), *Hall's Ireland*, vol. ii, p. 447. Ó Gráda, *Black '47*, p. 216.

18 Ní Dheá, 'Micheál Ó Raghallaigh', in *The Other Clare*, vol. xvi, p. 18. Buttimer, 'A Stone on the Cairn', in Morash and Hayes, *Fearful Realities*, p. 101. Coyne, *Scenery and Antiquities of Ireland*, p. 301.

19 Murphy, *Diocese of Killaloe 1800–1850*, pp. 280–300. Connolly, *Priests and People*, pp. 182–183.

20 Caesar Otway, *Sketches in Erris and Tyrawley* (1850), cited in Hickey and Doherty, *Dictionary of Irish History*, pp. 461–462.

21 Mathias, *First Industrial Nation*, p. 449. Lee, 'Pre-Famine Irish Censuses', in Goldstrom and Clarkson, *Irish Population*, p. 54. Kinealy, *Death-Dealing Famine*, p. 30.

22 Kinealy, *Death-Dealing Famine*, pp. 29–30; Thompson, *Making of the English Working Class*, p. 429. Mathias, *First Industrial Nation*, p. 449.

23 Donnelly, *Great Irish Potato Famine*, pp. 6–8; Dooher and Kennedy, *Fair River Valley*, pp. 167–168.

24 Hall and Hall, *Ireland*, 422. Coyne, *The Scenery and Antiquities of Ireland* (1842), p. 301.

25 Pelly and Tod, *Highland Lady*, p. 235. Ó Gráda, *Ireland Before and After the Famine*, p. 15.

26 Nicholls, *History of the Irish Poor Law*, pp. v, 153-154; Kinealy, *Great Irish Famine*, pp. 106-107.

27 Kinealy, 'The Role of the Poor Law during the Famine', in Póirtéir, *Great Irish Famine*, pp. 105-106; Kinealy, *Great Calamity*, pp. 13-16; Crawford, 'Cavan', in Gillespie, *Cavan*, p. 150, Ó Cathaoir, 'Wicklow', in Hannigan and Nolan, *Wicklow*, p. 516.

28 Cited in MacAtasney, *This Dreadful Visitation*, p. 6. Burke, *People and Poor Law*, p. 46.

29 Dooher, 'Growth and Development of Strabane', in Dooher and Kennedy, *Fair River Valley*, p. 166. Ó Murchadha, *Sable Wings*, p. 24. McAtasney, *This Dreadful Visitation*, p. 4. O'Brien, 'New Poor Law', in *Irish Economic and Social History*, vol. xii, p. 39.

30 McArthur, 'Medical History', in Edwards and Williams, *Great Famine*, p. 292. Kinealy, *Great Calamity*, p. 25. McDowell, 'Ireland on the Eve of Famine', in Edwards and Williams, *Great Famine*, p. 49.

31 Bourke, *Visitation*, pp. 27-29; Ó Grada, *Ireland Before and After the Famine*, pp. 12-14. Bourke, *Visitation*, pp. 22, 39-42.

32 Eiríksson, 'Food Supply and Food Riots', in Ó Gráda, *Famine 150*, pp. 75-76. Ó Gráda, *Ireland Before and After the Famine*, p. 5; Ó Murchadha, 'Years of the Great Famine', in Lynch and Nugent, *Clare: History and Society*, p. 245.

Notes to Chapter Two: A Long Farewell to the White Potatoes: The Coming of the Blight

1 Killen, *Famine Decade*, pp. 30-31, 33, cited in Woodham-Smith, *Great Hunger*, p. 38; Swords, *In Their Own Words*, p. 21. Ó Murchadha, *Sable Wings*, p. 29; Woodham-Smith, *Great Hunger*, p. 38; Grace, *Nenagh*, p. 41; O'Neill, 'Famine in Offaly', in Nolan and O'Neill, *Offaly*, p. 684.

2 Nelson, *Cause of the Calamity*, p. 5; Dowley, 'Potato and Late Blight', in Ó Gráda, *Famine 150*, p. 57. O'Neill, 'Administration of Relief', in Edwards and Williams, *Great Famine*, p. 210; Swords, *In Their Own Words*, pp. 18-19. Parkhill, 'Famine in Londonderry', in Kinealy and Parkhill, *Famine in Ulster*, p. 147.

3 Grace, *Nenagh*, p. 41. O'Neill, 'Famine in Offaly', in Nolan and O'Neill,

Offaly, pp. 685, 721. O'Regan, 'First Responses to Blight', in Cowman and Brady, *Famine in Waterford*, p. 33.

4   Swords, *In Their Own Words*, p. 20; Ó Murchadha, 'Onset of Famine', p. 46. Swords, *In their Own Words*, pp. 19, 25; Grace, *Nenagh*, p. 43; Conaghan, *South-West Donegal*, p.16. Swords, *In Their Own Words*, pp. 18–19.

5   Swords, *In their Own Words*, p. 19. Killen, *Famine Decade*, p. 37; Conaghan, *South-West Donegal*, p. 16.

6   Dooher, *Strabane*, in Dooher and Kennedy, *Fair River Valley*, pp. 170–171; Grant, 'Tyrone', in Dillon and Jefferies, *Tyrone*, p. 587. Kinealy and Parkhill, *Famine in Ulster*, p. 5. Bourke, *Visitation*, p. 157. Swords, *In Their Own Words*, pp. 19, 20.

7   Hickey, *West Cork*, pp. 142–144; Ó Murchadha, *Sable Wings*, p. 34; O'Brien, *Mullingar*, p. 13. Pelly and Tod, *Highland Lady*, p. 205. O'Neill, 'Famine in Offaly', in Nolan and O'Neill, *Offaly*, p. 685.

8   Swords, *In Their Own Words*, pp. 23–25, 129–131; Conaghan, *South-West Donegal*, pp. 21, 23, 26. Nolan, *Callan*, p. 80.

9   Swords, *In Their Own Words*, p. 22. Hickey, *West Cork*, pp. 142–145. Ó Murchadha, *Sable Wings*, p. 34.

10 Swords, *In Their Own Words*, p. 22. Hickey, *West Cork*, pp. 142–145. Ó Murchadha, *Sable Wings*, pp. 34, 38, 40.

11 Nowlan, *Politics of Repeal*, p. 96; Woodham-Smith, *Great Hunger*, pp. 48–49. Ó Murchadha, *Sable Wings*, p. 34.

12 Gray, *Famine, Land and Politics*, pp. 96, 104; Woodham-Smith, *Great Hunger*, pp. 41–43.

13 Gray, *Famine, Land and Politics*, pp. 96–97. Nelson, *Cause of the Calamity*, pp. 4–6; Ó Murchadha, *Sable Wings*, p. 37; Hickey, *West Cork*, p. 143. O'Neill, 'Administration of Relief', in Edwards and Williams, *Great Famine*, p. 210.

14 Conwell, *Galway Landlord*, p. 17. Ó Murchadha, *Sable Wings*, p. 38. O'Neill, 'Scientific Investigation', in *Irish Historical Studies*, vol. v, no. 18, p. 138.

15 O'Neill, 'Administration of Relief', in Edwards and Williams, *Great Famine*, pp. 213–215; Kinealy, *Death-Dealing Famine*, p. 57. Woodham-Smith, *Great Hunger*, pp. 54, 74–75; Donnelly, *Great Irish Potato Famine*, p. 49. Woodham-Smith, *Great Hunger*, p. 83.

16 Society of Friends, *Transactions*, p. 21. O'Neill, 'Administration of Relief', in Edwards and Williams, *Great Famine*, p. 215; Villiers-Tuthill, *Patient Endurance*, p. 18. Woodham-Smith, *Great Hunger*, p. 73.

17 Cunningham, *Galway*, p. 129; Villers-Tuthill, *Patient Endurance*, p. 17; Woodham-Smith, p. 73. O'Neill, 'Food Problems', in *Journal of the Royal Society of Antiquaries of Ireland*, pp. 102–104.

18 Cunningham, *Galway*, p. 129. *Illustrated London News*, 4 April 1846, cited in Killen, *Famine Decade*, p. 58. Villiers-Tuthill, *Patient Endurance*, p. 18.

19 Kinealy, *Great Calamity*, p. 50. Swords, *In Their Own Words*, pp. 44–47; Woodham-Smith, *Great Hunger*, p. 85.

20 O'Neill, 'Administration of Relief', in Edwards and Williams, *Great Famine*, pp. 216–217. O'Neill, 'Famine in Offaly', in Nolan and O'Neill, *Offaly*, p. 688. Curtin, *West Limerick*, p. 73; Grace, *Nenagh*, p. 64; Ó Murchadha, 'Years of the Great Famine', in Lynch and Nugent, *Clare History and Society*, p. 246.

21 O'Neill, 'Administration of Relief', in Edwards and Williams, *Great Famine*, p. 218; Swords, *In Their Own Words*, p. 34; Grace, *Nenagh*, p. 66. O'Neill, 'Administration of Relief', p. 216.

22 Parkhill, 'Famine in Londonderry', in Kinealy and Parkhill, *Famine in Ulster*, p. 151. Kinealy and MacAtasney, 'Famine in County Armagh', pp. 49–53. Gwinnell, 'Famine Years in Wexford', p. 39.

23 Kinealy, *Great Calamity*, p. 55. O'Neill, 'Administration of Relief', in Edwards and Williams, *Great Famine*, p. 219.

24 Connell, *Meath*, p. 179. O'Neill, 'Famine in Offaly', in Nolan and O'Neill, *Offaly*, p. 686. Grace, *Nenagh*, p. 44.

25 Swords, *In Their Own Words*, pp. 32–33. Gwinnell, 'Famine Years in Wexford', in *Journal of the Wexford Historical Society*, pp. 37, 38. Swords, *In Their Own Words*, p. 43.

26 Ó Murchadha, *Sable Wings*, p. 42; Ó Murchadha, 'Onset of Famine', in *The Other Clare*, vol. xix, p. 48.

27 Cunningham, *Galway*, pp. 126–127; Kerr, *Nation of Beggars*, pp. 60–63; Kerr, *Catholic Church and the Famine*, pp. 11–12; O'Brien, *Mullingar*, p. 13.

28 O'Neill, 'Famine in Offaly', in Nolan and O'Neill, *Offaly*, p. 686; Swords, *In Their Own Words*, pp. 29–31; O'Brien, *Mullingar*, pp. 13, 17.

29 Foynes, *Skibbereen*, p. 30.

30 Conaghan, *South-West Donegal*, pp. 27, 36. Ó Murchadha, 'Onset of Famine', in *The Other Clare*, p. 50. Killen, *Famine Decade*, p. 60.

31 Marnane, 'Famine in South Tipperary', Part One, in *Tipperary Historical Journal*, pp. 11–12; Woodham-Smith, *Great Hunger*, p. 80.

32 Gray, *Famine, Land and Politics*, p. 138.

33 Swords, *In Their Own Words*, p. 40. O'Brien, *Mullingar*, p. 18.

34 O'Neill, 'Administration of Relief', in Edwards and Williams, *Great Famine*, p. 220. Cunningham, *Galway*, p. 130. Hickey, *West Cork*, p. 146; Curtin, *West Limerick*, p. 19.

35 Grant, 'Aspects of the Great Famine', in Hughes and Nolan, *Armagh*, pp. 612–613; Woodham-Smith, *Great Hunger*, pp. 79–80. Ó Murchadha, *Sable Wings*, p. 62. Swords, *In Their Own Words*, pp. 41–45.

36 O'Neill, 'Famine in Offaly', in Nolan and O'Neill, *Offaly*, pp. 688, 722; Killen, *Famine Decade*, pp. 5, 62. Ó Murchadha, *Sable Wings*, pp. 67–68; Swords, *In their Own Words*, pp. 44–45.

37 Cited in Foynes, *Skibbereen*, p. 32. Both cited in O'Neill, 'Administration of Relief', in Edwards and Williams, *Great Famine*, pp. 221–222.

38 See Bourke, *Visitation*, p. 146; Gray, *Famine, Land and Politics*, p. 96.

39 *Return on an Order*, p. 21. Ó Tuathaigh, *Ireland Before the Famine*, p. 211.

40 Nowlan, *Politics of Repeal*, p. 106. Woodham-Smith, *Great Hunger*, p. 93. Swords, *In Their Own Words*, p. 65; Ó Murchadha, 'Onset of Famine', in *The Other Clare*, p. 50. Society of Friends, *Transactions*, pp. 69–70, 80.

41 Villiers-Tuthill, *Patient Endurance*, p. 20. Gallogly, 'Famine in County Cavan', in Kinealy and Parkhill, *Famine in Ulster*, p. 63.

42 Trevelyan, *Irish Crisis*, p. 48. Woodham- Smith, *Great Hunger*, p. 88; Nowlan, *Politics of Repeal*, p. 116.

43 MacAtasney, 'Famine in County Armagh', in Kinealy and Parkhill, *Famine in Ulster*, p. 39. Woodham-Smith, *Great Hunger*, p. 88; Swords, *In Their Own Words*, p. 21; O'Neill, 'Famine in Offaly', in Nolan and O'Neill, *Offaly*, p. 687.

44 Conaghan, *South-West Donegal*, p. 38. *Cork Examiner* cited in Foynes, *Skibbereen*, p. 31. *Freeman's Journal* cited in Woodham-Smith, *Great Hunger*, p. 89.

Notes to Chapter Three: One Wide Waste of Putrefying Vegetation: The Second Failure of the Potato

1 Ó Murchadha, *Sable Wings*, p. 64. *Clare Journal*, 16 July 1846. Swords, *In Their Own Words*, p. 51; Woodham-Smith, *Great Hunger*, pp. 92–93; Miller, *Emigrants and Exiles*, pp. 282–282. Hamrock, *Mayo*, p. 6.

2 Hannigan, 'Wicklow', in Hannigan and Nolan, *Wicklow*, p. 802. Trench, *Realities of Irish Life*, pp. 99–102. *Correspondence, Commissariat, July 1846–January 1847*, First Part, p. 4.

3 *Clare Journal*, 17 August 1846. Curtin, *West Limerick*, p. 20. Hamrock, *Mayo*, p. 6; Swords, *In Their Own Words*, p. 51.

4 *Correspondence, Commissariat, July 1846–January 1847*, First Part, p. 4. Lyne, *Lansdowne Estate*, p. 715. Barber, *Prendergast Letters*, p. 98. *Correspondence,*

Commissariat, July 1846–January 1847, p. 15; Donnelly, *Great Irish Potato Famine*, p. 65.

5   Gray, *Famine, Land and Politics*, p. 231. Woodham-Smith, *Great Hunger*, p. 87.

6   Nowlan, *Politics of Repeal*, pp. 114–115, 221; O'Neill, 'Administration of Relief', in Edwards and Williams, *Great Famine*, p. 223.

7   Woodham-Smith, *Great Hunger*, pp. 89–90; Kinealy, *Great Calamity*, pp. 51, 378. O'Neill, 'Administration of Relief', in Edwards and Williams, *Great Famine*, p. 221; *Correspondence from July 1846, Board of Works*, First Part, pp. 62, 74.

8   Woodham-Smith, *Great Hunger*, pp. 105, 106; O'Neill, 'Administration of Relief', in Edwards and Williams, *Great Famine*, pp. 223, 225. Trevelyan, *Irish Crisis*, p. 53; O'Neill, 'Administration of Relief', in Edwards and Williams, *Great Famine*, p. 223.

9   O'Neill, 'Administration of Relief', in Edwards and Williams, *Great Famine*, pp. 224–226. Woodham-Smith, *Great Hunger*, pp. 106–107; Kinealy, *Great Calamity*, pp. 76, 78.

10 O'Neill, 'Administration of Relief', in Edwards and Williams, *Great Famine*, p. 225. Donnelly, *Great Irish Potato Famine*, pp. 68–69. Kinealy, *This Great Calamity*, p. 76.

11 O'Neill, 'Administration of Relief', in Edwards and Williams, *Great Famine*, pp. 226, 227. Woodham-Smith, *Great Hunger*, p. 108.

12 Act 9 & 10 Vic., Cap. 107. O'Neill, 'Administration of Relief', in Edwards and Williams, *Great Famine*, p. 228; Grace, *Nenagh*, p. 72; Grant, 'Aspects of the Great Famine', in Hughes and Nolan, *Armagh*, p. 813; Grant, 'Great Famine in County Down', in Proudfoot, *Down*, pp. 355–356.

13 Trevelyan, *Irish Crisis*, p. 56; Kinealy, 'Workhouse System in County Waterford', in Nolan and Power, *Waterford*, p. 584.

14 Donnelly, *Land and People*, p. 174; Donnelly, *Great Irish Potato Famine*, p. 59. O'Neill, 'Famine in Offaly', in Nolan and O'Neill, *Offaly*, p. 693.

15 Hannigan, 'Wicklow', in Hannigan and Nolan, *Wicklow*, p. 804; O'Brien, *Mullingar*, p. 24. Foynes, *Skibbereen*, pp. 39–40. Grant, 'Aspects of the Great Famine', in Hughes and Nolan, *Armagh*, p. 812. Trevelyan, *Irish Crisis*, p. 56. Swords, *In Their Own Words*, p. 63.

16 Hamrock, *Mayo*, p. 12. Swords, *In Their Own Words*, p. 60; Villiers-Tuthill, *Patient Endurance*, p. 34. Hickey, *West Cork*, p. 146.

17 Kinealy, *Great Calamity*, p. 60; Eiríksson, 'Food Supply and Food Riots', in Ó Gráda, *Famine 150*, p. 78. Woodham-Smith, *Great Hunger*, p. 111. Griffith, *Board of Works*, p. 112.

18 Hamrock, *Mayo*, pp. 6, 8. Hickey, *West Cork*, p. 153; Donnelly, *Land and People*, p. 89. Villiers-Tuthill, *Patient Endurance*, p. 32.

19 Trevelyan, *Irish Crisis*, p. 57; Woodham-Smith, *Great Hunger*, p. 111. O'Neill, 'Famine in Offaly', in Nolan and O'Neill, *Offaly*, p. 687. Donnelly, *Land and People*, p. 89.

20 Donnelly, *Land and People*, pp. 90–91; Cowman, 'Some Local Responses', in Cowman and Brady, *Famine in Waterford*, p. 243. Fraher, 'Dungarvan Disturbances', in Cowman and Brady, *Famine in Waterford*, p. 139.

21 Murphy, *A People Starved*, p. 33. Cunnngham, *Galway*, pp. 134–135. Fraher, 'Dungarvan Disturbances', in Cowman and Brady, *Famine in Waterford*, p. 143.

22 Donnelly, *Land and People*, p. 91; Ó Murchadha, *Sable Wings*, pp. 81–83; Hannigan, 'Wicklow', in Hannigan and Nolan, *Wicklow*, pp. 804–805; Kinealy and MacAtasney, *Hidden Famine*, p. 63.

23 Cunningham, *Galway*, p. 134; Flynn, *Ballymacward*, p. 146. Hannigan, 'Wicklow', in Hannigan and Nolan, *Wicklow*, pp. 804–805. Ó Murchadha, *Sable Wings*, p. 82.

24 Cowman, 'Some Local Responses', in Cowman and Brady, *Famine in Waterford*, p. 245. Curtin, *West Limerick*, Ó Murchadha, *Sable Wings*, pp. 77–78; Eiríksson, 'Food Supply and Food Riots,' in Ó Gráda, *Famine 150*, pp. 82–83; Trevelyan, *Irish Crisis*, p. 79.

25 Eirikssen, 'Food Supply and Food Riots', in Ó Gráda, *Famine 150*, p. 84. Cowman, 'Some Local Responses', in Cowman and Brady, *Waterford*, pp. 242, 250; Ó Ciosáin, *Cnoc an Fhomhair*, p. 164.

26 Grant, 'Great Famine in County Tyrone', in Dillon and Jefferies, *Tyrone*, p. 592; Grant, 'Aspects of the Great Famine', in Hughes and Nolan, *Armagh*, p. 814; Grant, 'Great Famine in County Down', in Proudfoot, *Down*, p. 355.

27 O'Neill, 'Administration of Relief', in Edwards and Williams, *Great Famine*, p. 221; Grant, 'Aspects of the Great Famine', in Hughes and Nolan, *Armagh*, p. 816; Ó Murchadha, *Sable Wings*, pp. 71–73. Grant, 'Great Famine in County Down', in Proudfoot, *Down*, p. 356; Ó Murchadha, *Sable Wings*, p. 84. Kinealy, *Great Calamity*, p. 92.

28 Hamrock, *Mayo*, pp. 13–14. Ó Murchadha, 'Years of the Great Famine', in Lynch and Nugent, *Clare*, p. 248. Ó Gráda, *Black '47*, p. 38; O'Neill, 'Administration of Relief', in Edwards and Williams, *Great Famine*, p. 229; Hickey, *West Cork*, pp. 154–155.

29 Hamrock, *Mayo*, pp. 12–14. Swords, *In Their Own Words*, pp. 96, 99.

30 Swords, *In Their Own Words*, pp. 100, 101. Hamrock, *Mayo*, p. 15.

31 Swords, *In Their Own Words*, p. 101. Hamrock, *Mayo*, pp. 15–16.

32 See Ó Grada, *Black '47*, pp. 39, 241; Ó Murchadha, 'Sable Wings', pp. 27–28; Woodham-Smith, *Great Hunger*, p. 160. Kinealy, *Great Calamity*, p. 171.

33 O'Neill, 'Administration of Relief', in Edwards and Williams, *Great Famine*, p. 229; Ó Grada, *Black '47*, p. 38. Foynes, *Skibbereen*, p. 46.

34 Foynes, *Skibbereen*, p. 52. Woodham-Smith, *Great Hunger*, pp. 160–163. Hickey, *West Cork*, p. 164.

Notes to Chapter Four: The Blessed Effects of Political Economy: Public Works and Soup Kitchens

1 Trevelyan, *Irish Crisis*, pp. 58–59, 64. Griffith, *Board of Works*, p. 79. Clare, *Young Irishman's Diary*, p. 100.

2 Kinealy, *Galway*, p. 379. Clare, *Young Irishman's Diary*, pp. 99, 103. Swords, *In Their Own Words*, p. 151.

3 Grant, 'Aspects of the Great Famine', in Hughes and Nolan, *Armagh*, p. 820. O'Neill, 'Administration of Relief', in Edwards and Williams, *The Great Famine*, p. 230; Society of Friends, *Transactions*, p. 161.

4 Broderick, 'Famine in Waterford', in Cowman and Brady, *Famine in Waterford*, pp. 174–175. Donnelly, *Great Irish Potato Famine*, p. 79. Society of Friends, *Transactions*, p. 161. Cunningham, *Galway*, p. 136; Ó Murchadha, *Sable Wings*, pp. 95–96; Swords, *In Their Own Words*, p. 166.

5 Clare, *Young Irishman's Diary*, p. 103. MacAtasney, *Lurgan/Portadown*, pp. 101, 102; Ó Murchadha, 'Years of the Great Famine', in Lynch and Nugent, *Clare: History and Society*, p. 246; Cunningham, *Galway*, p. 130. *Sixteenth Report of the Irish Commissioners for Public Works*, cited in Killen, *Famine Decade*, p. 166.

6 Donnelly, *Great Irish Potato Famine*, p. 79. Clare, *Young Irishman's Diary*, p. 99. O'Neill, 'Administration of Relief', in Edwards and Williams, *The Great Famine*, p. 230. Swords, *In Their Own Words*, p. 188. Society of Friends, *Transactions*, pp. 188, 191.

7 O'Neill, 'Administration of Relief', in Edwards and Williams, *The Great Famine*, p. 229; Broderick, 'Famine in Waterford', in Cowman and Brady, *Famine in Waterford*, p. 174. Griffith, *Board of Works*, pp. 113–114, 117.

8 *Correspondence, Board of Works Series*, Second Part, p. 66. Ibid. pp. 60–67. Kinealy, *Great Calamity*, pp. 94–95.

9 Ó Murchadha, *Sable Wings*, p. 93. Grant, 'Tyrone', in Dillon and Jefferies, *Tyrone*, pp. 591, 595. *Correspondence, Board of Works Series*, Second Part, p. 66. Curtin, *West Limerick*, pp. 60–61.

10 Hannigan, 'Wicklow' in Hannigan and Nolan, *Wicklow*, p. 805. Murphy (ed.) and Nicholson, *Annals*, p. 39. Clare, *Young Irishman's Diary*, pp. 103–104.

11 Gordon, *Reminiscences of an Irish Land Agent*, p. 52. Hannigan, 'Wicklow' in Hannigan and Nolan, *Wicklow*, p. 805. Society of Friends, *Transactions*, p. 191. *Report of the Commissioners of Health*, p. 13.

12 Hannigan, 'Wicklow', in Hannigan and Nolan, *Wicklow*, p. 806. Hickey, *West Cork*, pp. 194, 267. Snell, *Letters from Ireland*, pp. 95–96.

13 O'Neill, 'Administration of Relief', in Edwards and Williams, *The Great Famine*, p. 234. Gray, *Famine, Land and Politics*, p. 262. Trevelyan, *Irish Crisis*, p. 63.

14 Donnelly, *Land and People*, p. 92; Donnelly, *Great Irish Potato Famine*, p. 79. O'Neill, 'Administration of Relief', in Edwards and Williams, *The Great Famine*, p. 227; Murray, *Galway: A Medico-Social History*, pp. 89–90; Cunningham, *Galway*, p. 140.

15 Act 10, Vic., Cap. 7. Kinealy, *Great Calamity*, pp. 143–145; O'Neill, 'Administration of Relief', in Edwards and Williams, *The Great Famine*, p. 239. Woodham-Smith, *Great Hunger*, pp. 172, 184–186.

16 Donnelly, *Great Irish Potato Famine*, p. 83. O'Neill, 'Administration of Relief', in Edwards and Williams, *Great Famine*, p. 239. Daly, 'Operation of Famine Relief', in Póirtéir, *Great Irish Famine*, p. 132.

17 O'Brien, *Mullingar*, pp. 28–31. Hannigan, 'Wicklow', in Hannigan and Nolan, *Wicklow*, p. 806; Curtin, *West Limerick*, p. 89; Swords, *In Their Own Words*, p. 165; Gwinnell, 'Famine Years in Wexford', in *Journal of the Wexford Historical Society*, p. 43.

18 Swords, In *Their Own Words*, p. 157. Hannigan, 'Wicklow', in Hannigan and Nolan, *Wicklow*, p. 807. Ó Murchadha, 'Sable Wings,' p. 31. Curtin, *West Limerick*, p. 62. Swords, *In Their Own Words*, p. 165.

19 O'Rourke, *Great Irish Famine of 1847*, p. 400. Cunningham, *Galway*, p. 141. Ó Gráda, *Black '47*, p. 72. Kinealy, *Great Calamity*, p. 145.

20 *Clare Journal*, 4 February 1847.

21 Swords, *In their Own Words*, p. 147. Ibid. p. 166. Woodham-Smith, *Great Hunger*, p. 158. Murphy, 'Captain A.E. Kennedy', in *The Other Clare*, p. 17. Miller, *Emigrants and Exiles*, p. 301.

22 Trench, *Realities of Irish Life*, p. 391. Murphy (ed.) and Nicholson, *Annals*, pp. 92, 94, 116–117. Morash, *Writing the Irish Famine*, p. 2. Hickey, *West Cork*, pp. 180, 192. O'Neill, 'Administration of Relief', in Edwards and Williams, *Great Famine*, p. 233. Hamrock, *Mayo*, pp. 112–116. O'Neill Daunt, *Life Spent for Ireland*, p. 62. Society of Friends, *Transactions*, p. 192.

23 McCavery, 'Famine in County Down', in Kinealy and Parkhill, *Famine in Ulster*, p. 98. MacAtasney, 'Famine in County Armagh', in Kinealy and

Parkhill, *Famine in Ulster*, pp. 40–41. Society of Friends, *Transactions*, p. 192.

24 Society of Friends, *Transactions*, p. 176, 193; Clarkson and Crawford, *Feast and Famine*, pp. 140, 144; Woodham-Smith, *Great Hunger*, pp. 195–196.

25 Hamrock, *Mayo*, p. 104. Murray, *Galway: A Medico-Social History*, p. 90. Murphy (ed.) and Nicholson, *Annals*, pp. 96–97. Swords, *In Their Own Words*, p. 385. O'Neill Daunt, *Life Spent for Ireland*, p. 62.

26 Society of Friends, *Transactions*, p. 175; Hamrock, *Mayo*, pp. 104–108; Villiers-Tuthill, *Patient Endurance*, p. 63. Cusack, 'Breaking the Silence', in *Ríocht na Midhe*, p. 172.

27 Murphy (ed.) and Nicholson, *Annals*, p. 63. Society of Friends, *Transactions*, pp. 182, 192, 252. Miller, *Emigrants and Exiles*, p. 291. Flynn, *Ballymacward*, p. 154. Society of Friends, *Transactions*, p. 178.

28 O'Neill, 'Administration of Relief', in Edwards and Williams, *The Great Famine*, p. 240. Woodham-Smith, *Great Hunger*, pp. 179, 295. *Second Report of the Relief Commissioners*, Appendix A, B, p. 6. Trevelyan, *Irish Crisis*, pp. 87, 88. Donnelly, *Great Irish Potato Famine*, p. 85. Kinealy, *Great Calamity*, pp. 149, 151. Grant, 'Down', in Proudfoot, *Down*, p. 370.

29 O'Neill, 'Administration of Relief', in Edwards and Williams, *The Great Famine*, p. 239. Grant, 'Tyrone', in Dillon and Jefferies, *Tyrone*, p. 587. Donnelly, *Land and People*, p. 93. Donnelly, *Great Irish Potato Famine*, p. 90.

30 Donnelly, *Great Irish Potato Famine*, p. 87. Society of Friends, *Transactions*, p. 181. O'Neill, 'Administration of Relief', in Edwards and Williams, *The Great Famine*, p. 240. Donnelly, *Great Irish Potato Famine*, p. 86.

31 Grace, *Nenagh*, pp. 103, 104. Woodham-Smith, *Great Hunger*, p. 295. Hannigan, 'Wicklow', in Hannigan and Nolan, *Wicklow*, p. 808. Connell, *Meath*, p. 199.

32 Grace, *Nenagh*, p. 104; Ó Murchadha, 'Sable Wings', pp. 29–30. Sullivan, *New Ireland*, pp. 61–62.

33 Trevelyan, *Irish Crisis*, pp. 89–90. *Report of the Commissioners of Health*, p. 22.

34 Hannigan, 'Wicklow' in Hannigan and Nolan, *Wicklow*, p. 808; Hickey, *Cork*, p. 889. Grant, 'Down', in Proudfoot, *Down*, p. 570.

35 Hickey, *West Cork*, pp. 204–205. Villiers-Tuthill, *Patient Endurance*, p. 62. Kinealy and MacAtasney, *Hidden Famine*, p. 82; Rogers, *Fr. Theobald Mathew*, p. 112.

36 O'Neill, 'Administration of Relief', in Edwards and Williams, *The Great Famine*, pp. 243–244. Robins, *Miasma*, pp. 128–129. Killen, *Famine Decade*, p. 148.

Notes to Chapter Five: Emaciated Frames and Livid Countenances: From Fever Pandemic to Amended Poor Law

1 Robins, *Miasma*, p. 116; Frogatt, 'Response of Medical Profession', in Crawford, *Famine*, pp. 135, 139; Ó Gráda, *Black '47*, p. 96. Cassell, *Medical Charities*, p. 66.

2 MacArthur, 'Medical History', in Edwards and Williams, *Great Famine*, pp. 268, 275–276. Clarkson and Crawford, *Feast and Famine*, p. 153; MacArthur, 'Medical History', pp. 265–266.

3 MacArthur, 'Medical History', in Edwards and Williams, *Great Famine*, pp. 267–268, 283. Clarkson and Crawford, *Feast and Famine*, pp. 152–153. Crawford, 'Poverty and Famine', in Gillespie, *Cavan*, pp. 156–158.

4 Geary, 'Famine, Fever and the Bloody Flux', in Póirtéir, *Great Irish Famine*, p. 77. MacArthur, 'Medical History', in Edwards and Williams, *Great Famine*, pp. 269, 285. Murray, *Galway, A Medico-Social History*, p. 92.

5 Clarkson and Crawford, *Feast and Famine*, pp. 149–150. Murray, *Galway, A Medico-Social History*, p. 92. MacArthur, 'Medical History', in Edwards and Williams, *Great Famine*, p. 469.

6 Crawford, 'Subsistence Crises and Famines in Ireland', in Crawford, *Famine*, p. 205. Frogatt, 'Response of Medical Profession', in Crawford, *Famine*, p. 136. Villiers-Tuthill, *Patient Endurance*, pp. 109–110. Trench, *Realities of Irish Life*, pp. 395, 399. Geary, 'Famine, Fever and the Bloody Flux', in Póirtéir, *Great Irish Famine*, p. 83.

7 Hickey, *West Cork*, pp. 211–215; Hickey, 'Famine in the Skibbereen Union', in Póirtéir, *Great Irish Famine*, p. 196; Hickey, *Cork*, p. 903. MacArthur, 'Medical History', in Edwards and Williams, *Great Famine*, p. 271.

8 MacArthur, 'Medical History', in Edwards and Williams, *Great Famine*, pp. 272–273. Ó Murchadha, *Sable Wings*, pp. 120–121. Miller, *Emigrants and Exiles*, p. 285.

9 MacArthur, 'Medical History', in Edwards and Williams, *Great Famine*, pp. 273, 274, Geary, 'Fever, Famine and the Bloody Flux', in Póirtéir, *The Great Irish Famine*, p. 82.

10 MacArthur, 'Medical History', in Edwards and Williams, *Great Famine*, p. 273. Kinealy, *Galway*, p. 378. Ó Cathaoir, 'Poor Law in County Wicklow', in Hannigan and Nolan, *Wicklow*, p. 541.

11 Act 9 Vic., Cap. 6. Frogatt, 'Response of Medical Profession', in Crawford, *Famine*, p. 142. Nicholls, *History of the Irish Poor Law*, p. 324.

12 Frogatt, 'Response of Medical Profession', in Crawford, *Famine*, p. 142. Kinealy, 'Role of the Poor Law During the Famine', in Póirtéir, *Great Irish*

Famine, p. 111. Grant, 'Great Famine in County Tyrone', in Dillon and Jefferies, *Tyrone*, p. 607.

13 Nicholls, *History of the Irish Poor Law*, pp. 324, 326. MacArthur, 'Medical History', in Edwards and Williams, *Great Famine*, p. 291.

14 Kinealy, 'Role of the Poor Law during the Famine', in Póirtéir, *Great Irish Famine*, p. 112. Grant, 'Great Famine in County Tyrone', in Dillon and Jefferies, *Tyrone*, p. 607. Ó Cathaoir, 'Poor Law in County Wicklow', in Hannigan and Nolan, *Wicklow*, p. 536. Grant, 'Great Famine in County Down', in Proudfoot, *Down*, p. 373.

15 Kinealy, 'Role of the Poor Law During the Famine', in Póirtéir, *Great Irish Famine*, p. 111; Kinealy, 'Administration in Crisis', in Crawford, *Famine*, p. 160. *Thirteenth Report of Poor Law Commissioners* (1847), cited in Killen, *Famine Decade*, pp. 85–86.

16 Ó Cathaoir, 'Poor Law in County Wicklow', in Hannigan and Nolan, *Wicklow*, p. 540. Durnin, 'Aspects of Poor Law Administration', in O'Brien, *Derry*, p. 544. Nicholls, *History of the Irish Poor Law*, p. 326. Woodham-Smith, *Great Hunger*, p. 198; Frogatt, 'Response of the Medical Profession', in Crawford, *Famine*, p. 142.

17 Act 10, Vic., Cap. 22. MacArthur, 'Medical History', in Edwards and Williams, *Great Famine*, pp. 297–298; Frogatt, 'Response of the Medical Profession', in Crawford, *Famine*, p. 142; *Report of the Commissioners of Health*, p. 16.

18 Frogatt, 'Response of the Medical Profession', in Crawford, *Famine*, pp. 143, 146. *Report of Commissioners of Health*, p. 4.

19 Nicholls, *History of the Irish Poor Law*, p. 336. Kinealy *Great Calamity*, p. 204. Act 10, Vic., Cap. 31.

20 Acts 10 & 11, Vic., Cap. 84. Acts 10 & 11 Vic., Cap. 90. Donnelly, *Great Irish Potato Famine*, pp. 92–94.

21 Kinealy, *Great Calamity*, p. 184; *Papers Relating to Proceedings*, Fourth Series, p. 268. Ó Gráda, *Black '47*, pp. 21, 23; Woodham-Smith, *Great Hunger*, p. 301.

22 Kinealy, *Great Calamity*, p. 186. Hickey, *West Cork*, pp. 207–208. Trevelyan, *Irish Crisis*, pp. 88–89.

23 Woodham-Smith, *Great Hunger*, pp. 303. *Seventh Report of the Relief Commissioners*, Supplementary Index, p. 20; Hickey, *West Cork*, p. 208.

24 Ó Murchadha, *Sable Wings*, p. 142–143; Broderick, 'Famine in Waterford', in Cowman and Brady, *Famine in Waterford*, pp. 192–193. Kinealy, *Great Calamity*, p. 194.

25 Murphy, *Diocese of Killaloe 1800–1850*, p. 214. Kinealy, *Great Calamity*.

pp. 196–197. Kinealy, 'Waterford', in Nolan and Power, *Waterford*, p. 586.

26   Kinealy, *Great Calamity*, pp. 195–196. Donnelly, *Land and People*, p. 99. Grant, 'Armagh', in Hughes and Nolan, *Armagh*, pp. 830, 832.

27   Connell, *Meath*, p. 212. Kinealy, *Great Calamity*, p. 196. O'Brien, *Mullingar*, pp. 36, 45.

28   *Papers Relating to Relief of Distress*, Sixth Series, pp. 73–74, 78, 80. Grace, *Nenagh*, pp. 137, 141.

29   Ó Murchadha, 'Limerick Union Workhouse', in *Old Limerick Journal*, p. 42. *Papers Relating to Relief*, Sixth Series, pp. 932–933. Kinealy, *Great Calamity*, pp. 187, 211. Murphy, *Tullamore Workhouse*, pp. 26–28.

30   Nicholls, *History of the Irish Poor Law*, p. 341. Kinealy, *Great Calamity*, pp. 193, 211. O'Brien, *Mullingar*, p. 37.

31   Marnane, 'Famine in South Tipperary', Part Two, in *Tipperary Historical Journal*, vol. x, pp. 142, 149. *Papers Relating to Relief*, Sixth Series, p. 92. *Papers Relating to Relief*, Sixth Series, pp. 90, 91.

32   *Papers Relating to Relief*, Sixth Series, pp. 94, 95, 96, 98; Ó Murchadha, 'Limerick Union Workhouse', in *Old Limerick Journal*, p. 43; Kinealy, *Great Calamity*, p. 201.

33   *Papers Relating to Relief*, Sixth Series, pp. 97, 103, 105.

34   Kinealy, *Great Calamity*, pp. 198–199, 205, 209. Nicholls, *History of the Irish Poor Law*, pp. 351–352. Grant, 'Armagh', in Hughes and Nolan, *Armagh*, p. 833.

35   O'Brien, *Mullingar*, p. 36; Ó Cathaoir, 'Poor Law in County Wicklow', in Hannigan and Nolan, *Wicklow*, pp. 538–539; Ó Cathaoir, *Carlow*, p. 699; Grace, *Nenagh*, pp. 137–138; Hamrock, *Mayo*, p. 88; Ó Murchadha, 'Limerick Union Workhouse', in *Old Limerick Journal*, vol. xxxii, p. 42. O'Neill, 'Famine in Offaly', in Nolan and O'Neill, *Offaly*, p. 695.

36   Walsh, 'The Famine, its Occurrence, its Effects', in O'Dwyer, *Famine in Kilkenny*, p. 52; Ó Murchadha, *Sable Wings*, p. 174.

Notes to Chapter Six: Asylum by the Neighbouring Ditches: The Famine Clearances

1   Norton, *Landlords, Tenants, Famine*, pp. 41, 198, 199. Donnelly, *Captain Rock*, p. 234; Donnelly, *Great Irish Potato Famine*, p. 134. Thomson and McGusty, *Irish Journals of Elizabeth Smith*, p. xviii.

2   Synnott, 'Marcella Gerrard's Estate', in *Journal of the Galway Archaeological*

and Historical Society p. 45; Broderick, 'Famine in Waterford', in Cowman and Brady, *Famine in Waterford*, pp. 182–182.

3 Synnott, 'Marcella Gerrard's Estate', in *Journal of the Galway Archaeological and Historical Society*, pp. 45, 46. *Hansard*, Third Series, 27 April 1846, pp. 1072, 1077. Woodham-Smith, *Great Hunger*, p. 183.

4 Jenkins, *Sir William Gregory*, pp. 71–73, 93; Gregory, *Autobiography*, pp. 133–136, 140–141. Kinealy, *Great Calamity*, pp. 226–227.

5 Connell, *Meath*, pp. 213–214. Kinealy, *Great Calamity*, pp. 221–222. Ó Murchadha, 'One Vast Abattoir', in *The Other Clare*, p. 64; Kinealy, *Great Calamity*, p. 223. Knightly, 'Godfrey Estate', in *Journal of the Kerry Archaeological and Historical Society*, p. 141. Donnelly, *Great Irish Potato Famine*, p. 111.

6 O'Neill, 'Famine Evictions', in King, *Famine, Land and Culture*, p. 48; Donnelly, 'Mass Evictions and the Great Famine', in Póirtéir, *The Great Irish Famine*, pp. 155–156. Osborne, *Gleanings in the West of Ireland*, pp. 256–257.

7 Donnelly, *Great Irish Potato Famine*, pp. 27, 156. Broderick, 'Famine in Waterford', in Cowman and Brady, *Waterford*, pp. 188–189, 211. *Galway Vindicator*, 18 December 1847. Hamrock, *Mayo*, p. 118.

8 *Illustrated London News*, 15 and 22 December 1849, 5 January 1850.

9 *Limerick and Clare Examiner*, 17 April 1850. Murphy (ed.) and Nicholson, *Annals*, p. 116. Kinealy, *Great Calamity*, p. 223. Murphy, *Diocese of Killaloe 1800–1850*, pp. 217–218; Grace, *Nenagh*, pp. 183–185.

10 Ó Cathaoir, 'Wicklow', in Hannigan and Nolan, *Wicklow*, p. 545; Connell, *Meath*, pp. 222, 232, 243; Gwinnell, 'Famine Years in Wexford', in *Journal of the Wexford Historical Society*, vol. ix, p. 53. Donnelly, 'Mass Evictions and the Great Famine', in Póirtéir, *The Great Irish Famine*, p. 158; Ó Gráda, *Black '47*, p. 59.

11 Swords, *In Their Own Words*, p. 380; Hamrock, *Mayo*, pp. 121, 130.

12 Swords, *In Their Own Words*, p. 390. Hamrock, *Mayo*, p. 135. Swords, *In Their Own Words*, pp. 282–283.

13 Donnelly, *Great Irish Potato Famine*, p. 158. Hamrock, *Mayo*, p. 122. Swords, *In their Own Words*, pp. 150, 331. Kinealy, *Great Calamity*, p. 224.

14 Lynch, 'Mass Evictions in Kilrush Poor Law Union', p. 25. Jordan, 'Famine and Aftermath in Mayo', in Morash and Hayes, *Fearful Realities*, p. 40. Ó Murchadha, *Sable Wings*, p. 7. Ó Murchadha, 'One Vast Abattoir', in *The Other Clare*, p. 59.

15 Osborne, *Gleanings in the West of Ireland*, p. 153. Ó Murchadha, 'Exterminator General', in Ó Murchadha, *County Clare Studies*, p. 174.

16 *Limerick and Clare Examiner*, 2 December 1848, 1 September 1849. Ó Murchadha, 'Exterminator General', in Ó Murchadha, *County Clare Studies*, p. 190. Osborne, *Gleanings in the West of Ireland*, p. 21.

17 Murphy, *A People Starved*, pp. 56, 61. Ó Murchadha, 'Years of the Great Famine', in Lynch and Nugent, *Clare: History and Society*, p. 259.

18 Ó Murchadha, 'One Vast Abattoir', in *The Other Clare*, p. 53. Hamrock, *Mayo*, p. 132.

19 Hamrock, *Mayo*, p. 134. Donnelly, *Cork*, p. 117. Grace, *Nenagh*, p. 184. Ó Murchadha, 'Exterminator General', in Ó Murchadha, *County Clare Studies*, p. 185.

20 Donnelly, *Cork*, p. 117; Grace, *Nenagh*, p. 185; O'Neill, 'Offaly', in Nolan and O'Neill, *Offaly*, p. 697–698; Ó Murchadha, 'Exterminator General', in Ó Murchadha, *County Clare Studies*, p. 186.

21 O'Neill, 'Famine Evictions', in King, *Famine, Land and Culture*, pp. 36, 67. Campbell, *Great Irish Famine: Words and Images*, p. 52.

22 Campbell, *Great Irish Famine: Words and Images*, pp. 48–50, 52.

23 Hamrock, *Mayo*, p. 118; Villiers-Tuthill, *Patient Endurance*, pp. 64–70: Murphy (ed.) and Nicholson, *Annals*, p. 99–100; Conaghan, *South-West Donegal*, p. 240; Cunningham, *Galway*, p. 143.

24 Hamrock, *Mayo*, p. 134. Norton, *Landlords, Tenants, Famine*, pp. 59, 60. Ó Murchadha 'Exterminator General', in Ó Murchadha, *County Clare Studies*, pp. 185–187; *Illustrated London News*, 29 December 1849.

25 *Reports and Returns Relating to the Kilrush Union*, p. 6. Ó Murchadha, 'Where Are the People Gone To?', in *The Other Clare*, vol. xxvi, p. 41. Conaghan, *South-West Donegal*, p. 242. Ó Murchadha, 'One Vast Abattoir', vol. xxi, in *The Other Clare*, p. 61.

26 Ó Ciosáin, *Cnoc an Fhomhair*, p. 183. Donnelly, *Cork*, p. 112; Conwell, *Galway Landlord*, p. 51. O'Neill, 'Famine Evictions', in King, *Famine, Land and Culture*, p. 51. Broderick, 'Famine in Waterford', in Cowman and Brady, *Famine in Waterford*, p. 188.

27 Jordan, *Land and Popular Politics*, pp. 111–112. Gwinnell, 'Famine Years in Wexford', in *Journal of the Wexford Historical Society*, p. 46. Swords, *In their Own Words*, pp. 114, 130.

28 Grace, *Nenagh*, p.182. Ó Murchadha, 'Exterminator General', in Ó Murchadha, *County Clare Studies*, pp. 171,172.

29 Grace, *Nenagh*, pp. 182–183. Ó Murchadha, 'Exterminator General', in Ó Murchadha, *County Clare Studies*, pp. 188–189. Donnelly, *Great Irish Potato Famine*, p. 161.

30 Acts 12 & 13 Vic., Cap. 77. Nowlan, *Politics of Repeal*, p. 219. Miller, *Emigrants and Exiles* p. 284.

31 Villiers-Tuthill, *Patient Endurance*, p. 143. Sullivan, *New Ireland*, pp. 138–139. Donnelly, *Great Irish Potato Famine*, p. 166.

32 Ó Néill, *Fiontan Ó Leathlobhair*, pp. 44–47, 122. Woodham-Smith, *Great Hunger*, p. 371.

33 Gray, *Famine, Land and Politics*, p. 192; Norton, *Landlords, Tenants, Famine*, p. 60. O'Neill, 'Offaly', in Nolan and O'Neill, *Offaly*, p. 713.

34 Pelly and Tod, *Highland Lady*, p. 425.

Notes to Chapter Seven: Leaving This Land of Plagues: The Famine Emigrations

1 Miller, *Emigrants and Exiles*, pp. 291, 316. Ó Gráda, *Black '47*, p. 228.

2 MacDonagh, 'Irish Catholic Clergy and Emigration', in *Irish Historical Studies*, vol. v, no. xx, pp. 288–293. Broderick, 'Famine in Waterford', in Cowman and Brady, *Famine in Waterford*, p. 200; Marnane, 'Famine in South Tipperary', Part Five, in *Tipperary Historical Journal*, vol. viii, p. 78.

3 Donnelly, *Great Irish Potato Famine*, p. 125. Hickey, *West Cork*, p. 229. Ó Murchadha, 'Years of the Great Famine', in Lynch and Nugent, *History and Society*, p. 260.

4 O'Neill, 'Offaly', in Nolan and O'Neill, *Offaly*, pp. 707–710; Donnelly, *Great Irish Potato Famine*, p. 182.

5 Miller, *Emigrants and Exiles*, p. 291. MacDonagh, 'Irish Overseas Emigration', in Edwards and Williams, *The Great Famine*, p. 319. O'Neill, 'Offaly', in Nolan and O'Neill, *Offaly*, p. 705.

6 Moran, *Sending out Ireland's Poor*, pp. 110–111. Hamrock, *Mayo*, p. 143; Marnane, 'Famine in South Tipperary', Part Five, in *Tipperary Historical Journal*, vol. xiii, p. 78. Ó Gráda, *Black '47*, p. 109. Donnelly, *Land and People*, p. 103.

7 Hickey, *West Cork*, p. 225. Curtin, *West Limerick*, p. 110. Miller, *Emigrants and Exiles*, p. 292; Woodham-Smith, *Great Hunger*, pp. 372–373.

8 Marnane, 'Famine in South Tipperary', Part Five, in *Tipperary Historical Journal*, vol. xiii, p. 78; *Prendergast Letters*, p. 138. Marnane, 'Famine in South Tipperary', Part Three, in *Tipperary Historical Journal*, vol. xi, p. 66.

9 Miller, *Emigrants and Exiles*, pp. 294–297, 303–304. Kinealy, *Great Calamity*, p. 309.

10　Moran, *Sending Out Ireland's Poor*, p. 89; Kinealy, *Great Calamity*, pp. 309–312; O'Mahony, 'Emigration from the Workhouses of the Mid-West', in *The Old Limerick Journal*, vol. xxxii, p. 171.

11　Grace, *Nenagh*, pp. 198–200; Moran, *Sending Out Ireland's Poor*, p. 38; Miller, *Emigrants and Exiles*, p. 304.

12　Moran, *Sending out Ireland's Poor*, p. 42; Rees, *Farewell to Famine*, pp. 24–25. Hannigan, 'Wicklow', in Hannigan and Nolan, *Wicklow*, p. 811.

13　Donnelly, *Great Irish Potato Famine*, pp. 140–141; Curtin, *West Limerick*, p. 110; Fitzpatrick, 'Emigration 1801–1870', in Vaughan, *New History of Ireland*, pp. 593, 597; Kinealy, *Great Calamity*, p. 313.

14　Moran, *Sending out Ireland's Poor*, pp. 105–107, 109–110, 119–120; MacDonagh, 'Irish Oversesas Emigration', in Edwards and Williams, *Great Famine*, pp. 336–337.

15　Ó Murchadha, 'Bad Times and Emigration', in *The Other Clare*, vol. xxvii, pp. 52–53. Fitzpatrick, 'Flight from Famine', in Póirtéir, *The Great Irish Famine*, p. 178; Kinealy, *Great Calamity*, p. 314; MacDonagh, 'Irish Overseas Emigration', in Edwards and Williams, *Great Famine*, p. 135. A.G.L. Shaw, *Convicts and the Colonies*; Costello, *Botany Bay*, p. 133.

16　Coleman, *Passage*, p. 167; Gray, *Famine, Land and Politics*, pp. 299–301; Moran, *Sending out Ireland's Poor*, pp. 83–87.

17　Fitzpatrick, 'Emigration 1801–1870', in Vaughan, *New History of Ireland*, p. 587. Coleman, *Passage*, pp. 254–257, 348–353.

18　*Census of Ireland for the Year 1851*, General Report, p. lvi; Kinealy, *Great Calamity*, p. 304.

19　Cited in O'Neill, 'Offaly', in Nolan and O'Neill, *Offaly*, p. 706. *Report Before Select Committee on Colonization from Ireland*, Appendix x, p. 129. 'State Aided Emigration Schemes c. 1850', in *Analecta Hibernica*, p. 391.

20　Fitzpatrick, 'Emigration 1801–1870', in Vaughan, *New History of Ireland*, p. 600. Moran, *Sending out Ireland's Poor*, p. 120. Curtin, *West Limerick*, p. 111. Grace, *Nenagh*, p. 194.

21　Kinealy and MacAtasney, *Hidden Famine*, pp. 81–82; O'Brien, *Mullingar*, p. 38. Hannigan, 'Wicklow', in Hannigan and Nolan, *Wicklow*, p. 812; Urwin, 'Effects of Great Famine', in *Journal of Wexford Historical Society*, vol. ix, p. 150.

22　Gwinnell, 'Famine Years in Wexford', in *Journal of Wexford Historical Society*, vol. ix, p. 44. McEvoy, 'Famine Days in Kilkenny', in *Old Kilkenny Review*, vol. xlix, p. 153. Ó Gráda, *Black '47 and Beyond*, p. 173.

23　Coleman, *Passage*, p. 22; Kinealy, *Great Calamity*, p. 297.

24　Miller, *Emigrants and Exiles*, p. 292. Cited in Killen, *Famine Decade*, p. 257.

Limerick Chronicle, 29 November 1848. Pelly and Tod, *Highland Lady*, p. 507. *Limerick and Clare Examiner*, 24 February 1849.

25 Hadfield and McVeagh, *Strangers to that Land*, p. 184. Robinson and Colville Scott, *Connemara after the Famine*, p. 6.

26 O'Donovan Rossa, *Recollections*, p. 142. Grace, *Nenagh*, p. 189. Woodham-Smith, *Great Hunger*, p. 216.

27 Ó Gráda, *Black '47*, p. 107. Woodham-Smith, *Great Hunger*, p. 217. Costello, 'Deer Island Graves', in Sullivan, *Meaning of the Famine*, p. 121.

28 Miller, *Emigrants and Exiles*, p. 300; Hollett, *Passage to the New World*, p. 42; Costello, 'Deer Island Graves', in Sullivan, *Meaning of the Famine*, p. 120.

29 Hickey, *West Cork*, p. 905. Hollett, *Passage to the New World*, p. 43. Coleman, *Passage*, p. 66.

30 Swords, *In Their Own Words*, p. 168. Coleman, *Passage*, p. 161. Fitzgerald, 'Great Hunger?', in Crawford, *Hungry Stream*, p. 109.

31 Fitzgerald, 'Great Hunger?', in Crawford, *Hungry Stream*, p. 109. Kinealy and MacAtasney, *Hidden Famine*, p. 143.

32 Kinealy, *Great Calamity*, pp. 339–340. Durnin, 'Aspects of Poor Law Administration and the Workhouse in Derry', in O'Brien, *Derry and Londonderry: History and Society*, pp. 543–544. Coleman, *Passage*, p. 164.

33 *Census of Ireland for the Year 1851*, General Report, p. lvii. Wittke, *Irish in America*, pp. 23–24. Coleman, *Passage*, p. 147.

34 Donnelly, *Great Irish Potato Famine*; p. 33; Miller, *Emigrants and Exiles*, p. 316; Fitzpatrick, 'Flight From Famine', in Póirtéir, *Great Irish Famine*, p. 179; Ó Gráda, *Black '47*, pp. 106–107.

35 Hollett, *Passage to the New World*, p. 148. Coleman, *Passage*, p. 146; Conaghan, *South-West Donegal*, p. 260.

36 Hollett, *Passage to the New World*, p. 148. Coleman, *Passage*, pp. 147–148; Gallman, *Receiving Erin's Children*, pp. 70–72.

37 Curtin, *Pauper Warren*, pp. 108–109; Coleman, *Passage*, p. 147. Costello, 'Deer Island Graves', in Sullivan, *Meaning of Famine*, p. 121. Ó Murchadha, 'Years of the Great Famine', in Lynch and Nugent, *Clare: History and Society*, p. 259.

38 McNeill, *Vere Foster*, p. 58; Coleman, *Passage*, pp. 120–122. Potter, *To the Golden Door*, p. 151.

39 McNeill, *Vere Foster*, pp. 58, 225–238. Mackay, *Flight from Famine*, pp. 134–135; Quigley, 'Grosse Île', in Crawford, *Hungry Stream*, pp. 25–27.

40 Quigley, 'Grosse Île', p. 26. Woodham-Smith, *Great Hunger*, p. 214.

41 Woodham-Smith, *Great Hunger*, pp. 216–217. Conaghan, *South-West Donegal*, pp. 252, 255. Hamrock, *Mayo*, p. 138.

42 Woodham-Smith, *Great Hunger*, pp. 214, 218. Coleman, *Passage*, p. 169. Hickey and Doherty, *Dictionary*, p. 194.

43 Coleman, *Passage*, pp. 171, 172. Hickey and Doherty, *Dictionary*, p. 194. Moran, *Sending out Ireland's Poor*, p. 95. Fitzpatrick, 'Emigration 1801–70', in Vaughan, *New History of Ireland*, p. 583.

44 Coleman, *Passage*, p. 172; Hickey and Doherty, *Dictionary*, pp. 194–1945.

45 Ó Laighin, 'Samhradh an Bhróin: Grosse Ile 1847', in Póirtéir, *Gneithe den Ghorta*, p. 223; O'Gallagher, 'Orphans of Grosse Île', in O'Sullivan, *Meaning of the Famine*, pp. 80–111.

46 MacKay, *Flight from Famine*, p. 272. Woodham-Smith, *Great Hunger*, p. 215. Costello, 'Deer Island Graves', in Sullivan, *Meaning of the Famine*, pp. 119–120. Kenny, *American Irish*, p. 104.

47 Hannigan, 'Wicklow', in Hannigan and Nolan, *Wicklow*, p. 812. MacDonagh, 'Irish Catholic Clergy and Emigration', in *Irish Historical Studies*, vol. v, no. xx, pp. 297–298. Rees, *Farewell to Famine*, pp. 71, 121.

48 Reid, *Decent Set of Girls*, p. 25. Miller, *Emigrants and Exiles*, pp. 297–299. Hollett, *Passage to New World*, p. 126.

49 Miller, *Emigrants and Exiles*, pp. 311–312.

Notes to Chapter Eight: Exiled from Humanity: The Later Years of the Famine

1 Donnelly, '"Irish Property Must Pay for Irish Poverty': British Public Opinion and the Great Irish Famine', in Morash and Hayes, *Fearful Realities*, p. 73. Trevelyan, *Irish Crisis*, p. 117; Kinealy, *Irish Famine: Impact, Ideology and Rebellion*, p. 73. Gray, '*Punch* and the Great Famine', in *History Ireland*, vol. 1, no. 2, p. 32.

2 Cited in Donnelly, 'Irish Property Must Pay', in Morash and Hayes, *Fearful Realities*, p. 63. Nowlan, *Repeal*, pp. 184–213. Davis, *William Smith O'Brien: Ireland 1848*, p. 21.

3 Sloan, *William Smith O'Brien and the Young Ireland Rebellion*, p. 276. Woodham-Smith, *Great Hunger*, pp. 353–354.

4 Sloan, *William Smith O'Brien and the Young Ireland Rebellion*, pp. 280, 285. Mitchel, *Jail Journal*, p. 72.

5 Sloan, *William Smith O'Brien and the Young Ireland Rebellion*, p. 276; Davis, *Revolutionary Imperialist*, p. 273.

6 Nolan, 'The Famine in Slieveardagh', in O'Dwyer, *Callan*, pp. 86–87. Pelly

and Tod, *Highland Lady*, p. 405. Murphy (ed.) and Nicholson, *Annals*, p. 119.

7   Woodham-Smith, *Great Hunger*, p. 362. Ó Murchadha, *Sable Wings*, p. 182. Villiers-Tuthill, *Patient Endurance*, p. 94. Gwinnell, 'Famine Years in Wexford', in *Journal of the Wexford Historical Society*, vol. ix, p. 51.

8   Kinealy, *Great Calamity*, p. 233. *Illustrated London News*, 26 August 1848, cited in Killen, *Famine Decade*, p. 204. Pelly and Tod, *Highland Lady*, pp. 409–410.

9   Kinealy, *Death-Dealing Famine*, pp. 137,139. Connell, *Meath*, p. 224; O'Brien, *Mullingar*, p. 44; O'Neill, 'Offaly', in Nolan and O'Neill, *Offaly*, p. 94. O'Brien, *Mullingar*, p. 40.

10 O'Brien, *Mullingar*, p. 44. Ó Cathaoir, 'Wicklow', in Hannigan and Nolan, *Wicklow*, pp. 539–540. Grant, *Armagh*, p. 833.

11 Ó Cathaoir, 'Wicklow', in Hannigan and Nolan, *Wicklow*, p. 544.

12 Kinealy, *Galway*, p. 387. Kinealy, 'Waterford', in Nolan and Power, *Waterford*, p. 587. Swords, *In Their Own Words*, p. 366.

13 Hamrock, *Mayo*, pp. 76–77.

14 Hamrock, *Mayo*, p. 54. *Limerick and Clare Examiner*, 7 April 1849; Murphy (ed.) and Nicholson, *Annals*, p. 138.

15 Ó Gráda, *Black '47*, p. 44. Grant, 'Down', in Proudfoot, *Down*, p. 376. Ibid., p. 379.

16 Cunningham, 'Famine in County Fermanagh', in Kinealy and Parkhill, *Famine in Ulster*, p. 141. MacAtasney, *Famine in Lurgan-Portadown*, p. 85. Kinealy, *Great Calamity*, p. 278.

17 Ó Murchadha, *Sable Wings*, p. 202. McArthur, 'Medical History', in Edwards and Williams, *Great Famine*, p. 307. Connell, *Meath*, p. 225. Marnane, 'Famine in South Tipperary', Part Three, in *Tipperary Historical Journal*, vol. xi, p. 63. Curtin, *West Limerick*, p. 27. O'Brien, *Mullingar*, p. 46. MacAtasney, *Lurgan/Portadown*, p. 82. Villiers-Tuthill, *Patient Endurance*, p. 115. McArthur, 'Medical History', in Edwards and Williams, *Great Famine*, p. 307.

18 Ó Murchadha, *Sable Wings*, pp. 171–173. Grace, *Nenagh*, pp. 186–187.

19 Ó Murchadha, *Sable Wings*, p. 173. Curtin, *West Limerick*, p. 110. Hannigan, 'Wicklow', in Hannigan and Nolan, *Wicklow*, p. 809. O'Brien, *Mullingar*, p. 43. Villiers-Tuthill, *Patient Endurance*, p. 130.

20 Kerr, *Nation of Beggars*, p. 203; Woodham-Smith, *Great Hunger*, p. 387. Rees, *Farewell to Famine*, p. 25.

21 Ó Murchadha, *Sable Wings*, p. 206. Nowlan, *Politics of Repeal*, p. 229. Woodham-Smith, *Great Hunger*, p. 397.

22 Woodham-Smith, *Great Hunger*, p. 391. Murphy (ed.) and Nicholson, *Annals*, p. 114; Kinealy, *Death-Dealing Famine*, p.140.

23 O'Brien, *Mullingar*, p. 47. Kinealy, *Great Calamity*, p. 284

24 Kinealy, *Great Calamity*, pp. 266–267. Ó Murchadha, *Sable Wings*, p. 216.

25 Kinealy, *Galway*, p. 388. Kinealy, *Great Calamity*, p. 285.

26 Nicholls, *History of the Irish Poor Law*, pp. 341, 360; Kinealy, *Great Calamity*, pp. 268–269. Kinealy, *Galway*, p. 389.

27 Curtin, *West Limerick*, p. 28. Ó Murchadha, 'Moloch of Landlordism', in *The Other Clare*, vol. xxv, p. 60. Sheedy, *Clare Elections*, p. 494.

28 *Limerick and Clare Examiner*, 8 December 1849. Ó Murchadha, 'Moloch of Landlordism', in *The Other Clare*, vol. xxv, pp. 61–62. Osborne, *Gleanings*, pp. 164–166.

29 Osborne, *Gleanings*, pp. 180–181, 156–184. Ó Murchadha, 'Moloch of Landlordism', in *The Other Clare*, vol. xxv, p. 67.

30 *Limerick and Clare Examiner*, 11, 15 May 1850. *Limerick and Clare Examiner*, 2 October, 27 November 1850; *Clare Journal*, 7 November 1850.

31 *The Times*, 31 March 1851.

32 Ó Murchadha, 'Where are the People Gone To?', in *The Other Clare*, vol. xxvi, p. 42. *Clare Journal*, 30 June, 20 October, 3 November 1851.

33 Kinealy, 'Poor Law in Mayo', *Cathair na Mart*, vol. 6, no. 1, p. 106. Marnane, 'Famine in South Tipperary', Part Three, in *Tipperary Historical Journal*, vol. xi, p. 72, Part Four, in *Tipperary Historical Journal*, vol. xii, p. 1.

34 Ó Murchadha, *Sable Wings*, pp. 228–229. *Census of Ireland, 1851*, General Report, p. xxi.

Notes to Chapter Nine: The Murdered Sleeping Silently: Aftermath

1 *Limerick and Clare Examiner*, 19 November 1851. O'Neill, 'Offaly', in Nolan and O'Neill, *Offaly*, p. 706. Fitzpatrick, *Oceans of Consolation*, pp. 289–290.

2 *Census of Ireland for the Year 1851*, General Report, pp. xv, xvi. Mokyr, *Why Ireland Starved*, cited in Donnelly, *Great Irish Potato Famine*, p. 171.

3 *Census of Ireland for the Year 1851*, General Report, pp. xxiii, xxiv. Robinson and Colville Scott, *Connemara after the Famine*, p. 30. Robinson, 'Connemara after the Famine', in *History Ireland*, vol. iv, p. 13.

4 McHugh, 'Famine in Irish Oral Tradition', p. 434. Robinson and Colville Scott, *Connemara after the Famine*, p. 50. Hunt, *Frock-Coated Communist*, pp. 232–233. Petrie, *Ancient Music of Ireland*, p. 55.

5 Sullivan, *New Ireland*, p. 68.

6   McHugh, 'Famine in Irish Oral Tradition', pp. 434–435. Vaughan and
    Fitzpatrick. *Irish Historical Statistics*, p. 3.

7   Clarkson and Crawford, *Feast and Famine*, p. 163. Nicholas Carolan, *Irish
    Times*, 16 March 1995. McHugh, 'Famine in Irish Oral Tradition', p. 397.

8   Whelan, 'Stigma of Souperism', in Póirtéir, *The Great Irish Famine*, p. 143.
    Trench, *Realities of Irish Life*, p. 406.

9   Whelan, 'Stigma of Souperism', in Póirtéir, *The Great Irish Famine*, pp. 145–146;
    Bowen, *Protestant Crusade*, p. 218. Villiers-Tuthill, *Patient Endurance*,
    pp. 132–138; Bowen, *Protestant Crusade*, p. 206.

10 Bowen, *Protestant Crusade*, p. 243.

11 Larkin, 'Parish Mission Movement', in Bradshaw and Swords, *Christianity
    in Ireland*, p. 200; Murphy, *Diocese of Killaloe 1850–1904*, pp. 267–270.

12 Whyte, *Tenant League and Irish Politics*, pp. 8–19. Miller, *Emigrants and
    Exiles*, pp. 288–230. Roche, 'Famine Years in Forth and Bargy', in *Journal
    of the Wexford Historical Society*, vol. xv, pp. 4–5. Sullivan, *New Ireland*,
    p. 68.

13 Lynch, 'Mass Evictions in Kilrush Poor Law Union', p. 109; Moloney, *Far
    from the Shamrock Shore*, p. 10. O'Rourke, *History of the Great Irish Famine*,
    p. XX.

14 Kinealy, 'Potatoes, Providence and Philanthropy', in O'Sullivan, *Meaning of
    Famine*, pp. 146, 151. Sarbaugh, 'Charity Begins at Home', in *History Ireland*,
    vol. ix, no. ii, p. 31.

15 Kinealy, 'Potatoes, Providence and Philanthropy', p. 163. Kinealy, 'Potatoes,
    Providence and Philanthropy', in O'Sullivan, *Meaning of Famine*, p. 150;
    Kerr, *Nation of Beggars*, pp. 55–56.

16 O'Neill, 'Administration of Relief', in Edwards and Williams, *Great Famine*,
    p. 255. Kinealy, 'Potatoes, Providence and Philanthropy', in O'Sullivan,
    Meaning of Famine, p. 142. Nowlan, *Repeal*, p. 107. Gray, 'Ideology and
    Famine', in Póirtéir, *Great Irish Famine*, pp. 86–103.

17 Gray, *Famine, Land and Politics*, p. 231. Kinealy, 'Role of the Poor Law
    During Famine', in Póirtéir, *Great Irish Famine*, pp. 105, 115, 121–122.

18 These issues are the subject of Professor Canny's *From Reformation to
    Restoration* and *Making Ireland British*; also Lenihan, *Consolidating
    Conquest*, p. 134; Gentles, *New Model Army*, p. 383.

19 Beckett, *Making of Modern Ireland*, p. 350. Bernstein, 'Liberals', in *Irish
    Historical Studies*, vol. xxxix, no. 116, p. 530. MacDonagh, 'Irish Overseas
    Emigration', in Edwards and Williams, *The Great Famine*, p. 336.

20 Gray, 'Punch and the Great Famine', in *History Ireland*, vol. i, no. ii, p. 31;
    Donnelly, "Irish Property Must Pay for Irish Poverty': British Public

   Opinion and the Great Irish Famine', in Morash and Hayes, *Fearful Realities*,
   p. 60.
21 Kerr, *Nation of Beggars*, p. 333; Kinealy, *Death-Dealing Famine*, p. 138.
   Osborne, *Gleanings*, pp. 255–25. *Census of Ireland for the Year 1851*, General
   Report, p. lviii.
22 Mitchel, *Last Conquest of Ireland*, p. 219.

Bibliography

NEWSPAPERS

Clare Journal
Cork Examiner
Freeman's Journal
Galway Vindicator
Illustrated London News
Irish Times
L'Illustration Journal Universel
Limerick and Clare Examiner
Mayo Telegraph
Times
Tipperary Vindicator
Tyrawley Herald

BRITISH PARLAMENTARY PAPERS AND DEBATES

Hansard's Parliamentary Debates, Third Series.
First Report from His Majesty's Commissioners for Inquiring into the Condition of the Poorer Classes in Ireland (Dublin, 1836).
Annual Reports of Poor Law Commissioners 1838–1865.
Return on an Order of the Honourable The House of Commons, dated 11 August 1846: A statement of the Total Expenditure for the Purpose of Relief in Ireland since November 1845, Distinguishing Final Payments from Sums which have been or are about to be repaid.
Correspondence from July 1846 to January 1847, Relating to the Measures Adopted for the Relief of the Distress in Ireland, Commissariat Series (London, 1847).

Correspondence from July 1846 to January 1847, Relating to the Measures Adopted for the Relief of Distress in Ireland, Board of Works Series (London, 1847).

Correspondence from January to March 1847, Relating to the Measures Adopted for the Relief of the Distress in Ireland, Board of Works Series, Second Part (London, 1847).

First Report of the Relief Commissioners, with Appendix (London, 1847).

Second Report of the Relief Commissioners, Constituted under the Act 10 Vic. Cap. 7, with Appendices (London, 1847).

Fifth, Sixth and Seventh Reports of the Relief Commissioners (London, 1847).

Papers Relating to Proceedings for the Relief of the Distress and State of the Unions and Workhouses in Ireland, Fourth Series, 1847 (London, 1847).

Seventh and Last Report of the Relief Commissioners (London, 1848).

Report Before Select Committee of the House of Lords on Colonization from Ireland, together with the Minutes of Evidence (London, 1848).

Digest of Evidence taken before Her Majesty's Commissioners of Inquiry into the state of the Law and Practice in respect to the Occupation of Land in Ireland. Two vols. (London, 1847 and 1848).

Papers Relating to Relief of Distress and State of Unions and Workhouses in Ireland, Sixth Series (London, 1848).

Reports and Returns Relating to the Kilrush Union (London, 1849)

Report of the Commissioners of Health, Ireland, on the Epidemics of 1846 to 1850 (Dublin, 1852).

Census of Ireland for the Year 1851 (Dublin, 1856).

OTHER PRINTED PRIMARY SOURCES

Barber, Shelley (ed.), *The Prendergast Letters: Correspondence from Famine-Era Ireland 1840–1850* (Boston, 2006).

De Beaumont, Gustave, *Ireland: Social, Political and Religious* (Paris, 1839). New edn., Tom Garvin and Andreas Hess, Cambridge, Mass. 2006.

Clare, Rev. Wallace (ed.), *A Young Irishman's Diary, Being Extracts from the Early Journal of John Keegan of Moate* (Dublin, 1928).

Coyne, J. Stirling, *The Scenery and Antiquities of Ireland* (London, 1842).

Fitzpatrick, David (ed.), *Oceans of Consolation: Personal Accounts of Irish Emigration to Australia* (London, 1994).

Gordon, Home (ed.) *The Reminiscences of an Irish Land Agent, being those of S.M. Hussey* (London, 1904).

Gregory, Lady Augusta (ed.), *Sir William Gregory, K.C.M.G, An Autobiography* (London, 1894).

Hadfield, Andrew and McVeagh, John (eds.), *Strangers to that Land: British Perceptions of Ireland form the Reformation to the Famine* (Gerrards Cross, 1994).

Hall, Samuel and Hall, Anna Maria, *Ireland, its Scenery, Character. Etc.*, 3 vols. (London, 1843).

Hamrock, Ivor (ed.), *The Famine in Mayo, 1845–1850: A Portrait from Contemporary Sources* (Castlebar, 2004).

Hooper, Glen (ed.), *The Tourist's Gaze: Travellers to Ireland 1800–2000* (Cork, 2001).

Inglis, Henry, *A Journey through Ireland in the Spring, Summer and Autumn of 1834*, 5th edn. (London, 1838).

Killen, John (ed.), *The Famine Decade: Contemporary Accounts 1841–1851* (Belfast 1995).

Kissane, Noel (ed.), *The Irish Famine: A Documentary History* (Dublin, 1995).

Larkin, Emmet (ed.), *Alexis de Tocqueville's Journey in Ireland, July–August, 1835* (Dublin, 1990).

Mitchel, John, *The Last Conquest of Ireland (Perhaps)* (London, 1861).

—— *Jail Journal* (Dublin, 1913).

Murphy, Maureen (ed.), Asenath Nicholson, *Annals of the Famine in Ireland* (Dublin, 1998).

—— (ed.), Asenath Nicholson, *Ireland's Welcome to the Stranger* (Dublin, 2002).

Nicholls, George, *A History of the Irish Poor Law* (London, 1856).

Ó Ceallaigh, Seán (eag.), *Filíocht na gCallanán: Peatsaí Ó Callanáin, 1791–1865 agus Marcas Ó Callanáin, 1789–1846* (Baile Atha Cliath, 1967).

O'Donovan Rossa, Jeremiah, *Rossa's Recollections* (New York, 1898).

O'Neill Daunt, William J, *A Life Spent for Ireland* (London, 1896).

Osborne, Rev. Sidney Godolphin, *Gleanings in the West of Ireland* (London, 1850).

Pelly, Patricia and Tod, Andrew (eds.), *The Highland Lady in Ireland: Elizabeth Grant of Rothiemurchus: The Highland Lady in Ireland, Journals 1840–1850* (Edinburgh, 1990).

Petrie, George, *The Ancient Music of Ireland* (Dublin, 1855).

Robinson, Tim (ed.), Thomas Colville Scott, *Connemara After the Famine: Journal of a Survey of the Martin Estate 1853* (Dublin, 1995).

Scott, Michael (ed.), *Hall's Ireland: Mr and Mrs Hall's Tour of 1840*, 2 vols. (London, 1984).

Society of Friends, *Transactions of the Central Relief Committee of the Society of Friends During the Famine in Ireland in 1846 and 1848* (London, 1852).

Snell, D.K.M. (ed.), Alexander Somerville, *Letters from Ireland during the Famine of 1847* (Dublin, 1994).

'State Aided Emigration Schemes c. 1850', *Analecta Hibernica*, vol. xxii (1960), pp. 331–393.

Sullivan, A.M., *New Ireland: Political Sketches and Personal Reminiscences of Thirty Years of Public Life*, 7th edn. (Edinburgh, 1877.)

Swords, Liam (ed.), *In Their Own Words: The Famine in North Connacht 1845–49* (Dublin, 1999).

Thackeray, William, *The Irish Sketchbook of 1842* (London, 1843, new ed. Dublin 2005).

Thomson, David and McGusty, Moyra (eds.), *The Irish Journals of Elizabeth Smith 1840–1850* (Oxford, 1980).

Trench, William Steuart, *Realities of Irish Life* (London, 1868).

Trevelyan, Charles Edward, *The Irish Crisis* (London, 1848).

SECONDARY SOURCES

Bartlett, Thomas, *The Fall and Rise of the Irish Nation: The Catholic Question 1690–1830* (Dublin, 1992).

Beckett, J.C., *The Making of Modern Ireland 1603–1923* (London, 1966).

Bernstein, George L., 'Liberals, the Irish Famine and the Role of the State', in *Irish Historical Studies*, vol. xxxix, no. 116 (November 1995).

Bourke, Austin, *'The Visitation of God'?: The Potato and the Great Famine* (Dublin, 1993). Ed. Jacqueline Hill and Cormac Ó Gráda.

Bowen, Desmond, *The Protestant Crusade in Ireland 1801–1870* (Dublin, 1978).

Bradshaw, Brendan and Swords, Liam (eds.), *Christianity in Ireland: Revisiting the Story* (Dublin, 2002).

Broderick, Eugene, 'The Famine in Waterford as Reported in the Local Newspapers', in Cowman and Brady, *The Famine in Waterford. 1845–1850: Teacht na bPrátaí Dubha*.

Burke, Helen, *The People and the Poor Law in Nineteenth Century Ireland* (Dublin, 1987).

Buttimer, Neil, 'A Stone on the Cairn: The Great Famine in Later Gaelic Manuscripts', in Morash and Hayes, *Fearful Realities: New Perspective on the Famine*.

Campbell, Stephen J., *The Great Irish Famine: Words and Images from the Famine Museum Strokestown Park, County Roscommon* (Strokestown, 1994).

Canny, Nicholas, *From Reformation to Restoration: Ireland 1534–1660* (Dublin, 1987).

—— *Making Ireland British* (Oxford, 2001).

Cassell, Ronald D., *Medical Charities, Medical Politics: The Irish Dispensary System and the Poor Law, 1836–1872* (Rochester, NY, 1997).

Clarkson, L.A., and Crawford, E. Margaret, *Feast and Famine: A History of Food and Nutrition in Ireland 1500–1920* (Oxford, 2001).

Coleman, Anne, *Riotous Roscommon: Social Unrest in the 1840s* (Dublin, 1999).

Coleman, Terry, *Passage to America: A History of Emigrants from Great Britain and Ireland to America in the mid-Nineteenth Century* (London, 1972).

Conaghan, Pat, *The Great Famine in South-West Donegal* (Killybegs, 1997).

Connell, Peter, *The Land and People of County Meath 1750–1850* (Dublin, 2004).

Connolly, S.J., *Priests and People in Pre-Famine Ireland 1780–1845* (Dublin, 1982).

—— (ed.), *The Oxford Companion to Irish History* (London, 1998, 2nd edn. 2002).

Conwell, John Joseph, 'Clanricarde and the Great Famine,' in Forde *et al.*, *The District of Loughrea.*

—— *A Galway Landlord during the Great Famine: Ulick John de Burgh, First Marquis of Clanricarde* (Dublin, 2003).

Costello, Con, *Botany Bay: The Story of the Irish Convicts Transported from Ireland to Australia, 1791–1853* (Cork, 1987).

Costello, Francis, 'The Deer Island Graves,' in Sullivan, *The Meaning of the Famine.*

Cowman, Des, 'Some Local Response to the Famine, 1846–48', in Cowman and Brady, *The Famine in Waterford 1845–1850: Teacht na bPrátaí Dubha.*

Cowman, Des and Brady, Donald *The Famine in Waterford 1845–1850: Teacht na bPrátaí Dubha* (Dublin, 1995).

Crawford, E.M. (ed.), *Famine, The Irish Experience 900–1900: Subsistence Crises and Famines in Ireland* (Edinburgh, 1989).

—— 'Subsistence Crises and Famines in Ireland: A Nutritionist's View', in Crawford, *Famine: The Irish Experience 900–1900: Subsistence Crises and Famines in Ireland.*

—— 'Poverty and Famine in County Cavan', in Gillespie, *Cavan: Essays on the History of an Irish County* (Dublin, 1995).

—— (ed.), *The Hungry Stream: Essays on Emigration and Famine* (Belfast, 1997).

Cunningham, John, 'The Famine in County Fermanagh', in Kinealy and Parkhill, *The Famine in Ulster.*

—— *Galway; 'A Town Tormented by the Sea'* (Galway, 2004).

Curtin, Gerard, *A Pauper Warren: West Limerick 1845–1849* (Cork, 2000).

Cusack, Danny, 'Breaking the Silence: The Poets of North Meath and the Great Famine', *Ríocht na Midhe*, vol. xix (2008).

Daly, Mary, E. 'The Operation of Famine Relief, 1845–47', in Póirtéir, *The Great Irish Famine.*

Davis, Richard, *William Smith O'Brien: Ireland–1848–Tasmania* (Dublin, 1989).

—— *Revolutionary Imperialist: William Smith O'Brien 1803–1864* (Dublin, 1998).

Dillon, Charles, and Jefferies, Henry A. (eds.), *Tyrone: History and Society* (Dublin, 2000).

Donnelly, James S. (Jr.), *Landlord and Tenant in Nineteenth Century Ireland* (Dublin, 1973).

—— *The Land and People of Nineteenth Century Cork: The Rural Economy and the Land Question* (London, 1975).

—— 'The Whiteboy Movement 1761–1765', in *Irish Historical Studies*, vol. xxi (1978).

—— 'Mass Evictions and the Great Famine', in Póirtéir, *The Great Irish Famine.*

—— '"Irish Property Must Pay for Irish Poverty": British Public Opinion and the Great Irish Famine", in Morash and Hayes, *Fearful Realities.*

—— *The Great Irish Potato Famine* (Stroud, 2001).

—— *Captain Rock: The Irish Agrarian Rebellion of 1821–1824* (Cork, 2010).

Dooher, John, 'The Growth and Development of Strabane, 1800–1850', in Dooher and Kennedy, *The Fair River Valley; Strabane Throughout the Ages.*

Dooher, John, and Kennedy, Michael (eds.), *The Fair River Valley: Strabane Throughout the Ages* (Belfast, 2000).

Dowley, Leslie, 'The Potato and Late Blight in Ireland', in Ó Gráda, *Famine 150: Commemorative Lecture Series.*

Durnin, Patrick, 'Aspects of Poor Law Administration and the Workhouse in Derry 1838–1948', in O'Brien, *Derry and Londonderry: History and Society: Interdisciplinary Essays in the History of an Irish County.*

Durnin, Patrick, *The Workhhouse and the Famine in Derry* (Derry, 2001).

Edwards, R. Dudley and Williams, D.E., *The Great Famine: Studies in Irish History 1845–1852* (Dublin, 1956).

Eiríksson, Andrés, 'Food Supply and Food Riots', in Ó Gráda, *Famine 150: Commemorative Lecture Series.*

Fitzgerald, Patrick, "'The Great Hunger?' Irish Famine: Changing Patterns of Crisis", in Crawford, *The Hungry Stream: Essays on Emigration and Famine.*

Fitzpatrick, David, 'Emigration, 1801–1870', in Vaughan, *A New History of Ireland, vol. v, Ireland Under the Union I, 1801–1870.*

—— 'Flight from Famine', in Póirtéir, *The Great Irish Famine.*

Flynn, John, *Ballymacward: The Story of an East Galway Parish* (Galway, 1991).

Forde, Joseph, *et al.* (eds.), *The District of Loughrea* (Galway, 2003).

Foynes, Peter, *The Great Famine in Skibbereen* (Skibbereen, 2004).

Fraher, William, 'The Dungarvan Disturbances of 1846 and Sequels', in Cowman and Brady, *The Famine in Waterford, 1845–1850: Teacht na bPrátaí Dubha.*

Frogatt, Peter, 'The Response of the Medical Profession to the Great Famine', in Crawford, *Famine, The Irish Experience 900–1900: Subsistence Crises and Famines in Ireland.*

Gallman, J. Matthew, *Receiving Erin's Children, Philadelphia, Liverpool and the Irish Famine Migration, 1845–1853* (Chapel Hill, 2000).

Gallogly, Fr. Dan, 'The Famine in County Cavan', in Kinealy and Parkhill, *The Famine in Ulster.*

Geary, Lawrence, 'Famine, Fever and the Bloody Flux', in Póirtéir, *The Great Irish Famine.*

Gentles, Ian, *The New Model Army in England, Ireland and Scotland, 1645–1653* (Oxford, 1992).

Gillespie, Raymond and Moran, Gerard, *A Various Country: Essays in Mayo History 1500–1900* (Westport, 1987).

Gillespie, Raymond (ed.), *Cavan: Essays on the History of an Irish County* (Dublin, 1995).

Goldstrom, J.M. and Clarkson, L.A. (eds.), *Irish Population, Economy and Society: Essays In Memory of the Late K.H. Connell* (Oxford, 1981).

Grace, Daniel, *The Great Famine in the Nenagh Poor Law Union, Co. Tipperary* (Nenagh, 2000).

Grant, James, 'The Great Famine in County Down', in Proudfoot, *Down: History and Society, Interdisciplinary Essays on the History of an Irish County.*

—— 'The Great Famine in County Tyrone', in Dillon and Jefferies, *Tyrone: History and Society.*

—— 'Aspects of the Great Famine in County Armagh', in Hughes, A.J., and Nolan, William (eds.), *Armagh: History and Society: Interdisciplinary Essays on the History of an Irish County.*

Gray, Peter, 'Punch and the Great Irish Famine', in History Ireland, vol. i, no. ii (1993).

—— 'Ideology and the Famine', in Póirtéir, The Great Irish Famine.

—— Famine, Land and Politics: British Government and Irish Politics 1843–1850 (Dublin, 1999).

Griffith, A.R.G., The Irish Board of Works, 1831–1878 (New York, 1987).

Gwinnell, Mary, 'The Famine Years in Wexford', in Journal of the Wexford Historical Society, vol. ix (1982–1983).

Hannigan, Ken, 'Wicklow Before and After the Famine', in Hannigan and Nolan, Wicklow: History and Society.

Hannigan, Ken and Nolan, William (eds.), Wicklow: History and Society: Interdisciplinary Essays of the History of an Irish County (Dublin, 1994).

Hickey, D.J. and Doherty, J.E., A New Dictionary of Irish History from 1800 (Dublin, 2003).

Hickey, Patrick, 'Famine, Mortality and Emigration: A Profile of Six Parishes in the Poor Law Union of Skibbereen, 1846–1847', in O'Flanagan and Buttimer, Cork: History and Society: Interdisciplinary Essays on the History of an Irish County.

—— 'Famine, Mortality and Emigration: A Profile of Six Parishes in the Poor Law Union of Skibbereen, 1846–1847', in O'Flanagan and Buttimer, Cork: History and Society: Interdisciplinary Essays on the History of an Irish County.

—— 'The Famine in the Skibbereen Union', in Póirtéir, The Great Irish Famine.

—— Famine in West Cork: The Mizen Peninsula, Land and People 1800–1852 (Cork, 2002).

Hollett, David, Passage to the New World: Packet Ships and Irish Famine Emigration (Abbergavenny, 1995).

Hughes, A.J. and Nolan, William (eds.), Armagh: History and Society: Interdisciplinary Essays on the History of an Irish County (Dublin, 2001).

Hunt, Tristram, The Frock-Coated Communist: The Life and Times of the Original Champagne Socialist (London, 2009).

Jenkins, Brian, Sir William Gregory of Coole: A Biography (Gerrards Cross, 1986).

Jordan, Donald E., Land and Popular Politics in Ireland: County Mayo from the Plantation to the Land War (Cambridge, 1994).

—— 'The Famine and its Aftermath in County Mayo', in Morash and Hayes, Fearful Realities: New Perspectives on the Famine.

Keating, John, Irish Famine Facts (Kilkenny, 1996).

Kennedy, Liam, Ell, Paul S. and Crawford, E.M., Mapping the Great Irish Famine: A Survey of the Famine Decades (Dublin, 1999).

Kenny, Kevin, The American Irish: A History (New York, 2000).

Kerr, Donal, 'A Nation of Beggars'? Priests, People and Politics in Famine Ireland 1846–1852 (Oxford, 1994).
—— The Catholic Church and the Famine (Dublin, 1996).
Kinealy, Christine, 'The Administration of the Poor Law in Mayo 1838–1898', Cathair na Mart, vol. 6, no. 1 (1986).
—— 'The Poor Law during the Great Famine: An Administration in Crisis', in Crawford, Famine, the Irish Experience 900–1900: Subsistence Crises and Famines in Ireland.
—— 'The Workhouse System in County Waterford, 1838–1923', in Nolan and Power, Waterford: History and Society: Interdisciplinary Essays in the History of an Irish County.
—— This Great Calamity (Dublin, 1994).
—— 'The Role of the Poor Law During the Famine', in Póirtéir, The Great Irish Famine.
—— 'The Response of the Poor Law to the Great Famine in County Galway', in Moran and Gillespie, Galway: History and Society, Interdisciplinary Essays on the History of an Irish County.
—— 'Potatoes, Providence and Philanthropy: the Role of Private Charity During the Irish Famine', in O'Sullivan, The Meaning of the Famine.
—— A Death-Dealing Famine: The Great Hunger in Ireland (London, 1997).
—— The Great Irish Famine: Impact, Ideology and Rebellion (London, 2002).
Kinealy, Christine and MacAtasney, Gerard, The Hidden Famine: Hunger, Poverty and Sectarianism in Belfast (London, 2000).
Kinealy, Christine and Parkhill, Trevor, The Famine in Ulster (Belfast, 1997).
King, Carla (ed.), Famine, Land and Culture in Ireland (Dublin, 2000).
Knightley, John, 'The Godfrey Estate During the Great Famine' in Journal of the Kerry Archaeological and Historical Society, Series ii, vol. v (2005).
Larkin, Emmet, 'The Parish Mission Movement 1850–1880', in Bradshaw and Swords, Christianity in Ireland: Revisiting the Story.
Lee, Joseph, 'On the reliability of Pre-Famine Irish Censuses', in Goldstrom and Clarkson, Irish Population, Economy and Society: Essays In Memory of the Late K.H. Connell.
Lenihan, Pádraig, Consolidating Conquest: Ireland 1603–1727 (London, 2008).
Lynch, Matthew, 'The Mass Evictions in Kilrush Poor Law Union', unpublished M.A. thesis, University of Limerick, 2000.
Lynch, Matthew, and Nugent, Patrick (eds.), Clare: History and Society; Interdisciplinary Essays on the History of and Irish County (Dublin, 2008).
Lyne, Gerard, J., The Lansdowne Estate in Kerry under the Agency of William Steuart Trench 1849–72 (Dublin, 2001).

MacArthur, William P., 'Medical History of the Great Famine', in Edwards and Williams, *The Great Famine: Studies in Irish History*.

—— 'The Famine in County Armagh', in Kinealy and Parkhill, *The Famine in Ulster*.

MacAtasney, Gerard, *This Dreadful Visitation: The Famine in Lurgan/Portadown* (Belfast, 1997).

McCabe, Desmond, 'Social Order and the Ghost of Moral Economy', in Gillespie and Moran, *A Various Country*.

McCavery, Trevor, 'The Famine in County Down' in Kinealy and Parkhill, *The Famine in Ulster*.

—— 'The Irish Catholic Clergy and Emigration during the Great Famine,' in *Irish Historical Studies*, vol. v, no. xx (September 1947).

MacDonagh, Oliver, 'Irish Overseas Emigration during the Great Famine', in Edwards and Williams, *The Great Famine: Studies in Irish History*.

McDowell, R.B., 'Ireland on the Eve of the Famine', in Edwards and Williams, *The Great Famine: Studies in Irish History, 1845–1852*.

McEvoy, Frank, 'A Glimpse of Famine Days in Kilkenny, in *The Old Kilkenny Review*, vol. xlix (1997).

McGrath, Thomas (ed.), *Carlow: History and Society, Interdisciplinary Essays on the History of an Irish County* (Dublin, 2008).

McHugh, Roger, 'Famine in Oral Irish Tradition', in Edwards and Williams, *The Great Famine: Studies in Irish History*.

Mackay, Donald, *Flight from Famine: How the Irish Came to Canada* (Toronto, 1990).

McMahon, Richard, 'Homicide Rates in Ireland, 1831–1850', in *Irish Economic and Social History*, vol. xxxvi (2009).

McNeill, Mary, *Vere Foster, 1819–1900: An Irish Benefactor* (Belfast 1971).

Marnane, Denis, 'South Tipperary on the Eve of the Great Famine,' in *Tipperary Historical Journal*, vol. viii (1995).

—— 'The Famine in South Tipperary,' Part One, in *Tipperary Historical Journal*, vol. ix (1996).

—— 'The Famine in South Tipperary', Part Two, in *Tipperary Historical Journal*, vol. x (1997).

—— 'The Famine in South Tipperary', Part Three, in *Tipperary Historical Journal*, vol. xi (1998).

—— 'The Famine in South Tipperary', Part Four, in *Tipperary Historical Journal*, vol. xii (1999).

—— 'The Famine in South Tipperary', Part Five, in *Tipperary Historical Journal*, vol. xiii (2000).

Mathias, Peter, *The First Industrial Nation: An Economic History of Britain 1700–1914* (London, 1969).

Miller, Kerby, *Emigrants and Exiles: Ireland and the Irish Exodus to North America* (New York, 1985).

Mokyr, Joel, *Why Ireland Starved: A Quantitative and Analytical History of the Irish Economy 189–1850* (Boston, 1983).

Moloney, Mick, *Far from the Shamrock Shore: The Story of Irish-American Emigration through Song* (New York, 2002).

Moran, Gerard, and Gillespie, Raymond (eds.), *Galway: History and Society, Interdisciplinary Essays on the History of an Irish County* (Dublin, 1996).

Moran, Gerard, *Sending out Ireland's Poor: Assisted Emigration to North America in the Nineteenth Century* (Dublin, 2004).

Morash, Chris, *Writing the Irish Famine* (Oxford, 1995).

Morash, Chris and Hayes, Richard (eds.), *Fearful Realities: New Perspectives on the Great Famine* (Dublin, 1996).

Murphy, Ignatius, 'Captain A.E. Kennedy, Poor Law Inspector and the Great Famine in Kilrush Union 1847–1850', in *The Other Clare*, vol. iii (1979).

—— *The Diocese of Killaloe, 1800–1850* (Dublin, 1992).

—— *The Diocese of Killaloe, 1850–1904* (Dublin, 1995).

—— *Before the Famine Struck: Life in West Clare 1834–1845* (Dublin, 1996).

—— *A People Starved: Life and Death in West Clare 1845–1851* (Dublin, 1996).

Murphy, Michael, *Tullamore Workhouse: The First Decade 1842–1852* (Tullamore, 2007).

Murray, James P., *Galway: A Medico-Social History* (Galway, n.d.).

Nelson, E. Charles, *The Cause of the Calamity: Potato Blight in Ireland, 1845–1847, and the Role of the National Botanic Gardens, Glasnevin* (Dublin, 1995).

Ní Dheá, Éilis, 'Micheál Ó Raghallaigh: Scríobhaí Ó Inis Díomáin', in *The Other Clare*, vol. xvi (1992).

Nolan, William, 'The Famine in Slieveardagh' in O'Dwyer, *The Famine in the Kilkenny/Tipperary Region: A History of the Callan Workhouse and Poor Law Union 1845–1852*.

Nolan, William and Power, Thomas (eds.), *Waterford: History and Society: Interdisciplinary Essays in the History of an Irish County* (Dublin, 1992).

Nolan, William, and O'Neill, Timothy P. (eds.), *Offaly: History and Society: Interdisciplinary Essays on the History of an Irish County* (Dublin, 1998).

Norton, Desmond, *Landlords, Tenants, Famine: The Business of an Irish Land Agency in the 1840s* (Dublin, 2006).

Nowlan, Kevin B., *The Politics of Repeal: A Study in the Relations between Great Britain and Ireland 1841–1850* (London, 1965).

Nowlan, Kevin B, 'The Political Background,' in Edwards and Williams, *The Great Famine; Studies in Irish History.*

O'Brien, Gerard, 'The New Poor Law in Pre-Famine Ireland,' in *Irish Economic and Social History*, vol. xii (1985).

—— (ed.), *Derry and Londonderry: History and Society: Interdisciplinary Essays on the History of an Irish County* (Dublin, 1999).

O'Brien, Seamus, *Famine and Community in Mullingar Poor Law Union 1845–1849: Mud Huts and Fat Bullocks* (Dublin, 1999).

Ó Caithnia, Liam, *Scéal na hIomána* (Baile Átha Cliath, 1980).

Ó Cathaoir, Eva, 'The Poor Law in County Wicklow,' in Hannigan and Nolan, *Wicklow: History and Society, Interdisciplinary Essays on the History of an Irish County.*

Ó Cathaoir, Eva, 'The Poor Law in County Carlow 1838–1923,' in McGrath, *Carlow: History and Society, Interdisciplinary Essays on the History of an Irish County.*

Ó Ciosáin, Micheál, *Cnoc an Fhomhair* (Magh Nuat, 1988).

Ó Ciosáin, Niall, 'Boccoughs and God's Poor: Deserving and Undeserving Poor in Irish Popular Culture,' in Tadhg Foley and Seán Rider (eds.), *Ideology and Ireland in the Nineteenth Century* (Dublin, 1998).

O'Dwyer, Michael (ed.), *The Famine in the Kilkenny/Tipperary Region: A History of the Callan Workhouse and Poor Law Union, 1845–1852* (Kilkenny, 1998).

O'Flanagan, Patrick and Buttimer, Cornelius (eds.), *Cork: History and Society: Interdisciplinary Essays on the History of an Irish County* (Dublin, 1993).

O'Gallagher, Marianna, 'The Orphans of Grosse Île: Canada and the Adoption of Irish Famine Orphans,' in O'Sullivan, *The Meaning of the Famine.*

Ó Gráda, Cormac, *The Great Irish Famine* (Dublin, 1989).

—— *Ireland Before and After the Famine: Explorations in Economic History 1800–1923* (Dublin, 1988, new edn. 1993).

—— *An Drochshaol: Béaloideas agus Amhráin* (Baile Atha Cliath, 1994).

—— (ed.), *Famine 150: Commemorative Lecture Series* (Dublin, 1997).

—— *Black '47 and Beyond: The Great Famine in History, Economy and Society* (Princeton, 1999).

—— *Ireland's Great Famine* (Dublin, 2005).

Ó Laighin, Pádraig Breandán, 'Samhradh an Bhróin: Grosse Ile 1847,' in Póirtéir, *Gneithe den Ghorta.*

O'Mahony, Chris, 'Emigration from the Workhouses of the Mid-West 1848–1849' in *The Old Limerick Journal*, vol. xxxii (1995).

Ó Murchadha, Ciarán, 'Limerick Union Workhouse during the Great Famine' in *The Old Limerick Journal*, vol xxxii (1995).

—— 'The Onset of Famine: County Clare 1845–1846,' in *The Other Clare*, vol. xix (1995).

—— 'Sable Wings over the Land: County Clare 1846–1847', in *The Other Clare*, vol. xx (1996).

—— 'One Vast Abattoir: County Clare 1848–1849' in *The Other Clare*, vol. xxi (1997).

—— *Sable Wings over the Land: Ennis, County Clare and its Wider Community During the Great Famine, 1845–1852* (Ennis, 1998).

—— (ed.), *County Clare Studies: Essays in Memory of Gerald O'Connell, Thomas Coffey, Sean Ó Murchadha and Pat Flynn* (Ennis, 2000).

—— 'The Exterminator General of Clare: Marcus Keane of Beech Park, 1815–1883, in Ó Murchadha, *County Clare Studies: Essays in Memory of Gerald O'Connell, Thomas Coffey, Sean Ó Murchadha and Pat Flynn*.

—— 'The Moloch of Landlordism: County Clare 1849–1852, in *The Other Clare*. vol. xxv (2001).

—— 'Where Are the People Gone To?': County Clare 1850–1851' in *The Other Clare*, vol. xxvi (2002).

—— 'The Bad Times and Emigration: County Clare 1850–1852', in *The Other Clare*, vol. xxvii (2003).

—— 'The Ballycoree Monster Meeting', in *The Other Clare*, vol. xxxii (2008).

—— 'The Years of the Great Famine,' in Lynch and Nugent, *Clare: History and Society: Interdisciplinary Essays on the History of an Irish County*.

O'Neill, T.P. 'The Scientific Investigation of the Failure of the Potato Crop in Ireland, 1845–1846' in *Irish Historical Studies*, vol v, no. 18 (September 1946).

—— 'The Society of Friends and the Great Famine,' in *Studies*, xxxix, 213 (June 1950).

—— 'Food Problems during the Great Irish Famine', in *Journal of the Royal Society of Antiquaries of Ireland*, vol. lxxxii (1952).

—— 'The Administration of Relief', in Edwards and Williams, *The Great Famine: Studies in Irish History*.

—— 'The Famine in Offaly,' in Nolan and O'Neill, *Offaly, History and Society: Interdisciplinary Essays on the History of an Irish County*.

—— 'Famine Evictions' in King, *Famine, Land and Culture in Ireland*.

Ó Néill, Tomás, *Fiontan Ó Leathlobhair* (Baile Átha Cliath, 1962).

O'Regan, Ted, 'First Responses to Blight', in Cowman and Brady, *Famine in Waterford 1845–1850: Teacht na bPrátai Dubha*.

O'Rourke, John, *The History of the Great Irish Famine of 1847, with Notices of Earlier Irish Famines* (Dublin, 1874, new edition, 2007).

O'Sullivan, Patrick (ed.), *The Meaning of the Famine* (New York, 1997).

Ó Tuathaigh, *Ireland Before the Famine* (Dublin, 1972).

Parkhill, Trevor, 'The Famine in County Londonderry', in Kinealy and Parkhill, *The Famine in Ulster.*

Póirtéir, Cathal (ed.), *The Great Irish Famine* (Cork, 1995).

—— (ed.), *Gnéithe den Ghorta* (Baile Atha Cliath, 1995).

Potter, George, *To the Golden Door: The Story of the Irish in Ireland and America* (Boston, 1960).

Proudfoot, Lindsay (ed.), *Down: History and Society, Interdisciplinary Essays on the History of an Irish County* (Dublin, 1997).

Quigley, Michael, 'Grosse Ile; 'The Most Important and Evocative Great Famine Site outside of Ireland' in Crawford, *The Hungry Stream: Essays on Emigration and Famine.*

Quinn, John, *Father Mathew's Crusade: Temperance in Nineteenth Century Ireland and Irish America* (Boston, 2002).

Reader, John, *Propitious Esculent: The Potato in World History* (London, 2008).

Reid, Richard, and Cheryl Mongan, *'A Decent Set of Girls': the Orphans of the Thomas Arbuthnot* (Yass, 1998).

Rees, Jim, *A Farewell to Famine* (Arklow 1994).

Robins, Joseph, *The Miasma: Epidemic and Panic in Nineteenth Century Ireland* (Dublin, 1995).

Robinson, Tim, 'Connemara after the Famine: Thomas Colville Scott's Journal of the Survey of the Martin Estate', in *History Ireland*, vol. iv (Summer, 1996).

Roche, Richard, 'The Famine Years in Forth and Bargy', in *Journal of the Wexford Historical Society*, vol. xv (1994–1995).

Rogers, Patrick, *Fr. Theobald Mathew, Apostle of Temperance* (London, 1945).

Sarbaugh, Timothy J., "Charity beings at Home: the United States Government and Irish Famine Relief 1845–1849', in *History Ireland*, vol. ix, no. ii (Summer, 1996).

Shaw, A.G.L., *Convicts and the Colonies: A Study of Penal Transportation From Great Britain and Ireland to Australia and other Parts of the Empire* (London, 1966).

Sheedy, Kieran, *The Clare Elections* (Dublin, 1993).

Sloan, Robert, *William Smith O'Brien and the Young Ireland Rebellion of 1848* (Dublin, 2000).

Stout, Matthew, 'The Geography and Implications of Post-Famine Population Decline in Baltiboys, County Wicklow', in Morash and Hayes, *Fearful Realities: New Perspectives on the Famine.*

Synnott, David, 'Marcella Gerrard's Estate' in *Journal of the Galway Archaeological and Historical Society*, vol. lvii (2005).

Thompson, E.P., *The Making of the English Working Class* (London, 1966).

Urwin, Margaret, 'The Effects of the Great Famine (1845–1849), on the County Wexford Parish of Bannow/Ballynitty', in *Journal of the Wexford Historical Society*, vol. xvii (1996–1997).

Vaughan, W.E. and Fitzpatrick, A.J., (eds.), *Irish Historical Statistics: Population 1821–1971* (Dublin, 1978).

Vaughan, W.E. (ed.), *A New History of Ireland, vol. v., Ireland Under the Union I, 1801–1870* (Oxford, 1989).

Villiers-Tuthill, Kathleen, *Patient Endurance: The Famine in Connemara* (Dublin, 1997).

Walsh, John, 'The Famine, its Occurrence its Effects and the Response to it at Local Level' in O'Dwyer, *The Famine in the Kilkenny/Tipperary Region*.

Whelan, Irene, 'The Stigma of Souperism', in Póirtéir, *The Great Irish Famine*.

Whyte, *The Tenant League and Irish Politics in the Eighteen Fifties* (Dundalk, 1963).

Wilson, Robert, *The Life and Times of Queen Victoria* (London, 1887–1888).

Wittke, Carl, *The Irish In America* (New York, 1970).

Woodham-Smith, Cecil, *The Great Hunger* (London, 1962).

Index